THE IRISH DRAMA

The
IRISH DRAMA
by
ANDREW E. MALONE

Benjamin Blom

First published by Constable, London, 1929
Reissued by Benjamin Blom, Inc., 1965
Library of Congress Catalog Card No. 65–16243

Printed in U.S.A. by
NOBLE OFFSET PRINTERS, INC.
NEW YORK 3, N. Y.

FOR LILLIE
WHO WANTED TO KNOW

FOREWORD

A QUARTER of a century is an appreciable period in the life of any institution, and as the Abbey Theatre in Dublin will soon be celebrating the Silver Jubilee of its foundation, the time is opportune for a survey of its achievement. It is as such a survey that this book is offered to the public.

The work is based upon consistent, and almost continuous, attendance at the performances, and the author may claim that he has seen every play which the Abbey Theatre has staged, some of them many times. Simultaneously, as a student of the contemporary drama throughout the world, he has either seen or read hundreds of modern plays from every land, and has read almost every book which had the drama as its theme. To the authors of these books he acknowledges his debt, whether he has used their work consciously or unconsciously.

It is probable that readers will find the Appendix, which sets out the Complete List of the Plays performed at the Abbey Theatre and its Forerunners, of more than passing interest. It will give a bird's-eye view of the achievements of the Irish Theatre and Drama for the thirty years of its existence.

The author would like to acknowledge the great pleasure he has at all times derived from the Abbey Theatre, and would heartily thank the playwrights, actors and directors for the provision of recreation in the most literal sense of the word.

A. E. M.

CONTENTS

APPENDICES

CHAPTER I

THE NEED FOR IRISH NATIONAL DRAMA

Ireland was the last country in Europe to develop a National Drama—
The Political and Social conditions were not entirely responsible for
this—Late development of Drama in Scandinavia—The Irish
contribution to British Drama—No Irish equivalent to ninth century
English Tropes—The Irish Bards and Shanachies—No Miracle or
Mystery Plays in Ireland—The Puritanical fear of the Theatre—The
Dublin stage in the eighteenth and nineteenth centuries—Growth
of the English Drama in Irish towns—Patriotic melodrama : Boucicault and Whitebread—The turning point at the end of the last
century due to political disillusionment.

THE very prominent position which the Irish Drama has
secured during the first quarter of the twentieth century tends
to obscure the fact that until the end of the nineteenth century
Ireland had been without any national drama in either the
Irish or the English languages. It is certainly somewhat
peculiar that one of the oldest of the civilisations of Europe,
with a culture and a literature continuing almost without a
break from pre-Christian times, should never have attempted
to give expression to its hopes, its struggles, and its desires, in
the form of drama at an earlier date. Ireland had reached a
very high state of culture and civilisation at the time when the
dramatists of Greece and Rome were at the highest points of
their influence and power ; and it was due largely to the
efforts of Irish missionary scholars that the classical languages
and literatures had their revival in mediaeval Europe. But
the activities of the Irish scholars in Europe seem to have
left Ireland itself somewhat unaffected, and quite unmoved
towards emulation of the achievements of the other nations.
So Ireland remained almost impassive to that great movement
in European culture which is known as The Renaissance.

The revival of art and literature in Europe did not affect Ireland, and it is quite possible that Ireland remained unaware that the Latin races had brought Drama back to the world ; and that this drama had reached its apogee in the work of an English poet named William Shakespeare. It was not that all the people of Ireland were completely unacquainted with the revival of art and letters in Europe ; there is sufficient evidence to suggest that as great a proportion of the Irish population of the time was as literate, and as cultured, as any in the world. But there seems to have been a lack of curiosity, and a complete absence of that spirit of emulation, which is essential to the growth of literature. It would almost seem that Ireland had not belonged to the European system, and that its people were completely disinterested in anything that the peoples of Europe might do. Throughout the later Middle Ages there were plays in Greek and in Latin, in Italian and in French, in German and in English, but it was not until 1901 that there was a play in Irish. In modern times the drama flourished in all the countries, and all the languages, of Europe, with only short and localised interruptions due to transient conditions and circumstances in one country or another. In China and Japan the drama was, and is, a very important feature of the national life. But through the centuries Ireland was unaware of, or perhaps only very ostentatiously ignored, all that other countries seemed to value. Few people in Ireland had any interest in drama, and that few consisted in the main of the cosmopolitan, Anglo-Irish, population of Dublin and some other cities and towns. The mass of the people was not interested in the drama or in the theatre, and even during the more recent centuries was probably oblivious of anything but the wildest farce and the most bloodthirsty melodrama.

It is true that the political and social conditions in Ireland were not favourable to the development of the drama in any regular way ; but it may be doubted whether they were entirely responsible for its complete neglect, and entire non-existence as a part of the national culture. It is true that the history of Ireland is one long chronicle of war, pillage, confiscation, and repression. Before the coming of the Norsemen the men of Ireland were kept busy fighting each other ; the Norse invaders merely provided new combatants, and gave greater variety to the warlike combinations. In time the combinations became unfavourable to the Norsemen and they were defeated and expelled from any dominating position in the affairs of the country. From the Battle of Clontarf in 1014 to the coming of the Normans under Strongbow in 1169 there was a century and a half during which there was comparative peace, as much peace as was the norm of the age in Europe, but even then there was no attempt to develop on the lines of other countries. With Strongbow, Earl of Pembroke, came to Ireland many of those Normans whose people had so recently become the masters of England. These Normans in turn fought against, or allied themselves with, sections of the Irish people and provided new possibilities for war, and new groupings of the population. In time came the Plantations and expropriations of Elizabeth, the sanguinary fanaticism of Cromwell, and the tortuous wars of the Stuarts, followed by comparative calm for nearly two centuries. The little war at the end of the eighteenth century, and the complete engrossment of the people in famines and politics, with occasional bloodshed, throughout the nineteenth century, may complete a hurried survey of national unrest. For the greater part of the time the people of Ireland were helots and outlaws in their own land, even in their own homes, by the operation of penal laws against their national customs and their religious beliefs. But even when all this has been taken into account, and given due weight in the consideration, it is not quite sufficient to justify, or excuse, the absence of national drama. Europe as a whole was during the Middle Ages little different from, or any better than, Ireland. Throughout Europe emperors, kings, princes, dukes, doges, barons, bishops, and free cities, competed with each other in a bloody struggle for domination and power. All Europe, too, had its religious persecutions, its robberies, its burnings, plunderings,

butcheries, and helotry. But despite all these the arts flourished, in the main, and the drama had its allotted place in the
social life of large sections of the population. France, Italy,
Germany, Spain, and England, had their internal persecutions
and external wars, but these did not prevent the growth of
national drama, as the wars of the Greeks of an earlier age did
not prevent the growth of a drama that has flourished through
the ages to our own day. Throughout all the troubles and
disturbances of these countries a cultural standard was
maintained, and that cultural standard gave a difference and a
distinction to the nations which were otherwise but geographical, political, or racial differences. In Ireland, too, there
was maintained a cultural standard, but in the very main-
tenance of that standard there orginated a system which
probably more than any other single cause prevented the
growth of a distinctively national drama. That system
consisted of the poetry recitals given in the homes, and the
oral diffusion of stories and news by the hearthstone. This
system, which had its beginnings with the bards in the halls
of the nobles and the shanachies in the homes of the people,
had degenerated consistently until at the end of the nineteenth century it was but a public reading of the weekly
newspapers. And by that time it was only the windy
speeches of the politicians that were of interest to the people.

This peculiarity was not entirely confined to Ireland ; it
may be found in all the countries which it is now fashionable
to call Celtic. Scotland had no national drama until very
recent years, and Wales has only begun to take an interest in
national drama. Some there are who would ascribe the
absence of drama from these countries to the alleged dreami-
ness and otherworldliness of the Celt, which is supposed to
have prevented the entire race from mastering the mechanics
of stage representation. Those who advance such a theory to
account for the absence of drama from Celtic countries seem
to forget that in its beginnings the drama had no mechanics at
all. Drama began as an offshoot of religious rites, even
as a part of religious ritual, and observances. As it was

in classical Greece so it was in mediaeval France, Germany, Italy, and England, and there was no apparent obstacle to prevent the comparatively simple people of these lands from performing, understanding, and enjoying the dramatic representations which were sometimes complex and sophisticated but which were generally simple tales presented very simply. The Catholic Church actively aided the growth and spread of this simple drama throughout Europe ; and in England as early as the ninth century *tropes*, or additional texts to ecclesiastical music, in dramatic form, seem to have been fairly common. They were invariably composed by monks or nuns and performed by selected members of the congregations. In the beginning these *tropes* were part of the actual religious service, but gradually they became detached and were presented separately as drama with a definitely religious purpose. Gradually, too, in the different countries fragments of the native speech came to be inserted in the Latin text, and the drama began to move definitely towards the people and to be shaped by the genius of the different nations and races. As in classical Greece song had developed into acted drama ; or at least the beginnings of drama, the germ from which the drama was to develop as a separate art distinct from religious observances and distinct from song. In Ireland there was no such development. Song there seems to have been in abundance, but there were no *tropes* to give the people that turn towards representation which produced the drama in other countries. In Ireland song remained song, and the singers remained just singers ; the song never developed into acted drama, the heroic poems of the bards were only recited, though they would probably have gained considerably in effect had they been acted in the presence of those whose feats of valour or kindness they were intended to celebrate. But no such representation was ever attempted, and a promising basis for drama seems to have passed unobserved. Also, there seems to have been no association between the religious rites and celebrations of the people with the dramatic form such as may be found in other Catholic countries. The earliest forms of

Druidic worship in Ireland must have contained some element which would nowadays be called dramatic, but all traces of these ceremonies seem to have passed from the popular mind at an early period of the Christian era. So from neither of its religious systems did Ireland receive any impulse towards dramatic form ; the impulse which other Christian countries felt at an early time never affected the Irish people, and those early forms of drama which are such a conspicuous feature in the drama of other countries are without any equivalent in Ireland.

In Ireland recitation took the place taken by representation in other European countries. The nobles and the aristocracy maintained the bards, and the ordinary folk maintained the shanachies, or storytellers, to provide recreation and instruction. The spoken word was of the greatest importance, and the imagination of the listener supplied all the dramatic action that was needed. The epic poem when recited by the bard in the halls of the nobility, or the story when told by the cottage fireside, brought to all sections of the people that dramatic excitement which their natures desired. In these recitals the fine word was of the utmost importance, and the use of the fine word was governed by a technique that is probably the most finished and elaborate that mediaeval Europe can show. The manner of delivery, too, had to be of the very highest standard if the significance of the fine word were to be recognised by the audience, and full value to be had by them of the dramatic content of the poem or story. These technical details of manner have left a very deep impression on the Irish mind, an impression that is probably as deep to-day as it was in any period of the national history. It is certainly of some significance to-day that the manner of a speech, its wording and the form in which it is delivered, is of much greater importance than the idea or the thought that it may contain. It is a frequent occurrence in the everyday experience of anyone who has to make speeches in Ireland to be congratulated, or the reverse, upon the manner of his speech, while never a word will be said of the ideas which the speech may have embodied, and no effort will be made to discuss the ideas or to put them into effect. A speech in Ireland is just a speech—a form of artistic exercise to be enjoyed or endured in accord with the mood of the listener and the virtuosity of the performer. That is something which Irish politicians understand almost instinctively ; and it is certainly not accidental that most Irish political speeches are calculated to thrill rather than to instruct. In England the speech of a politician will be judged by the practicability and the commonsense of the ideas which it may embody ; in Ireland it will be judged by artistic standards only, on a basis of ' art for art's sake.' In a way these speeches of the politicians, particularly during the nineteenth century, gave to the people all the artistic entertainment which they could either secure or understand ; and the politician had to compete with the travelling circus as a purveyor of popular entertainment. Since the bards recited no more, and the shanachies read only the weekly newspapers where they survived at all, the orator in the market-place had to take the places of both in an effort to supply instructive recreation to the populace. He had to give his audience an emotional thrill, or be rated a failure. Those who heard Irish politicians only in the unemotional atmosphere and surroundings of the Palace of St. Stephen at Westminster can have only the very remotest conception of the oratorical flights which they were capable of taking. At Westminster the work that had to be done was so different from that which had to be done in Ireland that there was only a very slight resemblance in the speeches delivered in both places by the same man. At Westminster there had to be reasoned argument to bring conviction to listeners ; in Ireland it was necessary to be flamboyantly rhetorical, with a richness of highly coloured metaphor and a copiously generous supply of adjectives. In fact, every speech delivered in Ireland had to be ' a sermon in crude melodrama ', complete with the well-known and gener-ally recognised goodness of all things Irish and the obviously hopeless badness of everything that was not Irish. Cinderella is supposed to be an excellent theme for modern dramatists, but the nineteenth century politicians of Ireland anticipated by more than half-a-century that discovery of dramatic critics, as every speech was but a slight variation upon that single theme. In every speech that had any interest for the people the history of Ireland and its social conditions were dramatised as the story of Kathleen ni Houlihan, or the Sean Bhean Bhoct, or Dark Rosaleen, or some other fanciful name. But it was always the story of Cinderella awaiting the coming of her Prince who would deliver her from rags and bondage. So throughout the nineteenth century, when the countries of Europe were turning to realism in the theatre, the only form of drama with which the people of Ireland were generally too familiar was that supplied by the dramatisation of political conditions in the speeches of politicians. But these politicians knew their work, and there are few in the history of that century who are comparable with the long line of Irish political orators from O'Connell to Redmond ; they really were spell-binders who kept their audiences hanging upon their every word, and when they had finished there remained only the impression of a *morceau* executed by a master-musician. But their style has left its mark upon the mind of the country ; it may be noted in the work of many Irish dramatists, and it is obvious in all Irish audiences.

The ' mystery ' and the ' miracle ' plays had no place in the life of Ireland, they were as unknown as the *trope* of an earlier age. The craft and trade guilds which gave these early efforts at dramatic representation their important places in the history of the drama in England had but small influence in Irish life at any time. They were not Irish—the Irish craftsman had an entirely different form of organisation and regulation, something more akin to an artistic hierarchy than a trading body. The craft guilds and the merchant guilds came into Ireland from England, and their membership was composed mainly of people from England. These people acted in their Irish guilds as their brethren acted in cognate guilds in England. In Dublin, and the few other Irish towns

where guilds were established, they gave displays of the ' mys-
teries ', evidently the same versions as were being acted in
England, and adopted patron saints ; but at no time did they
become Irish in thought or outlook. When the cleavage came
in the religious life of Europe, and divergence became
marked by the changes of Henry VIII and Elizabeth, the
guilds in Ireland became Protestant and the Catholic Irish
were generally debarred from membership. This religious
cleavage probably prevented the guilds from becoming Irish,
as they must have become in course of time if there had been
no external interference. The guilds might have been
governed by a majority of Irish members and they would
probably have been adapted to suit the circumstances and
conditions of Irish life. As it was they remained English, and
definitely Protestant in outlook, and there was no Irish
organisation to perform similar functions for the Catholic
Irish until the trades union movement came into prominence
at a much later date. Too great emphasis cannot be placed
upon the religious cleavage in its relation to the development
of thought and activity in Ireland generally. The cleavage
between Catholic and Protestant may be noted in every form
of activity and in every phase of Irish life. Probably the wars
and the persecutions in the name of religion, rather than the
religious differences themselves, may account for this
phenomenon.

Certain it is, however, that Catholic Ireland had, and to
some extent still has, the same idea of the theatre that Jeremy
Collier had of the Restoration Drama in England. The
theatre is ' bad ', just as novels are ' bad ', and no really
' good ' person can have intercourse with either form of
artistic expression. This fact is all the more remarkable in
Ireland when it is remembered how much the drama, and the
theatre, in other Catholic countries owe to the sympathy and
active encouragement of the Catholic Church and clergy.
In these other countries the earliest dramatists were usually
either priests or nuns, and it is hardly too much to say that
without this active encouragement of the Church there would

have been no drama until a much later time than that in which it actually had its beginnings. In France, in Italy, in Spain, in Germany, and in England the active encouragement of the Church seems to have been willingly, even enthusiastically, given ; in Ireland it was withheld. Germany might have a dramatist nun in Hrotswitha of Gandersheim, who wrote a series of religious plays in the tenth century. " There are many Catholics ", she notes in her preface, " and we cannot acquit ourselves of the charge, who, attracted by the polished elegance of the style of pagan writers, prefer their works to the Holy Scriptures. There are others who, although they are deeply attached to the Sacred Writings and have no liking for most pagan productions, make an exception in favour of the works of Terence, and, fascinated by the charm of the manner, risk being corrupted by the wickedness of the matter, Wherefore I . . . have not hesitated to imitate in my writings a poet whose works are so widely read." The ' mystery ' and the ' miracle ' plays reached their highest point in excellence and popularity in the fourteenth century after their performance had been conditioned and regularised by the decree of Pope Urban IV in 1264, and made operative by the Council of Vienne in 1311. On Corpus Christi these plays, which had hitherto remained disconnected, were to be bound together into more or less formal cycles dealing with the incidents of the Old and New Testaments so that they should present to the eager crowds the whole story of the world from the creation of Adam to the Resurrection of Christ. These centuries were centuries of war in Ireland, but so they were in Europe, and the good intentions of the Pope made little difference to the Catholics of Ireland in so far as drama was concerned. In other Catholic countries the young drama was Catholic in atmosphere, Catholic in the personnel of its authors and actors, and sometimes national in its language. In Ireland it remained Catholic in atmosphere only so long as the membership of the guilds remained Catholic. When the guilds became Protestant the drama became Protestant also ; and at no time was the young drama in Ireland national in its language. But even when the guilds were Catholic there seems to have been no active encouragement from the Catholic Church for the drama ; and, of course, when the guilds became Protestant there was no intercourse with the Catholic clergy at all. It is not at all improbable that the later coldness of the attitude of the Catholic Church in Ireland towards the drama was induced by the Protestantism of the guilds in those formative early years. In the other Catholic countries of Europe there was no break in the transmission of religion and culture from one generation to another. In Ireland both religion and national culture were relegated to an inferior position in the nation, and such drama as there was developed on English lines and under Protestant patronage. In Dublin, and in some other Irish cities where the theatre existed at all, it was under Protestant patronage and control, and the plays presented were as English as if they had been presented in London. To this fact may almost certainly be ascribed the later puritanical attitude of Irish Catholics towards the theatre ; an attitude which persists in diminished severity to this day. As to why the Catholic Church in Ireland neglected the earlier ' mystery ' folk drama it may be impossible now to discover, and it will probably suffice to say that to that neglect is due the late development of drama in the Irish language. But even now there are thousands of people in Ireland who, though they may enter a theatre at odd times, are quite certain that the theatre is an evil thing and an unwholesome influence in the life of any community.

All these influences and circumstances acted and reacted upon each other in such ways as to prevent, until a very late period, the growth of a native drama in Ireland. In Scandinavia, where the influence and fundamental conditions were somewhat similar, the development of the drama was also slow. There it was not until the first quarter of the eighteenth century that Holberg began his career as a dramatist under the inspiration of the plays of Molière ; and a century-and-a-half had to elapse ere the drama of Scandinavia came to magnificent fruition in the work of Ibsen, Bjornsen, and Strindberg. With Ibsen and Strindberg the Scandinavian drama burst forth in revolt. When Irish drama came, about the same time, there was little of revolt in it, it resembled the drama of Holberg rather than that of Ibsen. This was because the drama in Ireland was something alien imposed upon the people from above rather than a spontaneous outgrowth from the ordinary life of the people. The theatre in Ireland was a foreign thing, divorced from the national life, whereas in the Scandinavian lands it had grown in the culture of the several peoples. In the eighteenth century the theatre in Dublin was of considerable importance, and could boast that plays were presented upon its stage before they were seen in London. The standards of staging and acting were at least as good as those prevailing in London at the time, and many plays which were first performed in Dublin were afterwards staged in London. But even this fact is of small significance to the development of the drama in Ireland because the Dublin theatre of that time was the theatre of an English colony which had its capital in London, and in its plays it followed the mode of the London theatre. It may be said boldly as a fact that all drama in Ireland until the beginning of the twentieth century was English drama, and that the impulse towards the representation of plays upon the stage in Ireland came always from outside.

In the larger Irish towns where there had been any attempt to stage plays at all the conditions were the same as those of Dublin. The theatre was something of a special preserve for the resident aristocracy which took its standards from London, and rarely did the community take even a remote interest in its doings. The theatre was in fact a foreign thing which was looked upon with suspicion. The plays enacted had no connection whatever with either the thought or the life of the mass of the Irish people ; they depicted a civilisation which was not only alien but definitely hostile to that of Ireland. So far as the aristocracy, the landlord class, was concerned the position was exactly reversed. The members of that class were, in the main, the descendants of the Anglo-Norman, or other English, settlers who had confiscated the lands they held, and who lived apart from the people in whose midst, and on whose lands, they dwelt. Their country was England, their capital was London, their civilisation was English, and they were provincials who aped the life of their capital to the greatest extent of their opportunities. They presented literature with the types made familiar by the novels of Charles Lever, Samuel Lover, and Maria Edgeworth, and social economics with the problem of the absentee landlord. Much has been said and written against these people, but in their favour it must be said that they maintained their own standards and their own civilisation though they were but a small minority of the population of the country in which they lived. From this class came the long line of dramatists which gave to the world Irish dramatists rather than Irish drama. It is doubtful that if this class had not existed there would have been any theatrical development in Ireland. In other countries the drama was the most democratic of the arts, drawing its patronage and sustenance from the masses, but in Ireland the theatre depended almost solely upon this alien aristocracy.

The class which patronised the theatre in Ireland did very little until the beginning of the twentieth century to develop a native Irish drama, but it made a great contribution to the drama in England. It is no exaggeration to say that the tradition of comedy on the English stage since the seventeenth century has been maintained by dramatists of Irish birth or of Irish training. William Congreve, the greatest of the Restoration dramatists, though not born in Ireland was educated at Trinity College in the University of Dublin, and that University is entitled to claim at least some of the credit for the fact that Sir Edmund Gosse could say, " No one, perhaps, in any country, has written prose for the stage with so assiduous a solicitude for style ". George Farquhar left the stage of a Dublin theatre to give to the drama in England the benefit of what Pope aptly termed his ' pert, low dialogue ' and his robust wit. Since the days of Congreve and Farquhar the tradition has been continued by a long line of comedy writers of which the most brilliantly conspicuous have been Oliver Goldsmith, Richard Brinsley Sheridan, Oscar Wilde, and George Bernard Shaw, but which contains also the names of many others whose plays are certainly not inferior to most of the comedies which bring fame and fortune to their authors from the theatres of England and America to-day. Between the time of Sheridan and that of Wilde the writing of comedy in English was almost lost as an art ; the very word had almost come to mean the adaptations which were made from French farces by a host of industrious mediocrities. It has been the fashion for some time to decry the merit of Wilde's comedies, but it is an indisputable fact these comedies represent at its best the English drama of the later nineteenth century. When compared with the insipid work of his contemporary English comedy writers the work of Wilde is living and charming. It can hardly be contended that the playgoers of continental Europe esteem the work of Wilde so highly only because they are unacquainted with the plays of his contemporaries. The fact is that English comedy was on the verge of death when Wilde revived it, and rescued the English stage from fatuity. No history of the English drama can fail to accord to Wilde's comedies an important, if not a very high, place in the evolution of the comedy in the English language. Sheridan and Goldsmith have been given their places as classics of the English stage, which means that they are relegated to the mercies of provincial amateur societies, and Bernard Shaw carries their tradition into the theatre of our own time. All these writers have in common a perfection of dialogue which is quite distinctively Irish ; and they all have that wit which is no less a distinguishing mark of the Irishman. They are all satirists, viewing English life with a somewhat disapproving smile. In all their comedies it is the life of the English people that is satirised, there is nothing of Ireland in them but the pert dialogue and the ironic wit which are characteristic of their countrymen at large. Comedies by English writers tend to be humorous and sentimental, while comedies by Irishmen tend to be witty and ironic. Had it not been for the line of Irish writers from Farquhar to Shaw English comedy would have been almost entirely deficient in that satiric content without which comedy loses much of its savour. It is somewhat unfortunate that Ireland should occupy such an inconspicuous place in the work of all these writers, and that they gave so little attention to the development of the drama in their own country. They had at their disposal in Dublin, and elsewhere throughout the country, good theatres and good acting, but the lure of London was irresistible, and England gained what Ireland lost : a gain and a loss to which Ireland has become accustomed in other branches of activity than those of the theatre and the drama. But perhaps, as Bernard Shaw once said to the *Daily Mail*, it is only because "Ireland would see through him in ten minutes, and he made a living in England ".

During the eighteenth century the theatre flourished in Dublin and in some of the provincial towns, and even during the nineteenth century it maintained some vigour. Then the drama in England languished and almost died, and good acting alone made the theatre tolerable during an arid period. The actor became supreme; the star actor became the custom, and the path was made clear for the dominating influence of the actor-manager. The star actors, and the actor-managers, of London toured in Ireland, and they were invariably rewarded by profitable journeys. But they killed the old stock companies and brought the theatre in Ireland into dependence upon London for its acting no less than for its plays. It used to be said that these star actors found in Dublin an audience which was at once more appreciative and more critical than any audience to be found elsewhere in either island. The advent of Tom Robertson as the leading dramatist in England completed the break in Ireland. The interest of Irish audiences in English plays began to wane, and even the finest acting of a play by Robertson failed to

rouse an Irish audience to interest. It is a curious sidelight
upon the mentality of the audiences of both islands that the
work of this dramatist should have marked a turning-point
in the theatre in Ireland as in England. Robertson is now
generally regarded by English critics and historians of the
drama as the man who brought ' realism ' to the English
stage, and his plays are said to mark the revival of the English
drama. But Robertson's definitely English plays never
interested an Irish audience. They were too localised, too
domestic, to be understood by those who were not intimately
associated with the fine points of the life they depicted. The
little snobberies and petty jealousies upon which they were
built were not understood in Ireland, and the very pedestrian character of the dialogue was much below what Irish
audiences expect in the theatre. Into the gap which was left
in the Dublin theatre there came Dion Boucicault from
America. He had discovered an audience for his plays among
the Irish population of America, and it was reasonable to
suppose that what was interesting, and gave pleasure, to
people who had not long left Ireland would prove equally
interesting and pleasing to those who had remained at home.
His supposition was accurate, and for nearly half a century
the plays of Boucicault, and the plays of a host of imitators,
continued to be popular on the Dublin stage. *The Colleen
Bawn*, *Arrah-na-Pogue*, *The Shaughraun*, and several others
maintained their popularity until very recent years, when
changes in other aspects of Irish life began to manifest themselves in the theatre. In the plays of Dion Boucicault the
Irish people found what they could never find in the plays of
Tom Robertson. They found colour, romance, high-sounding
words, deeds of daring, and the spirit of sacrifice. Those who
may be disposed to sneer in a condescending way at Boucicault's plays would do well to examine them and take note of
the care with which they are constructed. The well-made
play for which American critics examine the work of Scribe
and Sardou can be examined more domestically in the work
of Boucicault, if they will but take the trouble to examine it.

It is easy to laugh at his melodrama ; but look how carefully he works for his effects, and how well he achieves them ! He brought the Irish masses into the theatre by giving them drama they could understand and characters with whom they could sympathise, and for that alone he deserves to be remembered. His work was continued by J. W. Whitebread in a series of patriotic melodramas which continued to fill his theatre almost to the outbreak of the Great War. The type of stage Irishman which these two playwrights managed to popularise was an amalgam of all the patriotic virtues which the Irishman liked to think were his own exclusive property ; and the self-satisfied audiences were given really heartless villains whom they could hiss to their heart's content, and heroes who were really heroes and died for the liberation of their country. Wolfe Tone, Robert Emmet, Lord Edward Fitzgerald, Napper Tandy were but a few of the patriotic heroes who roused the enthusiasm of Dublin audiences in the plays of Whitebread and his associates. These plays were Irish in theme and mood as Robertson's were English, and almost for the first time gave to Ireland a drama which had some connection with the life and thought of the people. They were poor plays, mainly melodrama of the most vivid kind, but they made history real for many thousands of people.

Meanwhile melodrama had invaded life in the turmoil of the Parnell controversy, and after Parnell had been deserted and vilified by those who should have been his most ardent and constant supporters the bottom seemed to fall out of Irish life. Then it was that attention was turned to those cultural movements which have since remade the life of the country. The Gaelic League was founded, and the Irish Literary Society. Standish O'Grady published his history of Ireland, and John O'Leary enthused his youthful listeners with his high mind and deep feeling. The wranglings of the politicians seemed as if they would never cease, and as they consisted mainly of personal abuse they held nothing of hope for the future. Thus the minds of many of the younger men

were turned from politics to literature, and the Irish Literary
Renaissance began. At the same time the theatre was having
a renaissance in Scandinavia, and the work of Ibsen was being
brought to the notice of the world in Free Theatres, Independent Theatres, and Little Theatres in many of the capitals
of Europe. George Bernard Shaw carried the campaign
against the older drama to London and waged incessant
warfare against the commercial theatre as it was then
constituted. When the Independent Theatre was founded
in London many of its chief supporters were Irishmen, and
it actually produced the first plays of Bernard Shaw, William
Butler Yeats, and George Moore. To one of these three
came the idea that Ireland ought to have a national drama,
and when that idea came to W. B. Yeats the Irish Dramatic
Movement was conceived. He discussed the matter with
George Moore and Edward Martyn, and these three with
Lady Gregory founded the Irish Literary Theatre. When
that theatre gave its first performance in Dublin in 1899 the
Irish national theatre was born, and a new national drama was
added to the world. Hitherto everything that Ireland had
given to drama was given to English drama, now and hence-
forth it would have a drama of its own which would represent
it to the world in somewhat nobler guise than the plays of
Boucicault and Whitebread, and more worthily voice the
culture which it had so long striven to make vocal. Ireland
had come at last to be represented in the theatre of the world,
and a new language was added to those in which drama is
clothed.

CHAPTER II

THE IRISH LITERARY THEATRE : 1899-1903

The theatre of commerce not sufficient—Neglect of the Poetic Drama—
The coming of Ibsen—Free Theatres : Paris, Berlin, London—
Irish interest in the Independent Theatre—Shaw's struggle for
Ibsenism—A literary renaissance in Ireland—The Gaelic League—
The Literary Societies—Douglas Hyde and Standish O'Grady—
Literature and Patriotism—W. B. Yeats thinks and Lady Gregory
plans—The Irish Literary Theatre in being—Dublin is roused—
English Players in Irish Plays—An Irish Company discovered by
' A.E.'—Miss Horniman helps.

DURING the second half of the nineteenth century the theatre
in England had become almost entirely an institution for the
making of profits. This was, perhaps, inevitable in an age
and a country when and where everything was judged upon
its capacity to pay. The only question to be asked about
anything was ' Will it pay ? " And if that question could not
be answered in the affirmative the matter was dismissed as
unworthy of further consideration by sensible people. Profits
were idolised, and the theatre, in common with most of the
desirable things of life, was offered in sacrifice to the idol.
Vain was the protest of Art for Art's Sake made in the
nineties, such a protest could only be treated as a joke by a
practical people. No community of hard-headed business
people could be expected to treat such a creed with any degree
of respect ; and so it was treated as a joke, even as an
obscene joke after the condemnation of Oscar Wilde. With
the downfall of Wilde any little hope there ever had been for
the success of the revolt of art against its own commercialisa-
tion faded away, and the merchants again reigned undisturbed.
In the theatre the practical men were actor-managers, and the
London successes, often even the London failures, became

the theatrical fare of the English provinces. Ireland had
since the decline of its local stock companies become for
theatrical purposes just a part of the English provinces, and
despite a continuous protest against the political domination
of Great Britain hardly a voice was raised against the dependence of the Irish theatre upon touring companies from
England, and the domination of the Irish stage by the London
actor-managers. As England had turned to commerce and
profits so Ireland had turned to politics ; and as art had to
make profits to be tolerated in England so had it to be political
to be tolerated in Ireland. Writing of every kind in Ireland
tended towards political journalism and propaganda, and it
kept its eyes upon the freedom of Ireland as in England it had
to keep its eyes upon the movements of the Stock Exchange.
Obviously such a preoccupation with extraneous matters
could not be good for the drama in either country, and as a
consequence the drama languished in both. Henrik Ibsen
had come with new life for the drama in Europe, but the stage
in England and in Ireland was fully occupied by such
playwrights as Robertson and Grundy, the one with his
home-made, even home-spun, plays and the other with
anglicised versions of the Paris modes. But crying somewhere in the wilderness was the powerful voice of George
Bernard Shaw. That powerful voice was, however, without
anything positive to say until Sir Edmund Gosse and the late
William Archer brought the plays of Ibsen within the reach
of speakers and readers of English.

Bad as was the position of the prose drama that of poetic
drama was infinitely worse, as for all practical purposes poetry
had gone from the English stage. Shakespeare was left, but
left in such a form that his work would hardly have been
recognisable even by himself. The ' fat part ' for the actor-
manager was considered as of greater importance than the
verse of Shakespeare, and sumptuously gorgeous production
of greater value than the beauty of speech. Shakespeare
was made into a spectacle so that people in the theatre might
not be reminded that he was in reality a poet. True, the poets

of nineteenth century England were generally poor dramatists, but that was not the reason for driving the verse play from the stage. The public taste had been debauched, and then the debauched taste was pandered to on its lowest level. A play was produced with an eye on the box-office and the hope of a long run, and in the then existing state of the popular taste poetic drama could not satisfy these hopes and desires. Shakespeare might in his time have been satisfied with a week's run for a new play, and in 1728 when *The Beggar's Opera* ran for a month it could be regarded as an extraordinary achievement. But spectacular shows made the long run essential if theatre managers were to escape bankruptcy, and even with long runs they very often failed. The elaboration of scenery and its increasing cost, by making production expensive, retarded the advent of the newer drama. Ownership of the theatres, too, had some influence upon the kind of drama that was produced. When Drury Lane and Covent Garden theatres lost their monopoly in 1834 new theatres began to be built mainly by men who were in no way interested in the drama but entirely as commercial speculations. But beyond all these was, perhaps, the real reason for the departure of poetry from the English stage. Criticism of a scientific kind was beginning to make itself felt, and as a consequence changes in dramatic technique became inevitable. The researches of scholars such as Sir E. K. Chambers and Mr. W. J. Lawrence had shown the intimate connection of the form of the Elizabethan stage with the technique of the Elizabethan drama, and this suggested many changes. Dramatists were shown the reason for many stage conventions, and they saw why these conventions should be abandoned when the necessity for them no longer existed. They were given the materials from which new theories of drama might be constructed, and they were enabled to look beyond the heavy splendours of the stage spectacles of their time. They began to question whether drama could not be more effective upon a simple stage which would make a call upon the imaginative powers of audiences, and release the spoken word

from thraldom to scenery. The gorgeous stage effects of the
actor-manager might be questioned, but despite everything
to the contrary his influence and his traditions linger into this
second quarter of the twentieth century.

But perhaps the principal reason for the absence of poetic
drama was the fact that the age was itself essentially prosaic.
The nineteenth century in England was largely under the
sway of the economists and the utilitarian philosophers, and
the minds of men were very much concerned with the
emerging problems of sociology and the physical sciences.
The Industrial Revolution had been a revolution indeed. It
had changed the minds of men no less than the methods of
manufacture, and the great spectacular heroes were displaced
by the rise of the middle classes and the misery of the
proletariat. Even emperors and kings had been taught that
they must live and reign within the limits prescribed for them
by law. Laws and constitutions, economics and utilitarianism, are all horrible traps for the feet of poets whose thoughts,
and whose creations, might be disposed to defy not only the
laws but the very gods themselves. But when it has been
shown that material prosperity is dependent upon compliance
with the laws the good citizen is likely to be ruthlessly
opposed to the rebel whom he believes to be mad. So
Shelley and Tennyson, Browning and Swinburne, were each
and all failures in the theatre. The practical man had become
so hard-headed that he declined to take poetic drama
seriously ; and the poets had not yet accustomed themselves
to the changed social conditions. The poets had not yet
realised that men and women of heroic mould might be found
in coalmines or steelworks, in suburbs and in slums, no less
than on battlefields or duelling-grounds, in castles and
courts. Even to-day the poets have not completely realised
that the days of bloodthirsty monarchs have gone for ever,
and that romance now or in the future can have nothing to
do with them. The aspirations of the people have changed
fundamentally, so that in our day kings may blush to find their
fame. The Great War hastened the downfall of the old-time

conception of the hero, and probably no artificial respiration can ever revive it again. The swaggering, swashbuckling, bloody hero is now only a curiosity for the cinema, which audiences may study dispassionately and casually as they would study the specimens in a museum. The poets had not begun to recognise, much less to accept, the new conditions in the theatre or in the world ; they had not yet begun to ' sing the song of steam '. But the critics were beginning to see, and to tell the public, that to be a poet it was not necessary to write in verse.

The plays of Robertson had to some extent prepared the English theatre for the reception of a new technique. He had brought the middle classes, and even the workers, on to his stage without caricature or burlesque. But the great ' dramatist of the suburbs ', and portrayer of the average, had to come from abroad. Not in the petty adaptations which Grundy made from French comedies and farces, but from a country almost unknown for its drama. It is possible, even probable, that such a dramatist would have come out of England itself, or out of Ireland, in time, but his coming was anticipated by the emergence of Henrik Ibsen from Norway. With the coming of Ibsen begins the revival of the drama in Europe. He was destined to become the greatest force the theatre had known for centuries. Ibsen began his career as a dramatist in 1855 as the writer of historical and symbolical plays, and passed through his two great dramatic poems, *Brand* (1866) and *Peer Gynt* (1867), to that series of ethical and social dramas by which he first became known to the English-speaking peoples. In Ibsen the theatre discovered the master mind that it so badly needed, and the argument that raged about his plays aroused a new interest in the theatre. From 1869 to 1899 he wrote the series of plays for which he took his themes and his characters from his surroundings and from the life of his time. His technical novelties passed with little notice at the time because he focussed attention upon the ethical and social problems which were clamant for attention. Without in any way attempting to convert audiences to his views he roused their indignation through emotional experience.

The technical novelty consisted mainly in identifying action with exposition. " What we might have learned from Ibsen ", says Bernard Shaw, " was that our fashionable dramatic material was worn out so far as cultivated modern people are concerned : that what really interests such people on the stage is not what we call action—meaning two well-known rather short-sighted actors pretending to fight a duel without their glasses, or a handsome leading man chasing a beauteous leading lady round the stage with threats, obviously not feasible, of immediate rapine—but stories of lives, discussions of conduct, unveiling of motives, conflict of characters in talk, laying bare of souls, discovery of pitfalls— in short *illumination* of life." Ibsen illuminated life in the series of plays which began with *The League of Youth* in 1869 and ended with *The Master Builder* in 1892. In the ten plays which he wrote between those two dates he treated the major ethical, social, and political problems of the time, sometimes outraging feeling, sometimes smashing accepted opinion, but at all times presenting the problems in a new light. His own countrymen were somewhat scandalised by his plays, and for a considerable period Ibsen lived away from Norway, mainly in Italy. His detailed, illuminating, exposure of modern civilisation, with its venerable and sometimes out-worn conventions and institutions, its shallow ideals, its ready-made morality, its hypocrisy, weakness, and pettiness, was pitiless in exactitude. " My vocation is to question, not to answer ", he said. So he caught as in the air the thought-currents of revolt and gave them adequate expression. Of course he was attacked as an ' immoral ' writer, and only the blameless rectitude of his life could counter the charge. Truly was it said at the time that the drama could never be the same again since Ibsen had lived and written. But the English theatre as an institution was not ready to receive his work with enthusiasm.

The actor-managers had no place for the work of Ibsen, so

it became necessary to organise societies and to found theatres in which the ' new ' drama might be produced. The first sign of revolt against the organised theatre came from Paris when André Antoine founded the Théâtre Libre in 1887. Antoine did not found his theatre expressly for the purpose of producing the plays of Ibsen ; rather was it founded to provide the stage for the Naturalistic dramatists of France. The desire for change was manifest, and Antoine provided the younger dramatists of France with their opportunity. " It is Antoine's chief glory ", said Eugène Brieux at a later date, " to have felt this desire, and to have been the first to bring it to its full fruition. From the moment he made his first appearance in the obscure little theatre in the Passage de l'Elysée des Beaux-arts dramatists brought him plays in which they, too, had endeavoured to do away with the old conventions, and in which they tried to affect the men and women of their day through sincere work reflecting more clearly than ever before the life of their time. All these authors *existed*, no doubt, but their works were not produced, their manuscripts were not even read." As it was in France so was it also in England and in Germany ; the authors existed and wrote plays, but their plays were ignored, unread and unacted. The Théâtre Libre gave to the young drama-tists of France a chance of which they were glad to avail themselves to the fullest extent, and it introduced the work of many dramatists who afterwards achieved world-renown. But Antoine did more than that when he opened his little theatre ; he gave to Paris playgoers their first opportunity to become acquainted with the plays of Ibsen, Strindberg, Tolstoi, Hauptmann, Heijermanns, Björnsen, and Verga, thus bringing a new current of thought and ideas into the French theatre. In 1889 the example of Antoine was followed in Berlin by Otto Brahm who, in that year, founded the Free Stage Society, and in his theatre produced the work of such notable dramatists as Gerhart Hauptmann, Herman Sudermann, Otto Hartleben, Johannes Schlaf, and Arno Holz, for the first time, in addition to plays by such foreigners as

Ibsen, Zola, and Tolstoi. In 1891 London followed the example of Paris and Berlin when Mr. J. T. Grein founded his theatre of revolt under the name of The Independent Theatre. This theatre, too, wanted plays that were different from the plays of the theatre of commerce, and it got them mainly from Ibsen and Bernard Shaw, but it got plays also from George Moore and W. B. Yeats. In a letter to Mr. J. T. Grein Bernard Shaw thus summarised the achievements of The Independent Theatre : " It is now very close on 30 years since you madly began an apparently hopeless attempt the bring the English theatre into some sort of relation with contemporary culture. Matthew Arnold had suggested that step : but nobody in the theatre took the slightest notice of him, because nobody in the theatre knew of the existence of such a person as Matthew Arnold. . . . When you first desperately stuck an advertisement into the papers to say that an unheard-of enterprise called the Independent Theatre would on a certain Sunday night and Monday afternoon perform an unheard-of play. . . . When the paper thereon declared that the manager of the theatre ought to be prose-cuted for keeping a disorderly house, and that you and the foreign blackguard named Ibsen who was your accomplice, should be deported as obvious undesirables, you made a hole in the dyke ; and the weight of the flood outside did the rest. When you declared that you would bring to light treasures of unacted English drama grossly suppressed by the managers of that day, you found that there was not any unacted English drama except two acts of an unfinished play (begun and laid aside eight years before) by me ; but it was the existence of the Independent Theatre that made me finish that play. . . . Everything followed from that : the production of *Arms and the Man*. . . . Miss Horniman's establishment of Repertory Theatres in Dublin and Manchester, the Stage Society, Granville Barker's tentative matinees at the Court Theatre, the full-blown management of Vedrenne and Barker, Edie Craig's Pioneers, and the final relegation of the nineteenth century London Theatre to the dustbin by Barrie ".

As usual, Bernard Shaw both exaggerates and anticipates. It is true that the establishment of a Repertory Theatre in Dublin by Miss Horniman may be traced to the Independent Theatre, as the Independent Theatre itself may be traced to Antoine's Théâtre Libre, but there were other forces at work which were more intimately and immediately concerned with the theatre in Ireland. It will be borne in mind that both George Moore and W. B. Yeats were interested in the Independent Theatre. That Theatre produced Yeats' play *Land of Heart's Desire* for the first time in 1894, and George Moore's *Strike at Arlingford* in 1893. So the first plays of three Irish authors who were destined for world-fame were staged by the Independent Theatre in its first seasons. Shaw became immersed in his work as the champion of Ibsen and Ibsenism in England, and with his own plays of contemporary English life, and the foundation of an Irish Theatre was left to George Moore and W. B. Yeats. The realisation of the idea in the Irish Literary Theatre was mainly the work of W. B. Yeats alone.

While Free Theatres were being founded in Paris, London, and Berlin a new ferment of a very different kind had come into the life of Ireland. Parnell had died and politics had lost all attraction for the younger men, who now turned to-wards literature. The old-fashioned, somewhat patronising, Society for the Preservation of the Irish Language had given place to the Gaelic League, a more popular and virile body which had for its object the restoration of Irish as the spoken language of Ireland. The Gaelic League was founded in 1893 by a small group of scholars and poets of which Douglas Hyde, David Comyn, Father Eugene O'Growney, Eoin MacNeill, and T. O'Neill Russell were the most prominent members. Almost at once it attracted to itself all that was active and virile in Irish intellectual life. The Gaelic League struck a chord in the Irish temperament which had been very long ignored and neglected, and the response of the people was even more ready and enthusiastic than had been antici-pated. Throughout the nineteenth century the language of

Ireland had been left out of consideration by all sections of the community ; the politicians ignored it, the Church rather spurned it, the British Government kept it out of the schools, with the inevitable result that the language had almost ceased to be used by any considerable section of the people. Ireland was being Anglicised, was becoming, as the phrase of the time named it, West Britain, and it was felt that some desperate effort was needed to rescue the language from inevitable death. Attention was turned towards the Irish language as a medium for literature : Edward Martyn thought of writing his plays in Irish, and George Moore toyed with Irish as a possible way of escape from an English that was being cheapened and weakened by the growth of the popular press. Douglas Hyde published his *Love Songs of Connacht*, and *Religious Songs of Connacht*, in the original Irish with an English translation. The beauty of the English used in the translations brought the Irish idiom into literary English, and to this source may be traced much of the charm of dialogue which so captivated all who heard Irish actors in Irish plays during the first memorable season in London. An interest in literature was aroused, but it was still somewhat difficult to divorce literature from patriotic politics. Irish Literary Societies were founded in Dublin and in London : a library of Irish books was planned, and many volumes actually published, by a well-known London publisher ; and generally there was a distinct movement for what John Eglinton afterwards called ' The De-Davisisation of Irish Literature ', which meant the release of literature from political bias and a preoccupation with political patriotism. In this movement W. B. Yeats took an initiating and a leading part.

These Irish Literary Societies in Dublin and in London may be said to have had their origin in the Southwark Irish Literary Club, which was founded in 1883 as a literary and social centre for Irish people resident in London. Through its lectures and discussions this club revived interest in the work of many Irish writers, and by its ' original nights ' had

brought to light many new writers whose very existence had
been unsuspected. To the meetings of this Club had come
W. B. Yeats, Douglas Hyde, John Todhunter, and many
others whose work afterwards became familiar to the world
of letters. And from its ' original nights ' was born the idea
for the organisation of societies for the cultivation and spread
of Irish literature in the English language. As usual it was
W. B. Yeats who took the initiative, and at a meeting in his
house in London in 1891 it was decided to form Literary
Societies in London and Dublin. In 1892 these Societies
actually began to function. In the London Society was
gathered the best of the Irish poets of the time, Lionel
Johnson, Katherine Tynan, Alice Milligan, William Larminie,
John Todhunter, T. W. Rolleston, and Stopford Brooke. In
the membership of the Dublin Society was included the
names of W. B. Yeats, George Sigerson, Douglas Hyde,
Standish O'Grady, William Larminie, and many of the
younger men and women writers whose work was then
unknown outside a very narrow circle in Ireland. The
declared purpose of these Societies was to foster the growth of
a new and distinctively Irish literature in English, and to that
end it organised lectures and discussions on Irish literary
topics, aided the publication of the work of neglected Irish
writers, and gave opportunities to the younger writers who
were striving to have themselves heard. In 1893 Stopford
Brooke delivered the inaugural lecture to the London Society,
taking as his subject ' The Need and Use of getting Irish
Literature into the English Tongue.' In this lecture may be
found what amounts to a manifesto of what afterwards came
to be known as the Irish Literary Revival. He pointed out
that the use of English need not necessarily hamper the
expression of the Celtic spirit, nor interfere with the continuance of the Gaelic tradition. To ensure this, however, it was
essential that Irish writers should work upon the material left
to them by their Gaelic ancestors. Pointing to the work to
be done he mentioned the translation and publication of the
Gaelic texts, the moulding of the mythological cycles into

imaginative unities, the treatment in verse of the tales of the
ancient heroes, and the collection of Irish folk-tales and folk-
songs. The subsequent development of a distinctively Irish
literature in the English language, for a considerable time,
proceeded upon the lines suggested in this lecture. A society
was formed, in London, for the translation and publication
of the early Irish texts ; anthologies of poems translated from
Irish were compiled and published ; the heroic tales began
to be worked upon by poets and dramatists, and to be re-
moulded into connected narratives ; and there began that
systematic collection of folk-tales and folk-songs which still
continues with unabated vigour.

All this work had a very marked effect upon Irish literature and drama. Probably the most important, and deep,
influence upon the creation of the new Anglo-Irish literary
idiom, which was later to become so novel a feature of the
Irish drama when it first came to London, was Douglas Hyde,
a native of Roscommon and a graduate of Trinity College,
Dublin. He had been from his earliest years an enthusiast
for the revival of Irish as the spoken language of the Irish
people. He spoke to one of the Literary Societies on ' The
Necessity of De-Anglicising the Irish Nation ', and he was
sure that the Irish language was the only instrument by
which de-Anglicisation could be effected. But he also shared
Stopford Brooke's belief in the ' necessity for getting Irish
literature into the English tongue ' as a necessary preliminary
to the creation of a new Irish literature in either the Irish or
the English languages. So in addition to being one of the
founders of the Gaelic League he began the systematic
collection, translation, and publication of the folk-tales and
songs of the West of Ireland. His *Love Songs of Connacht*,
published in 1893, may be marked as the beginning of the
use of the Irish idiom in literary English. That idiom had
been always in use by Irish speakers of English ; it is said to
be the result of speaking in one language and thinking in
another, but its use is not by any means confined to bilingual
speakers, and it is just as likely to be encountered in speakers

whose native language is English. Douglas Hyde introduced that idiom into literary English, using it for the notes as well as the text of his works, with generally satisfactory, though sometimes monotonous, effects.

Another whose influence was great in those early days is Standish James O'Grady, sometimes called the Father of the Irish Literary Revival. He has a strong claim to the title if it could be conferred upon any one person, because it was his work that gave the first inspiring push to the young poets and dramatists to go to the past and to link themselves with the Gaelic literary tradition. Back to the Heroic Tales, said O'Grady in effect, and to aid in the return he wrote his famous *History of Ireland* (1878-1880), which is generally referred to as the *Bardic History*. The publication of this great work was undoubtedly an epoch-marking event in the literary history of modern Ireland, as from its pages came much of the inspiration of the younger school of poets which was just then about to come into being, but which would probably have taken a different direction had O'Grady's *Bardic History* not been available. In this work O'Grady undertook, as he says, " the reconstruction by imaginative processes of the life led by our ancestors in this country ", and he reduced to its artistic elements the heroic period of Irish history as it is revealed in the Bardic literature. The work has all the characteristics of an epic poem ; it is primitive in its energy, wide in its sweep, and Homeric in its simplicity. History and legend mingle with each other so that to O'Grady " Achilles and Troy appear somehow more real than Histoeus and Miletus ; Cuculain and Emain Macha than Brian Boromh and Kincorah ". So the gods and the demi-gods, the heroes and the kings of ancient Irish history and mythology come alive as the past lives again in these vigorously brilliant pages. Maeve, Fergus, and Ferdia ; Conchobar, Laeg, and Cuculain ; and, of course, Deirdre, were brought to new life for the Ireland of our day, and to give renewed inspiration to a school of Irish poets in the English tongue. *The Spectator* in reviewing the work called it a rich mine of the virgin poetry of Ireland, and asked " Why does not someone arise among them (the Irish) aspiring to do for these legends what Tennyson has done for the legends of King Arthur and the Knights of the Round Table ? " The answer was forthcoming in the work of such poets as W. B. Yeats, George W. Russell ('A.E.'), and a host of lesser writers, as it is still forthcoming in the brilliant work of Austin Clarke. But, curiously enough, with the solitary exception of Deirdre, the dramatists have done little to bring the heroic figures upon the stage. Yeats, Synge, Russell, and Trench, have all been attracted by Deirdre ; Martyn by Maeve ; Lady Gregory and George Moore by Grania ; and there the dramatisation of the heroic legends ended for all except W. B. Yeats. So in reality only the founders and beginners of the Irish dramatic movement may be counted as directly traceable to the work of Standish O'Grady. With the non-dramatic poets it is otherwise, and by them he might be claimed as father ; O'Grady brought to their ears again the authentic voice of heroic and pagan Ireland in a work of epic grandeur.

But all this literary stirring did not pass unnoticed by those to whom politics and patriotism were synonymous terms. From the days of Thomas Davis and the Young Irelanders of the 1840's Irish ' poetry ' had consisted mainly of politics in verse, and that ' de-Davisisation of Irish literature ' which was very desirable was not to be effected without challenge, and without a very severe struggle. Those who preferred literature to politics were labelled ' Decadents ' or ' Pagans ', and these labels may still be found clinging to the criticism of Irish literature which appears in some ultra-Catholic journals and periodicals in Ireland even to-day. But the victory of the newer school was never in doubt to its members and adherents, and as early as 1901 W. B. Yeats could say : " Now we see a new generation in Ireland which discusses Irish literature and history in Young Ireland Societies, and societies with newer names, and there are far more than when I was a boy who would make verses for the people. They have the help, too, of a vigorous journalism, and this journalism sometimes urges them to desire the direct logic, the clear rhetoric, of ' popular poetry '.   It sees that Ireland has no cultivated minority, and it does not see, though it would cast out all English things, that its literary ideal belongs more to England than to other countries. . . .   Among all that speak English in Australia, in America, in Great Britain, are there many more than the ten thousand the prophet saw, who have enough of the written tradition education has set in room of the unwritten to know good verses from bad ones, even though their mother-wit has made them Ministers of the Crown or what you will ? Nor can things be better till the ten thousand have gone hither and thither to preach their faith that ' imagination is the man himself ', and that the world as imagination sees it is the durable world, and have won men as did the disciples of Him who

> " His seventy disciples sent
>   Against religion and government."
>   (*Essays*, pp. 13, 14.)

Some of the ten thousand went forth and did good work, but the end of the Grand Crusade is not yet.

The Irish poets were given a hearing and a welcome, better perhaps in other countries than in their own, and the Irish School became a recognisably different thing, a new thing, among the literatures of the world. Some of these poets became dramatists also at a later stage. But sufficient for the time was it that there was a definite literary impulse, and a new literary idiom, in Ireland while at the same time there was a resurgence of the drama in Europe. Three of the Irish writers were interested in the resurgent drama no less than in a revival of Irish literature—W. B. Yeats, George Moore, and Edward Martyn. The three were known to each other, but it was Lady Gregory who was to bring them together for the common endeavour to found an Irish Theatre. Readers of Mr. Moore's *Hail and Farewell* will be familiar with the diverting details which that work contains about the common adventure, but as that excellent work was classed by its publisher as ' fiction ' it will be better to go to Lady Gregory for statements of fact. " I was in London in 1898 and I find written (in her diary) ' Yeats and Sir Alfred Lyall to tea, Yeats stayed on. He is very full of playwriting. . . . He with the aid of Miss Florence Farr, an actress who thinks more of a romantic than of a paying play, is keen about taking or building a little theatre somewhere in the suburbs to produce romantic drama, his own plays, Edward Martyn's, one of Bridges', and he is trying to stir up Standish O'Grady and Fiona Macleod to write some. He believes there will be a reaction after the realism of Ibsen, and romance will have its turn'." It will be remembered that Yeats's *Land of Heart's Desire* had been already produced in London by the Independent Theatre at the Avenue Theatre in 1894, so that this interest in the theatre and playwriting was no new thing. But Lady Gregory did not know Yeats very well at that time and she probably thought that the interest was only beginning. Later in the same year, 1898, as Lady Gregory recounts in *Our Irish Theatre*, she had a further talk with Mr. Yeats on the subject. " I said it was a pity we had no Irish theatre where such plays could be given. Mr. Yeats said that had always been a dream of his, but he had of late thought it an impossible one, for it could not at first pay its way, and there was no money to be found for such a thing in Ireland. We went on talking about it, and things seemed to grow possible as we talked, and before the end of the afternoon we had made our plan. We said we would collect money, or rather ask to have a certain sum of money guaranteed. We would then take a Dublin theatre and give a performance of Mr. Martyn's *The Heather Field* and one of Mr. Yeats's own plays, *The Countess Cathleen*."

So a letter was drafted and sent out asking for guarantees to the extent of £300. In the letter it was stated, " We propose to have performed in Dublin in the spring of every year certain Celtic and Irish plays, which whatever be their degree of excellence will be written with a high ambition, and so to build up a Celtic and Irish school of dramatic literature.

We hope to find in Ireland an uncorrupted and imaginative audience trained to listen by its passion for oratory, and believe that our desire to bring upon the stage the deeper thoughts and emotions of Ireland will ensure for us a tolerant welcome, and that freedom of experiment which is not found in theatres of England, and without which no new movement in art or literature can succeed. We will show that Ireland is not the home of buffoonery and of easy sentiment, as it has been represented, but the home of an ancient idealism. We are confident of the support of all Irish people, who are weary of misrepresentation, in carrying out a work that is outside all the political questions that divide us ". Political divisions presented no barrier to the securing of the necessary guarantees, people of all classes and opinions readily gave their support to the scheme, though it must be remarked that the Anglo-Irish, Unionist and ' garrison ', landlord class was most conspicuous. Among the supporters will be found Aubrey de Vere, who thought Home Rule might make Ireland less homely than Devon, and John O'Leary, the aged Fenian ; Lord Ardilaun and Tim Healy ; Professor W. E. H. Lecky and William O'Brien ; the Duchess of St. Albans and John Dillon ; Lord Dufferin and Douglas Hyde ; Professor Mahaffy and John Redmond ; with Sir Horace Plunkett, Sir Peter O'Brien (the ' Peter the Packer ' of Nationalist Ireland), Jane Barlow, Emily Lawless, and many others little less prominent in some branch of human activity. So it was really an Irish scheme, supported by all sections of politics in Ireland at the time. The guarantors were never called upon to make any payment, as Mr. Edward Martyn defrayed all the initial expenses of the venture out of his own pocket. But the demonstration of active support, and faith in the feasibility of the scheme, was as welcome as it must have been unexpected. When it is remembered what the political divisions were in Ireland in 1898, and the bitterness of the personal animosities in Irish politics at the time, the support which was accorded to Lady Gregory and her fellow-venturers was little short of marvellous.

The necessary financial support having been assured a
further difficulty then presented itself. It was found
impossible to secure a Dublin theatre at the time required,
or at a sufficiently low price. There were then three theatres
in the city, but all were booked far ahead, as the promoters
would have known had they been experienced in theatrical
affairs. The Queen's specialised in Boucicaultian melodrama,
the Gaiety in musical comedy and the like, the Royal in
' straight ' plays and grand opera. Only the Gaiety remains
as it was thirty years ago, but it now takes ' straight ' drama
since the Royal has gone over to twice nightly variety shows.
This new difficulty in securing a theatre made resort to some
other device necessary. It was suggested that a society,
similar to the Stage Society, should be formed to give performances only for its members, but this suggestion was
rejected as unworthy of the beginnings of what was hoped
and believed would develop into a National Theatre. There
remained only the alternative of unlicensed halls, of which
there were many. Fortunately, just at that time the Irish
Local Government Bill was before the House of Commons
and Irish Members of all parties aided in securing its amend-
ment so as to empower the Lord Lieutenant " on the application of the Council for the County of Dublin or the County
Borough of Dublin to grant an occasional licence for the
performance of any stage play in any theatre, room, or
building " when the profits accruing were to be devoted to
public or philanthropic uses. So the first performance of the
Irish Literary Theatre was announced for 8th May, 1899, at
the Ancient Concert Rooms in Great Brunswick Street,
Dublin. The title of the enterprise was Mr. Martyn's, the
scheme was a modification of Mr. Yeats's original proposal
to Lady Gregory in London, the actual organising work was
mainly Lady Gregory's, and the assistance of Mr. George
Moore was sought and secured to assemble the company and
conduct the rehearsals in London.

The plays selected for the first performance were those
mentioned in the conversation which Lady Gregory had with

Mr. Yeats in her home in Galway the previous year, *The Heather Field* and *The Countess Cathleen*. *The Countess Cathleen* shocked Dublin and was the occasion of uproarious behaviour on the part of a section of the audience at its first performance. The play was attacked in a pamphlet entitled *Souls for Gold*, which had been extensively circulated before the performance, as being anti-Irish and anti-Catholic. There was no point in the attack, as the play shows only self-sacrifice of the noblest kind. But indignation had been aroused, and the noisy behaviour of the audiences concentrated attention upon the play and the venture of which it was a part. Young men from the University College were exhorted to attend at the Ancient Concert Rooms and make protest against ' this insult to their faith '. They went and protested to such an extent that the assistance of the police had to be secured. The police lined the gallery, and so the Irish Literary Theatre started its career under that most ill-omened thing in the Ireland of its day—police protection. But the critics who had been sent over by the London press, including Max Beerbohm, were generous in their praise, and this, perhaps, was some little compensation to the English actors and actresses who failed to gather what all the fuss was about. The mind of Mr. Martyn, too, had been disturbed by the suggestion that the play was anti-Catholic. He was a very orthodox, and a very fervent, Catholic, and the suggestion that he would be connected with anything which could be termed anti-Catholic affected him deeply. So his mind had to be eased, and it was only after the play had been submitted to, and passed by, a literary Catholic canon in England that his doubts were set at rest. The English may, as has been suggested, take their pleasures sadly, but it is long since they have taken their theatre seriously enough to be riotous about it. In Ireland things are different, and a riot in the theatre is always one of the possibilities.

In 1900 an English company was again brought to Dublin to produce three plays at the Gaiety Theatre. The plays selected were *Maeve*, by Edward Martyn, *The Bending of the*

Bough, by George Moore, and *The Last Feast of the Fianna*, by Alice Milligan. This time there was no disturbance, instead an enthusiastic audience greeted the plays and players. So pleased were the members of the company that they said they had never played to such an appreciative audience. They were, however, somewhat puzzled by bursts of applause at odd moments during the progress of the plays ; they were all ignorant of Irish history and politics, and consequently did not understand that what the audience cheered were invariably political allusions. George Moore's play was the first Irish play to deal with a vital problem of public affairs, a matter of political importance, and it was expected to cause some commotion. Moore himself thought it would cause a revolution, because no one could leave the theatre with the same ideas with which he had entered. In this he was disappointed ; the play caused no commotion, and though the revolution has been caused Moore's play was quickly forgotten. The honours of the evening went to Edward Martyn : *Maeve* simply captivated the audience, and its political suggestiveness gave it a topical savour which is never quite absent from Irish historical plays. And Ireland was very definitely patriotically Irish during the Boer War ! This was Martyn's only theatrical triumph. His heart was in the theatre, and he hoped to make a name for himself as a dramatist, but he was not destined to repeat this one great evening of unalloyed success.

For the third season in 1901 the work was undertaken by Sir Frank Benson's company, which produced *Diarmuid and Grania*, by George Moore and W. B. Yeats, at the Gaiety Theatre. This play has never been published and is now quite forgotten, but the evening of its production, 21st October, 1901, was made for ever memorable by the production of another play which ended a long silence and marked the opening of a new era. The event was the first production on any stage of a play in the Irish language, *Casad-an-Sugan* (*The Twisting of the Rope*), by Douglas Hyde. The principal part was acted by Dr. Hyde himself, and the entire company

consisted of Dublin amateurs.   This was the last occasion
upon which English actors appeared in any of the plays of the
new Irish theatre.   They had given many fine performances,
and had done much to give the enterprise a good start, but
it had always been felt that an Irish theatre could never really
be founded until there were competent Irish actors available.
Bernard Shaw had said in 1897 to the Irish Literary Society in
London, " and as to saying there are good Irish actors, there
are not, and there won't be until the conditions in Ireland
are favourable for the production of drama ".   It might be
thought that conditions in Ireland in 1901 were not very
favourable for the production of either drama or actors, but,
as the event was to prove, both were actually available and
both were of very high quality.

   It happened that there were then two brothers in Dublin
who were passionately fond of the theatre, and who both had
a genius for acting.   One was a comedian, and the other had
a marked predilection for verse plays.   They are both now
well known throughout the world ;   their names are Frank
and William Fay.   Frank Fay is now in Dublin again conducting a school of elocution and acting, while William
(W.G.) is the producer at the Birmingham Repertory Theatre.
George W. Russell ('A.E.') had discovered these two young
men, or rather they had discovered him by going to him and
asking that he should write a play for a small company of
amateur actors with which they were connected.   'A.E.'
agreed to write the play, and shortly afterwards he gave them
his *Deirdre*, and brought W. B. Yeats to see the company at
rehearsal.   From this meeting Yeats came away with an
admiration for the brothers Fay which induced him to give
them his *Kathleen ni Houlihan* for production by their company.   Thus it came about that on the 2nd April, 1902, the
Irish National Dramatic Company presented these two plays
at the Saint Teresa's Hall, Clarendon Street, Dublin.   This
performance marks the real beginning of the Irish National
Theatre :   for the first time the plays were written by Irish
playwrights, acted by an Irish company, and staged by an Irish

producer. Later in the same year another play by Mr. Yeats
was presented by the company, but 'A.E.' has never since
written the second play to which all eagerly looked forward.
During the year six plays were produced by the company,
and in 1903 it gave two plays by Mr. Yeats, and the first plays
of Lady Gregory, Padraic Colum, and John Millington Synge.
In May 1903 the company went to London for the first time,
and there caused something of a sensation. The acting no
less than the plays made such an impression on the critics
that the visit was easily the theatrical event of the year. The
unconventionality of the acting, in marked contrast to that
of the prevailing English school, and the sombre brilliance
of Synge's first play made such an impression that one critic
said they came like a refreshing breeze to jaded London.
The visit was a triumph for the young Irish players, and the
very fact that they could so impress the leading dramatic
critics of London strengthened their confidence and matured
their art. But that London visit did more for the Irish drama
than was at first anticipated, for it brought the company under
the notice of Miss A. E. F. Horniman, the Queen of Repertory
as Mr. Frank Vernon has so justly titled her, and the interest
which she afterwards took in the Irish theatre makes an
important contribution to the history of twentieth century
drama.

All the influences which had gone to bring the Irish drama
and the Irish theatre into being had at last met in convergence.
The impulse that had revived the drama in Europe had come
from Christiania (Oslo). It had affected Paris and Berlin, and
had given London that Independent Theatre from which all
that is notable in contemporary English drama may be said
to have sprung. It moulded the dream of an Irish poet in
London, and it inspired him to direct the disillusioned
enthusiasm of his compatriots towards dramatic literature
rather than towards the barrenness of political personalities
in the Ireland of their time. But in Ireland itself a new life
was stirring and a cultural ideal was being born in the work
of the Gaelic League. With all Irish cultural activities W. B.

Yeats had contact. His idea of ' a little theatre somewhere in the suburbs ' of London where romantic plays could be given was localised and made Irish by the plans of Lady Gregory, and the financial support of her friends. So the Irish Literary Theatre came into being. And when George Russell ('A.E.') brought Mr. Yeats into contact with the brothers Fay the Irish National Dramatic Company was formed of Irish actors. The visit to London was to provide the company with a permanent home in the Abbey Theatre, which was provided by the generosity of Miss A. E. F. Horniman. Curious that in this stream of causes the practical persons should be women, and the dreamers men. To Lady Gregory first, and to Miss Horniman in only slightly lesser degree, must go the credit for the Irish Theatre. They made it possible, but to W. B. Yeats, George Moore, Edward Martyn, George Russell ('A.E.'), and the brothers Frank and William Fay much of the credit must also be given.

> They shall be remembered for ever,
> They shall be alive for ever.

CHAPTER III

THE FOUNDERS AND THEIR IDEALS

(*a*) W. B. Yeats. (*b*) Lady A. Gregory. (*c*) Edward Martyn. (*d*) George Moore.

(*a*) W. B. YEATS

WHEN W. B. Yeats discussed his theatrical ambitions with Lady Gregory for the first time, in the early part of 1898, it will be remembered that he was thinking of ' taking or building a little theatre somewhere in the suburbs ' of London where romantic plays could be acted and fine words be spoken finely. It might have been the ideal of any London poet of the time, of any one of the young poets of the Rhymers' Club of which Mr. Yeats was a member. There was nothing distinctively Irish in the ideal, and it would seem that for the moment Ireland and its literary regeneration had been forgotten by the man who had undertaken to bring Ireland back into European letters. The fact is that there were two W. B. Yeats's : one was a fastidious poet and an artist of distinction : the other was a patriot and something of a politician. Irish patriotism was novel to Mr. Yeats, for despite his Irish birth he was probably less Irish in sympathy and outlook than his friend Lionel Johnson who was English, and born in England. It is true that Mr. Yeats had been to school in Dublin, and that before he disclosed his ambitions to Lady Gregory in her London drawing-room he had written and edited much that was Irish or of Irish interest. He had met, and been captivated by, John O'Leary, had contributed to the Parnellite paper, *United Ireland*, was a foundation-member of the Irish Literary Societies, and on intimate terms with the leading Irish literary and political personalities of the time. But despite all these connections it is probable that at the time Mr. Yeats was no more deeply attached to Ireland than was his friend Mr. George Moore. A latent attachment there certainly was, the love of Sligo and the peasant lore of its people, which suggestion and opportunity were to develop later into the dominating influence of the second half of his literary life. He had discovered the romance of the ships and people of Sligo when he had lived with his grandparents as a little boy, and the discovery had made an abiding impression on a particularly sensitive mind. He had read his Spenser and his Shelley on the Hill of Howth that overlooks the beautiful Bay of Dublin. It was in Dublin, too, that he had begun his studies in mysticism, and that his first youthful verses had received the praises of Edward Dowden. It was the company he had met in Dublin that had sent him to the study of Irish history and mythology, which gave him an heroic, and somewhat romantic, conception of Irish Nationality and Irish Nationalist politics. Possibly the personalities rather than the principles were in the beginning the great attracting force, because it is still a matter of doubt and dispute whether Mr. Yeats is politically an Irish Nationalist at all. But, meanwhile, he had to earn a livelihood in London, and it was there that his literary ideals had been formed and his genius first recognised.

Bernard Shaw has made two statements about Ireland which will aid in an understanding of Mr. Yeats. " The Church of Ireland was not so much a religion as a side in politics " ; and " I am a typical Irishman, my family came from Hampshire ". The family of W. B. Yeats was a Church of Ireland clerical family, and his mother's people had come from Cornwall. He was born in Dublin in 1865, his father being John B. Yeats the celebrated portrait painter, and his mother a member of the Pollexfen family of Sligo. The name is certainly not Irish, but Mr. Yeats's great-grandfather had been a Church of Ireland rector in Sligo, and his grandfather a rector in the County Down. His Pollexfen great-grandfather had come from Cornwall and had established a prosperous shipping and milling business in Sligo. Thus both of his parents had connections with Sligo, and it is that county which forms the background for his earliest recollections, and provides the material for some of his most beautiful, as also some of his most popular, poems. Mr. Yeats's father spent much of his life out of Ireland ; the earlier part of it was lived in London, and the later in New York, where he died in 1922. The outlook of John B. Yeats seems to have been entirely English, tempered only by the belief that the artistic creativeness of the English was worn out and that Ireland would be the new home of the arts in the British Isles. He had also a great admiration for Isaac Butt, the founder of the Home Rule Movement and the first leader of an Irish Nationalist Party in the British House of Commons. This admiration distinguished him from the majority of his class and creed in Ireland ; that majority was Unionist in politics and definitely anti-Irish in sympathy and outlook. " The artist inculcates no lesson and preaches no dogma"; wrote John B. Yeats in his essay *The Rationale of Art*, " yet often the noble become more noble for his companionship." This artistic creed of the father has been the creed of the son ; he has preached it and demonstrated it on every possible occasion as a poet, a dramatist, a propagandist, or, more recently, a politician. If the Irish bias of his father was slight the English bias of his grandfather's house in Sligo was also slight though more marked. " I had a little flagstaff in front of the house ", he writes in *Reveries* (page 15), " and a red flag with a Union Jack in the corner." This flag he floated from its staff every day, and its appearance must have given opportunities for some bitter comments from the country-people. For the Union Jack in the Ireland of the 1870's was no beloved emblem ; it was the flag of a party, of a ' side in politics ', the emblem of an alien race and a tyrannical Government. And at the time that the young W. B. Yeats was flaunting his Union Jack the man who had tried to break its power in Ireland, and who was afterwards to exercise such power over the poet's mind, John O'Leary, was serving his sentence as a prisoner of the British Govern-

ment. In that Sligo household there was a stable-boy who
" had a book of Orange rhymes, and the days when we read
them together in the hayloft gave me the pleasure of rhyme
for the first time. Later on I can remember being told, when
there was a rumour of a Fenian rising, that rifles had been
served out to the Orangemen, and presently, when I had
begun to dream of my future life, I thought I would like to
die fighting the Fenians " (*Reveries*, page 20). There was
nothing extraordinary about this childish dream ; it was the
everyday dream of every child of the class and creed to which
he belonged in the Ireland of the time. When he went to
school in London the dream may have faded, and when,
later, he mingled in the Dublin Metropolitan School of Art
with Fenians and the sons of Fenians the fear which had
conditioned the dream may have been banished for ever. In
the School of Art he made the acquaintance of George W.
Russell ('A.E.'), and began that intimate association which
has influenced contemporary Irish literature so much. In
1887 the Yeats family returned to London, and there W. B.
Yeats began to edit books about Ireland, such as his *Irish
Fairy and Folk Tales* and other collections of stories, for
London publishers, but his literary career had really begun
with the publication of *Mosada* in Dublin in 1886.

The early work of Mr. Yeats was not distinctively Irish
either in theme or in form. *Mosada* has its setting in Spain,
but he says himself that he preferred 'Arcadia and the India
of romance '. It seems to have been in London between 1886
and 1891 that Mr. Yeats began to meditate upon Ireland and
to be attracted by it, as between these dates ' the common
thought of the people ', of Sligo perhaps, began to colour,
and even to be the theme of, his poems. Some of his best
known poems were written during these years. In 1891 he
was back again in Dublin for a time, and he merged himself
in the storm that raged about the personality of Charles
Stewart Parnell ; it may be that he found the theme of his
Countess Cathleen in that epic struggle. He contributed to
the Parnellite organ *United Ireland*, and became acquainted

with the leading personalities, including Miss Anna Parnell and Miss Maud Gonne. It seems to have been about this time that he met John O'Leary, that noble man who had been sentenced to twenty years penal servitude for his part in the Fenian Rising of 1867, but who had been released after serving three years on condition that he lived abroad for the remainder of the term. He had spent the time in Paris but had returned to end his days in Ireland, where he died in 1905 without taking any further part in Irish politics. He took no active part in politics, but he was a most potent influence upon the leaders of the Sinn Fein Movement who were his friends and admirers. What Mr. Yeats says of Thomas Davis, O'Leary's teacher and prophet, applies with equal relevance to O'Leary himself : " All who fell under his influence took this thought from his precept and his example : we struggle for a nation, not for a party, and our political opponents who have served Ireland in some other way may, perhaps, be better patriots " (*New Ireland*, 17th July, 1915). From this time onward everything that he undertook had some thought for Ireland, and it was all conditioned and coloured by the influence of John O'Leary. " He belonged to the romantic conception of Irish Nationality on which Lionel Johnson and myself founded, so far as it was founded on anything but literature, our Art and our Irish criticism. . . . I learned much from him . . . and that ideal Ireland, perhaps from this out an imaginary Ireland, in whose service I labour will always be in essentials (his) Ireland." He was one of " the last to speak an understanding of life and Nationality, built upon the generation of Grattan, which read Homer and Virgil, and by the generation of Davis, which had been pierced through by the idealism of Mazzini, and of the European revolutionists of the mid-century " (*Essays*, pp. 304, 305). But Arthur Griffith carried the tradition of Davis, and Padraic Pearse the philosophy of O'Leary, into our own days, so that when Mr. Yeats wrote in *September* 1913,

Romantic Ireland's dead and gone,
It's with O'Leary in the grave,

he had failed to recognise the strength and influence of these two men, and the numbers of their followers. But at Easter 1916 they demonstrated that romantic Ireland was not dead and gone, as they rose in defiance of counsels of prudence, and attacking the might of the British Empire, then prepared for the greatest effort of its history, they proclaimed an Irish Republic which they knew could never be made a reality in world politics.

But the patriotism of Mr. Yeats was always subservient to his art. Had he not been one of the so-called ' decadents ' in the London of the ' 90's ' ? And had he not with them accepted as his motto 'Art for Art's Sake ' ? He had attacked Irish ' patriotic poetry ', and the counter-attack which he provoked has been so bitter and so prolonged that it has hardly ended yet. " Our attacks, more especially, on verse which owed its position to its moral or political worth, roused a resentment which even I find it hard to imagine to-day, and our verse was attacked in return, and not for anything peculiar to ourselves, but for all that it had in common with the accepted poetry of the world, and most of all for its lack of rhetoric, its refusal to preach a doctrine or to consider the seeming necessities of a cause " (*Essays*, p. 317). So he had " set to work to find a style and things to write about that the ballad writers might be the better". But the ballad-makers were none the better for his efforts, they were merely encouraged to write against Mr. Yeats and against everything for which they thought he stood. When he had desired to cultivate the best they made jests for the worst.

The literary tradition of Ireland, in so far as there may be said to have been any literary tradition at all, was, and still is largely, oral rather than written. The Irish people do not read very much, and when they do read it is mainly the newspapers. There is little bookish tradition such as may be found in European countries with a Latin culture, or such as now exists in the industrial civilisation of England and the United States. Irish people will listen for hours, but they will not read for minutes. So audiences will be found for

ballad-singers, story-tellers, and political orators ; for the
circus, the concert, or the drama ; for anything with action
and speech in it. But readers in Ireland are rare. The gradual
organisation of a library system throughout the country,
under the auspices of the Carnegie Trust and with the aid of
local governing bodies, may produce a change in time, as it
is making the people familiar with books and making the
written word of greater significance than that which is spoken.
But the written word is of small significance to the poet.
Verse is intended to be spoken, and the poets have little
cause to grumble when their books of verse are not read.
Perhaps the radio will bring back poetry to the hearts and ears
of the multitude by bringing recitation to the hearth instead
of doling it out in slim volumes over the counters of the
booksellers. Mr. Yeats has always maintained that his verse
should be spoken, and he has given considerable attention to
methods of speaking verse in general and his own verse in
particular. " Since I was a boy ", he wrote in 1907 (*Essays*,
p. 16), " I have always longed to hear poems spoken to a harp,
as I imagined Homer to have spoken his, for it is not natural
to enjoy an art only when one is by oneself. Whenever one
finds ·a fine verse one wants to read it to somebody, and it
would be much less trouble and much pleasanter if we could
all listen, friend by friend, lover by beloved ". Much of his
time and thought had been given to the proper speaking of
verse before he discovered his ideal in Miss Florence Farr, a
London actress of considerable repute and attainments. Of
Miss Farr's method of speaking verse he says, " I have just
heard a poem spoken with so delicate a sense of its rhythm,
with so perfect a respect for its meaning, that if I were a wise
man and could persuade a few people to learn the art I would
never open a book of verses again " (*Essays*, p. 15). As the
Irish people did not read, and as the art of speaking verse
seemed to be lost in England, a poet who desired to reach the
people, of Ireland first but others also, had to do something
almost desperate to reach its ears. That few people had to be
persuaded to learn the art of speaking verse ; and an audience

had to be found for them when they had learned it. Obviously a theatre had to be founded, as only in the theatre could verse be spoken finely to an audience consisting of ' friend by friend, lover by beloved '. So the foundation of a theatre was decided upon by Mr. Yeats, and as the ideal speaker of verse had been discovered in London, the theatre had to be founded in that city. Hence that ' little theatre somewhere in the suburbs ' of London in the management and control of which Miss Farr was mentioned to Lady Gregory as likely to participate.

But Mr. Yeats also held strongly to the opinion that cities were destructive to the arts of the drama. " The drama has need of cities ", he said in 1899 (*Essays*, p. 206), " that it may find men in sufficient numbers, and cities destroy the emotion to which it appeals, and therefore the days of the drama are brief and come but seldom. It has one day when the emotions of cities still remember the emotions of sailors and husband-men and shepherds and users of the spear and the bow ; as the houses and furniture and earthen vessels of cities, before the coming of machinery, remember the rocks and the woods and the hillsides ; and it has another day, now beginning, when thought and scholarship discover their desire. In the first day it is the Art of the people ; and in the second day, like the dramas acted of old times in the hidden places of temples, it is the preparation of a Priesthood. It may be, though the world is not old enough to show us any example, that this Priesthood will spread their Religion everywhere, and make their Art the Art of the People." Mr. Yeats would have drama return to the primitive emotions, and to the music of words, which is, like all intellectual emotions, exhausting. Acting, too, would have to return to a sophis-ticated simplicity. Actors spoke " as if they were reading something out of the newspapers. They forgot the noble art of oratory, and gave all their thought to the poor art of acting, that is content with the sympathy of the nerves ". Thus, he held, it was not so much that the contemporary poets of England were undramatic, but that the audiences of cities, and of an industrial and urban civilisation, had lost contact with those simple emotions which alone produce great drama; and that the actors who played before such audiences had become incapable of declaiming verse as it should be declaimed. " Mr. Swinburne's *Locrine* was acted a month ago (April 1899), and it was not badly acted, but nobody could tell whether it was fit for the stage or not, for not one rhythm, not one cry of passion, was spoken with a musical emphasis, and verse spoken without a musical emphasis seems but an artificial and cumbersome way of saying what might be said naturally and simply in prose " (*Essays*, pp. 207, 208). The comment of the average Londoner of the late nineties could hardly have been more completely put. Verse to such an audience did seem but a stilted, unnatural, and affected way of saying what could more plainly and simply be said in prose. But musical emphasis, and rhythm, are not in themselves enough for an audience that demanded above all else ' plain English '. As Mr. Yeats himself very plainly foresaw when he wrote (*Essays*, p. 209) : " Even if poetry were spoken as poetry, it would still seem out of place in many of its highest moments upon a stage, where the superficial appearances of nature are so closely copied ; for poetry is founded upon convention, and becomes incredible the moment painting or gesture reminds us that people do not speak verse when they meet upon the highway. The theatre of Art, when it comes to exist, must therefore discover grave and decorative gestures, such as delighted Rossetti and Madox Brown, and grave and decorative scenery, that will be forgotten the moment the actor has said ' It is dawn ', or ' It is raining ', or ' The wind is shaking the trees ' ; and dresses of so little irrelevant magnificence that the mortal actors and actresses may change without much labour into the immortal people of romance. The theatre began in ritual, and it cannot come to its greatness again without recalling words to their ancient sovereignty." Such a theatre, in the conditions of the late nineteenth and early twentieth centuries, could appeal to only a few people, and Mr. Yeats often seems to be contradictory when he speaks of an art for the people which is to be so elaborate and so sophisticated that it could only appeal to a very small and highly cultured section of a highly cultured community. It was an attempt to elaborate the ' folk ' in terms of the pre-Raphaelite teaching ; an attempt to say that the gestures of the uncultivated were ' grave and decorative ', while those of the cultivated urbanites were crude and gauche. In a word, it was the reaction of a very sensitive nature against the mechanisation of society, a mechanisation which threatened the arts and all the gracious things of life, but what everyone thought of as ' civilisation ' and ' progress '. But time and tide have been against Mr. Yeats, as they were against the pre-Raphaelites, and the mechanisation has not only gone on, it has gone much farther and much faster.

Even Western Ireland is still pretty much as it was thirty years ago, though there, too, mechanical civilisation is having its way. When Mr. Shaw placed his oracle in Galway (in *Back to Methuselah*) he was merely suggesting what seems likely to be an historical fact, oracles are likely to have their end there. Western Ireland is not all romance, as the novels of Lian O'Flaherty are now showing to a rather surprised world, but it was romance to one who had the culture of England and who was in the way of becoming ' more Irish than the Irish themselves ', as is the way of such people when once they succumb to the lure. So Mr. Yeats could say in 1899, " Mr. Bridges' *Return of Ulysses*, one of the most beautiful, and, as I think, dramatic of modern plays, might have some success in the Aran Islands, if the Gaelic League would translate it into Gaelic, but I am quite certain that it would have no success in the Strand " (*Essays*, p. 206). So " why should we thrust our works, which we have written with imaginative sincerity and filled with spiritual desire, before these quite excellent people who think that Rossetti's women are ' guys ', that Rodin's women are ' ugly ', and that Ibsen is ' immoral ', and who only want to be left at peace to enjoy the works so many clever men have made especially to suit them ? We must make a theatre for ourselves and our friends, and for a few simple people who understand from sheer simplicity what we understand from scholarship and thought. We have planned the Irish Literary Theatre with this hospitable emotion, and, that the right people may find out about us, we hope to act a play or two in the spring of every year ; and that the right people may escape the stupefying memory of the theatre of commerce which clings even to them, our plays will be for the most part remote, spiritual, and ideal " (*Essays*, p. 204). It will suffice to say that Ibsen is still regarded as ' immoral ' in Ireland, and that the plays which have been written in Ireland as the result of Mr. Yeats' efforts to found a theatre have generally been anything but ' remote, spiritual, and ideal '. Only his own plays have been written to his own requirements, and he has had no followers, nor has he founded a school. But his hopes were high thirty years ago, more high perhaps than they are to-day, and he enthused and energised a great experiment in dramatic art which, if it did not quite live up to his hopes and expectations, at least brought his country into the stream of European drama. In his artistic effort he failed, but in his patriotism the work has more than justified him. His patriotic ideal lives though he may now occasionally rend those who keep it living.

(b) LADY GREGORY

It was Lady Augusta Gregory who gave to the dreams and aspirations of W. B. Yeats and Edward Martyn for the creation of a literary theatre the practical shape which they seemed unable to give to them themselves. It was she who suggested the start of a literary theatre in Ireland, as it was she who secured the interest of her very large and influential circle of friends and acquaintances for the project. Yet it is somewhat strange that up to the time when she suggested this definite step, and undertook a large part of the organising work, she had never taken more than a passing and purely recreational interest in the drama or the theatre. Her husband, Sir William Gregory, had been an important official of the British Government ; he had been a Colonial Governor who had a knowledge of, and an interest in, art, which secured for him a Governorship of the National Gallery in London. In this way Lady Gregory had become intimately associated with the higher branches of the British political and diplomatic services, and with the literary and artistic society of London. These associations brought her into contact with all the important personalities of London life towards the end of the nineteenth century, and it was in this circle of acquaintances that she first met the young poet W. B. Yeats. She seems to have become deeply interested in his work almost from the first, and it was that interest, particularly in the verse plays, that brought Lady Gregory into the theatre where she was destined to become such a force, and such a leading personality. " The plays that I have cared for most all through, and for love of which I took up this work, are those verse ones by Mr. Yeats " (*Our Irish Theatre*, p. 78). So when Mr. Yeats is credited, as he rightly is, with the discovery and encouragement of J. M. Synge he must also be credited with the bringing of Lady Gregory into the theatre, and with some share, be it ever so little, of the gratitude which the people of Ireland owe to Lady Gregory for the self-sacrificing and nationally significant work which she has been doing for the past thirty years. Had Lady Gregory never become interested in the verse plays of Mr. Yeats the Irish Theatre and the Irish Drama might never have been ; Ireland might still have been without a national drama, the theatre of the world would have been without that spicily bitter drama which is the Irish contribution to its stage, and the long list of plays which Lady Gregory herself has contributed would never have been written.

But long before she had any interest in the verse plays of Mr. Yeats Lady Gregory had been in love with the peasantry of her native county of Galway, and that love was deeper as it was longer. She was born at Roxborough, County Galway, in 1859, a member of that Persse family which has given so many notable personalities to both England and Ireland.

The family was of English extraction, its culture was English, and its outlook and sympathies were English as its politics were Unionist. Her near neighbour was Edward Martyn who lived at Tillyra Castle, and a little more distant, at Moore Hall in the County Mayo, lived George Moore. Thus it will be noted that all the four founders of the Irish Literary Theatre, and of the national drama which derived from that Theatre, were intimately associated by birth or family ties with the province of Connacht. Of the four two were members of Catholic families, and two of Protestant ; but all four were of the Anglo-Irish rather than the Gaelic tradition, though doubtless there was considerable Gaelic blood intermixed with the original English or Norman. Connacht is very mixed in its blood, but it is nevertheless still the most Gaelic in thought and speech of the four provinces of Ireland. It is possible that Oliver Cromwell is responsible for this Gaelic survival, as it was he who offered Connacht to the people of the other provinces as an alternative to Hell. And the alternative is not so far-fetched as it may seem at first glance. Connacht is still as it was in Cromwell's time the wildest and the poorest of the Irish provinces ; it is awesome in the wild grandeur of its mountains and stony plains, its lakes, rivers, and castles, but is also pathetic in the squalid poverty of its people. It is a veritable paradise to the artist, but it is as veritably a hell to the social reformer and the statesman. The painter delights in its scenery, the poet revels in the wild and vividly-coloured phraseology of the people, the fisherman finds all he ever dreamed of in its rivers and lakes, but to the statesman and the sociologist Connacht is simply a ' congested district ', that is, not a densely populated district as might be supposed, but simply a place where the land is not fertile enough to provide sustenance and livelihood for the people who try to live upon it. Its scenic splendour and its poverty-ridden inhabitants are both primitive, recalling and realising for the twentieth century a time when the world was young and the slimy mark of the city had not been laid upon the civilisation of Europe.

So far as Connacht is concerned Greece and Rome might not have been, and the Industrial Revolution has only touched it to make it poorer.   Its chief cities, Galway and Sligo, were once great social and commercial centres ; great trading cities and shipping ports for the commerce of Ireland with Spain and continental Europe.   They are now but slovenly provincial market-towns dependent upon the fairs and petty trading of poor farmers ; they are but ghosts of their former selves, serving as disturbing memories of a great and prosperous past that has gone, maybe for ever.   So Connacht is a province of memories, as Leinster, Munster, and Ulster are provinces of hopes.   In Connacht the past still lives and is still vivid in speech, in stone, and in misery ; there the old stories linger and the old songs are sung, and the old customs are followed, in an environment that has changed but little in five hundred years.   Revolutions, social, political, industrial, and economic, have passed it by, leaving it with bitter memories of the east and with its hopes centred in the west. But the intellect of Connacht is still young and eager, as its speech is still quick and coloured, with a gravity and a sonority that newspapers and national schools have combined to take from the English of other places.   It can be easily and readily understood, then, why the new Irish literature in English should have begun in Connacht, as it can also be readily understood why the writers have not come directly from the old Gaelic stock.   This new literature is the impact of one civilisation upon the cultured people of another, and a different, civilisation.   To the Anglo-Irish landed ' gentry ' the life of the people about them presented a strangeness that was irresistibly attractive, and the four founders of the Irish Literary Theatre had all lived with and understood the strange attraction.   They sympathised with it and it became a part of themselves.

Lady Gregory has lived among the peasantry of her native Galway for the greater part of her life, and never has she been away from it for any very prolonged period.   In her early life she was attracted by the folk-stories and the folk-songs of the cottagers, and she commenced that systematic collection which has since been presented to the world in many forms, not the least notably as the material which is used in many of her plays. In this way her love for the people grew till it became almost a passion, and she in her turn became the beloved of her people. Her life became part of the life of the district, and her thoughts and speech became those of her people. It is true, of course, that her interest in, and her visits to the cottages of, the people were misinterpreted, and a construction placed upon her activities for which there was never even the slightest justification. But there are malicious folk in every community, and malicious folk are especially numerous and active in Ireland, and these malicious folk were bold enough to suggest that the interest which Lady Gregory took in the people amongst whom she lived was the interest of a proselytising Protestant endeavouring to undermine the Catholic faith of her poorer neighbours. Tales were circulated about the tracts she was supposed to have left in the cottages where she visited, and she was given the title of ' souper,' which was the name bestowed upon those who went to the Protestant soup-kitchens during the famine years of 1847-1849. As these tales had no basis in fact, and as they were circulated and credited mainly in districts where Lady Gregory was unknown personally, they may be set down as part of the propaganda to discredit the Irish Literary Theatre in its early years. At all events they did not deter Lady Gregory from the continuance of the work to which she has given her life, and for which Ireland is now so much indebted to her. There is in her attitude towards the people, and in some of her most popular plays, that touch of patronage and unconscious snobbery which is expected from the ' county ' landowning families, but nowhere in her life or in her work is there the faintest trace of religious bigotry. In her work the Catholicism of the people is always treated with the utmost sympathy and reverence. But Irish Catholics are sensitive and somewhat timid about their religion, apt to interpret as ironic any comments which non-Catholics may have to make, and to be suspiciously malicious about the actions of non-Catholics who take any interest in the welfare of their poorer neighbours.

It was folk-lore, not religion, that was the great interest of Lady Gregory's early life. It was that interest which brought her to learn the Irish language so that she could converse with the Irish-speaking peasantry of Galway on a basis of equality. As one of her own and her husband's closest friends she had Sir Frederick Burton, artist, archaeologist, and scholar, an Irishman who had been a personal friend of Davis and Petrie, had known John Mitchel, and had drawn the design for the title-page for *The Spirit of the Nation*, a volume which expressed in song the patriotic sentiments of the Young Ireland movement of the mid-century. But Burton was never a political Nationalist, nor was Lecky or the majority of Lady Gregory's very extensive circle of friends, and it is doubtful if she herself ever became a political Nationalist as that term was understood in the old days of Parnell, Gladstone or Redmond. Her early days had been made romantic, as she says, and somewhat thrilling by the spectre of

> An army of Papists grim
> With a green flag o'er them.
> Red coats and black police
> Flying before them.

Her home had been attacked by the Whiteboys, and the attack had been driven off by her father firing his gun from the window. Then she, too, met John O'Leary, the terrible Fenian leader of her childhood stories, and she also found him charming and lovable. So even revolutionary Nationalism lost its menacing aspect. She met Douglas Hyde at the house of her neighbour Edward Martyn, and in him she encountered a sympathetic spirit whose life-work was almost the same as her own. He had been collecting the folk-tales of the West, and had been collecting those songs which in translation so deeply influenced the Irish literary movement, and the dialogue of the new Irish drama. Thus she came to understand and sympathise with the Gaelic League, so that she could say later, " It was a movement for keeping the Irish language a spoken language, with, as a chief end, the preserving of our own Nationality. That does not sound like a revolution, yet it was one. It was the discovery, the disclosure of the folk-learning, the folk-poetry, the folk-tradition ". As this also was the one absorbing interest of Lady Gregory herself at that time it was an easy step for her to collaborate in the work of Dr. Hyde. But Dr. Hyde's interest in folk-lore was mainly philological or linguistic, as that of Mr. Yeats was mainly vague and mystical. Lady Gregory was interested in folk-lore for the sake of the folk, and for the aesthetic pleasure which she derived from it. She had no purpose that the study of folk-lore might be made to subserve, and she had no theories which it might be used to illustrate. She was the servant of the folk, its devotee, with no desire that it should serve any utilitarian purpose whatever either for herself or her design. For, in fact and in truth, she had then no design that it might be made to serve. Her friends in Ireland were all absorbed in efforts to ' do something for the country '; every person born in Ireland comes into the world with this desire as his inheritance, and not even emigration and years of life in other countries will ease the urge, it affects the descendants of the famine emigrants to the United States as it affected Bernard Shaw and George Moore. Lady Gregory did not escape it, unconsciously, perhaps, she had nourished it, and when her friends came to her with the project of a theatre she was ready for them—but she would not have the theatre ' somewhere in the suburbs ' of London. The theatre which Lady Gregory visualised at that critical interview in 1898 was a theatre which would be located in Ireland, would stage plays of Irish life and character, and which, because Ireland is mainly a peasant nation with a civilisation that is definitely rural, would be in reality a folk-theatre in the broadest sense of the word. Such a theatre could have no place in the theatrical or dramatic life of London : there it would be merely a freak. But in Ireland it would be real, and it might in time give the necessary stimulus to the creation of a school of drama that would be the revelation of the folk mind of Ireland.

So she set to work, and it was mainly from the circle of her friends and acquaintances that the supporting guarantees for the creation of the Irish Literary Theatre were secured. She used her great persuasive powers to their very fullest extent, and to the best advantage, as she used also that capacity for organisation which till then she was probably unaware that she possessed. The circular letter that was drafted in her house in Galway in the autumn of 1898 bears the impress of her personality, as the list of those to whom it was sent was compiled largely from her personal address-book. In this way she had grown from the little girl whose childish fears were emphasised by the tales she had heard of Fenian ‘ atrocities ’ to the woman who loved her Catholic neighbours, who collected and cherished their stories and their songs, the woman who talked to them in their own Irish tongue. Her greatest phase began when she undertook the organisation of a theatre for Ireland. When she began that work she entered upon a career which was to make her name known throughout the world. She was then in her fortieth year, but even then she seems to have had no ambition to write plays herself. But it is as a writer of delightful little comedies that she is best known to the world to-day. Her greatest work, and her most lasting achievement, however, is in that theatre which she did so much to establish. Of Lady Gregory more than any other single one of the four who founded the Theatre it may be said, the Irish Theatre is hers and she made it. Because not only did she provide the necessary organising ability in the initial stages, but she also moulded its policy and its plays in ways that will be demonstrated in these pages from its very earliest days. She has been a Director of the Theatre from the first, and she remains to-day as keenly and as actively interested in its management and in its welfare as she was in the beginning.

When Lady Gregory became immersed in the work of organising an Irish Theatre she was not deeply interested in the drama, and she had no theories about either the theatre or the drama. One of the objects of the Theatre, as stated in the original circular letter, was, " to build up a Celtic and Irish school of dramatic literature ". But Lady Gregory admits that the word ' Celtic ' conveyed little or nothing to her. " I think the word ' Celtic ' was put in ", she says (*Our Irish Theatre*, p. 9), " for the sake of Fiona Macleod, whose plays, however, we never acted, though we used to amuse ourselves by thinking of the call for ' author ' that might follow one, and the possible appearance of William Sharp in place of the beautiful woman he had given her out to be, for even then we had little doubt they were one and the same person. I myself never quite understood the meaning of the ' Celtic Movement ' which we were said to belong to. When I was asked about it, I used to say that it was a movement meant to persuade the Scotch to begin buying our books, while we continued not to buy theirs." That reply was characteristic of everything that Lady Gregory is or has done. She has never been given to theorising about the theatre or anything else, always she has been the practical person, the realist. She has taken her work where she found it, she had done the work that needed to be done, and has passed on to something else. With her plays it has been the same ; she has no theories of drama to expound at length when opportunity offers, nor does she make opportunities to expound them. A theatre was needed, so she set out to found a theatre : plays were needed when that theatre had been founded, so she started to write plays. It is probable that during the thirty years during which she has been actively connected with the direction of a theatre she has accumulated thoughts and ideas about theatres, plays, and players, but she has been silent about these and is content to continue the work in the way and in the spirit in which she began it.

(c) EDWARD MARTYN

So lifelike is the portrait of Edward Martyn, 'dear Edward', given by Mr. George Moore in *Hail and Farewell* that readers might easily be pardoned for believing that he was merely a somewhat eccentric and charming character imagined by the novelist to give verisimilitude to his work. *Hail and Farewell* is a tale that was highly polished and varnished ere it left the hands of its author, and Edward Martyn is one of its characters upon whom little of the varnish has been lavished. Edward Martyn was the kind of man whom novelists delight to invent, but he had not to be invented by Mr. Moore, he really existed and was there ready to hand, stolid and solid, to be used as a foil for the brilliant conversation of the chronicler. Edward Martyn was one of the very rare Irishmen who had no gift for the limelight, as he had neither the desire nor the capacity to make himself conspicuous. He lived in the most secluded manner, frugal almost to the point of misery, and intimate with only a small number of people. His life was almost monastic in its austerity, and there was in him almost everything that would have made an exemplary member of a contemplative order. He was a man of some wealth who chose to live as one of the poor. A landlord in the County Galway he had no sympathy with his class in their treatment of, nor in their struggle with, their tenantry ; his sympathies were very probably on the side of the struggling small farmers who found it impossible to comply with the demands of the landlords when faced with the competition of the new lands across the oceans, and by the development of transport. He was a Deputy Lieutenant for his county who actively opposed recruiting for the British Army at the time of the Boer War. He was a very devout Catholic who was, nevertheless, one of the earliest to discover Ibsen and to recognise and proclaim his greatness ; as he was also one of the few Irishmen of his time who kept close contact with the ideas and the literature of continental Europe. He was a political Nationalist by instinct and conviction, but it was only with the greatest reluctance that he was persuaded to take a prominent position in the Sinn Fein movement in its early days, but he retained the presidential chair of that organisation for only a very short time, though he is believed to have supported it liberally with funds. An enthusiast for mediaeval church music and the founder of a Palestrina choir in the Catholic Cathedral in Dublin, on an endowment of £10,000, he was no less an enthusiastic admirer of Wagner's genius and a regular visitor to the festivals at Bayreuth. Despite the variety of his interests and the wide range of his ideas Edward Martyn never seemed to have any constant or continuous contact with the ordinary affairs of daily life, nor did the ordinary life of his time seem to have any reality for him. He seemed to live in a world of his own with the ideas and abstractions which he loved and could understand, but from the raw, crude, hustling, materialistic, daily life of the modern world he shrunk, and he avoided contact with it as much as possible. Generous and charitable in all things and to all men he proved himself a true and worthy kinsman to that 'Humanity' Martyn who had striven so long and so valiantly in the British Parliament for the humane treatment of animals.

Edward Martyn was born in Ireland and educated in England. He was educated at Oxford and when he went down from that University he continued to live in London, and it was there that he definitely formulated his aesthetic creed. He had been born in Tillyra, County Galway, in 1860, but he lived so long in London that his name was almost unknown in Dublin, as in his native county. So when his name appeared as one of the founders of the Irish Literary Theatre, and the author of one of the plays which were to be produced in 1899, the literary people of Dublin were taken by surprise. They had never heard of Edward Martyn as an author, yet he had already written, and destroyed, a volume of verse, and had published under a pseudonym in 1890 a prose work of quite an unusual type. This prose work, a novel perhaps it would be called to-day though it is not in any sense a novel, *Morgante the Lesser*, was largely a satirically analytical commentary upon the civilisation of the time somewhat after the manner of Swift or Rabelais. Morgante, and his followers the Enterists, while reminding one at times of Gulliver and Gargantua, have lives and entities of their own, as they have also a significance which would do credit to either Swift or Rabelais. Morgante is distinctly modern in his mentality, but coldly detached, even isolated, in his ideas, and from the heights of his isolation he subjects the civilisation of late nineteenth-century England to a series of tests the results of which provide a good deal of quiet humour. The passing fads and fancies of the times are not the only aspects of society which attract the attention of Morgante. He is especially concerned with the more fundamental and permanent ideas and institutions, and he subjects Religion, Science, and Education to detailed examination in a bitter and somewhat grotesque manner which is amazingly well sustained throughout a lengthy narrative. But quite definitely obtruding itself through the multitudinous details of the long book is Edward Martyn's conception of the never-ending conflict between materialism and idealism, between the utilitarian and the artistic. This struggle was to be the dominating theme of Edward Martyn's life and work, it coloured his thoughts and his actions, and was for him the most absorbing conflict which was presented by the world in general, and by England in particular, for human contemplation. He was, himself, very definitely on the side of the artists and against the utilitarians, whom he thought would destroy all that was fine and romantic in life. This struggle decided his politics as it provided the themes for his plays. Always and everywhere he was on the side of the soul in that eternal struggle between " brother ass and his rider ". Very often his partisanship is carried to such extremes that the body seems to be denied any rights at all. He cared very little for his own physical comfort, being always content with little, and when he died in 1923 he directed that his body should be given to a medical school for use and afterwards buried in the cheapest possible way. It was the last gesture of a spirit that had always been in revolt against that materialism which is dictated by the needs of the body, and which makes the world the preserve of mass-production millionaires instead of the abode of beauty and romance which all the mediaevalists like Edward Martyn or G. K. Chesterton picture to themselves with satisfaction.

Edward Martyn was an aesthete and a connoisseur who just fell short of being an artist. George Moore is of the opinion that it was Martyn's soul which prevented him from being an artist, but it was more probably his wealth which was the real barrier. He was not by any means a man of energy who would work for the sake of work, and it is possible that a slight economic pressure, which is the spur to most people who develop into materialists afterwards, would have developed in him that steady application which he so conspicuously lacked. The artist in him would have been liberated by a closer contact with the ordinary life which he seemed to treat with a lofty disdain, and with something like a sniff of contempt. It would, too, have made him easier to work with and have given him somewhat greater respect for the apprenticeship period which is necessary even for artists. Of all the persons who came into the Irish Literary Theatre movement he alone refused to learn the technique of the drama from others ; Mr. Yeats and Lady Gregory were content to take lessons where and when they were given, but Martyn remained to the end what he was in the beginning—a gifted amateur. Ideas he had in abundant profusion, in greater profusion perhaps than any of his Irish contemporaries, as he had also a closer contact and a wider acquaintance with the ideas of the Continent. His culture was essentially continental, and he had a sympathetic understanding of the newer forces in music and drama which were then stirring in Germany, Russia, and Scandinavia. He did not think that England would respond to these new forces, as he thought that England had become too much concerned with material prosperity and with the forms of progress that would be

easily demonstrable in statistical tables, and that nothing else
was likely to be of more than passing interest to the English
people for many generations to come. He had a deep interest
in, and a wide knowledge of, the contemporary drama of
Europe, being especially attracted to the work of Ibsen and
Strindberg, both of whom he thought, rightly as time and
events have since proven conclusively, were alien in spirit from
all that was essentially English. But he foresaw that these
two dramatists would regenerate the drama in Europe and
dictate its form for a considerable time, and it was a tragic
thought that England was not ready to receive them. The
materialism of the English people was a tragedy for Edward
Martyn, who believed that the England of Shakespeare and
Johnson was the real England, as it was the England that he
loved. His interest in Ireland was, at that time, not very
marked, and he seems to have known little or nothing of what
was passing there. He was out of sympathy and touch with
the members of his own landowning class, and he had formed
no point of contact with the peasantry. He had never any
outstanding regard for the peasantry, whom he did not understand, and never tried to understand. This is all the more
remarkable when it is borne in mind that Edward Martyn was
of the same Catholic faith as the vast bulk of his peasant
neighbours at Tillyra, while Lady Gregory, who is a Protestant,
shared their minds, understood them completely, and was
trusted by them. But peasants had no attraction for Martyn,
and he made no attempt to understand them or to come into
contact with their minds. His own mind, his thoughts, and
his aspirations, led him in quite a different direction. It may
be that the materialism which so revolted him in England was
also the basis of his estrangement from the peasantry of his
native county. An urban materialism may develop some
admirable points which may even succeed in securing the
approval of the artist, but rural materialism is so mean and
grasping, so cruel and greedy, that only those who like ugly
things would find it attractive. Even the estimable John
O'Leary could find little that was good to say in favour of the

small peasant farmers of Ireland. They have been satirised and castigated by almost every writer who knows Ireland, but they are still oblivious that anything they do is not wholly admirable, and the complacency with which they assume, and accept the assurance from those who use them as grindstones, almost drives reformers to despair. But the peasantry is Nationalist as Martyn was a Nationalist! Not quite so, however : Martyn was a Nationalist only in politics, he was European in culture, as his collaborators in the Irish Literary Theatre were Unionist, or of Unionist tradition, who were Irish and Nationalist in culture and aspirations. But as George Moore has said, " the drama brings strange fowls to roost ".

Edward Martyn was a man of the theatre to his very finger-tips. All his ambitions were concentrated in the theatre, but the very defects of his qualities prevented him from ever realising these ambitions. He has studied Ibsen's works with the greatest care, and followed his career with the closest attention, getting, perhaps, closer to the mood and spirit of Ibsen than any of his contemporaries who were writing plays. He had known the Théâtre Libre in Paris, the Freie Bühne in Berlin, and the Independent . Theatre in London, following their work with the closest attention, as in these experimental theatres he saw the only hope for the literary drama. The " vast cosmopolitanism and vulgarity " of English theatre audiences made him despair of any future for intelligent drama in England, and even the Independent Theatre did not offer much scope for the kind of play he had hoped to see on its stage. The ' daring ' play which was likely to be banned by the Censor had no attractions for him, and he was sadly grieved when his revered Ibsen was mistaken for, and treated as, a ' daring ' dramatist and a preaching moralist. Martyn had never the slightest desire to preach or to reform anyone or anything ; he was content when a human conflict was presented on the stage in intelligent terms and in fitting language. His charge against the theatre of commerce was that it was intellectually dishonest and vulgar, and thus far he was in agreement with Bernard Shaw and most critics of his time. It was when the language of the drama came to be discussed that he parted company with them. He thought that the language of the stage must not be the commonplace language of everyday life, but must be literary in form and elevating in effect ; in this he was at one with W. B. Yeats and George Moore. He held that in the commercial theatre there could be no adventure of spirit or intellect ; there could be nothing but petty meanness treated with vulgarity. But the Independent Theatre was likely to be little better, and George Moore's criticism of that movement was probably shared in by Edward Martyn. In his preface to *The Heather Field* Mr. Moore very ironically narrates his adventures with William Archer and others who professed to be interested in the literary drama. He says that the collapse of the theatre of ideas in London was due mainly to the indiscriminate enthusiasm of the critics, and their public, for any play that seemed to depart from the Sardou ' well-made ' success of the commerical theatre. Sir Arthur Pinero in particular is accused by Mr. Moore of having demoralised audiences by inducing them to take his suburban audacities for advanced ideas, and his literary melodrama for a new technique. In an atmosphere such as Mr. Moore describes there was little hope for the plays of Martyn, and neither managers nor critics could be found to see anything worthy in them. They were published in 1890, nearly ten years before the first of them was produced in Dublin.

It is almost certain that Martyn would have preferred to have his plays produced in London, but as London was unwilling he turned to Dublin. He thought of an Irish Literary Theatre, perhaps, because he thought there was " in Irish audiences an idealism founded upon the ancient genius of the land ". He hoped to find in Ireland an audience which had not been debauched and spoiled by the theatre of commerce, and the cheap emotionalism in which it dealt. Like Yeats he sought an audience unspoiled but receptive, and when he despaired of finding such an audience in London he sought for it in Dublin. His plays were ready but he had no theatre where they could be acted, and a theatre had to be founded for the purpose. But it must not be the private theatre of an individual ! Martyn was wealthy enough to have financed the production of his own plays had he so desired ; but he did not desire anything especially for himself which was not equally available to others. His great desire was for drama of an intelligent kind which was true to humanity and to literature. So when the project for an Irish Literary Theatre was discussed by Lady Gregory and Mr. Yeats, at Lady Gregory's home in Galway in the autumn of 1898, it was an easy matter to enlist the active support and encouragement of Edward Martyn. He was one of the first guarantors, and it was he who afterwards defrayed the entire cost of the experimental seasons. The story was, as George Moore says in *Ave*, disappointingly short and simple. " When Yeats had said that he had spent the summer at Coole with Lady Gregory I saw it all. Coole is but three miles from Tillyra ; Edward is often at Coole ; Lady Gregory and Yeats are often at Tillyra ; Yeats and Edward had written plays ". In effect that is the whole story, at least in so far as Edward Martyn is concerned. Certain it is that he entered the combination without any conscious desire ' to do something for the country ', or to do anything for himself. He knew what the next phase of the drama was likely to be, and he may have had some desire that Ireland would take its part in the earliest stages of the new developments, since England probably would not. But it was on the drama that his mind was centred all the time. He was little concerned with Ireland, with peasants, or with the development of folk-drama. He was concerned very much with the drama of ideas, with its form, its dialogue, and its presentation, as with its content, and it was upon this drama that he laboured all his life. He had no desire that Ireland should concentrate upon itself to the exclusion of European ideas and culture ; on the contrary, he was certain that Ireland should open itself as widely as possible to the reception of all that was best in

Europe.   The belief of Edward Martyn was summarised by the late T. M. Kettle when he told Ireland that, " in order to become truly Irish she must first become European ".   It was in this spirit that Edward Martyn wrote his plays, as it was in this spirit that he became one of the founders of the Irish Literary Theatre.

(d) GEORGE MOORE

George Moore is the greatest novelist Ireland has yet given to the world, and probably the greatest writer of the English language now living, but his interest in his native country has never been either deep or prolonged.   He is a Connachtman, born in the County Mayo in 1853, and his native province will be found in all its grandeur, in all its primitiveness, and with all its seductive charm in his novel *The Lake* (1905), which is the outstanding work, if *Hail and Farewell* be excepted, of his last Irish period, that is of his last prolonged residence in Ireland.   But any adequate understanding of George Moore can conceive him as being Irish only in part. He is not Irish in sympathy, he has never had any interest in the Irish political struggle except to oppose it mildly, though his family has been prominent in Irish politics for several generations, and his brother is now a Senator of the Irish Free State with somewhat marked inclinations towards Gaelicism and Republicanism.   Senator Colonel Maurice Moore is not quite an extremist but he is quite definitely Irish in his thoughts and sympathies.   But George Moore is not Irish in thoughts or sympathics ; anything of George Moore that in 1899 was not French was very distinctively English, so that there is some reason for the opinion that *Esther Waters* (1894) is ' the most English of novels '.   He had spent his early manhood in France, and it was there that he had served his literary apprenticeship in the Naturalistic school of Émile Zola. ' Shocking the *bourgeois* ' is a difficult and protracted operation in France, where the *bourgeois* has had so many attempts to shock him that he became almost impervious to further shocks.   But in the England of the

Victorian Jubilee it was so easy that the easy-going Mrs.
Grundy almost invited the daring young men to shock her.
The young Thomas Hardy had shocked her so badly that she
never quite recovered her vigour ; and she never forgave him
because in shocking her he had also presumed to lecture her
and to show her better ways. George Moore shocked her—
but he never lectured her. He did not attempt to act as a
chorus to his own imagined Fates. Thomas Hardy grimaced
with pain, he was hurt by that which shocked Mrs. Grundy ;
but George Moore smiled the gay impish smile that has been
preserved to him throughout his literary life. He was serious,
yes, but not too serious ; and he was always careful to dis-
claim any intention to impart any moral lessons. He did not
attempt to become a god in a book, so he extracted no lessons
from betting or bastardy, from mummers or from nuns. He
was ' daring ', but he never became ungentlemanly. In a
word, he was English. He had gauged the English temper
and environment, as he had himself been absorbed by the
English atmosphere in which he lived. Despite his aesthetic
preoccupation George Moore has a great deal in common with
the English Utilitarians, his philosophic outlook is not so very
different from that of Jeremy Bentham. He is aristocratic,
even autocratic, fond of a luxurious comfort, and as utilitarianism in practice has resolved itself into an easy chair and
a smoke in the evening, George Moore may be classed among
the utilitarians. Perhaps he is an Epicure, but then Utilitarianism is merely Epicureanism for the masses. Few
Irishmen have either accepted, or been attracted by, the
philosophy of Utilitarianism, for the Irishman it is a coldly
materialistic creed, and though bread may be more sustaining
than stones the stones are apt to have the greater charm and
variety of colour and shape. So neither France nor England
quite eradicated all that was Irish from George Moore. He
retained, and still retains, that temperament which is peculiar
to the Irishman. He has something of a swagger, he trails
his coat provocatively, he is not without his stock of the little
tricks of the showman and the ' publicity ' merchant, he is

arrogant and dogmatic, and he has that streak of malice without which no good Irishman is complete. He has also retained those abiding influences of the Irishman, a country and a religion. It is, of course, true that George Moore has spent much of his time, and shown a great deal of his temper, in reviling both the country and the religion of his birth ; but revile as he may he has never succeeded in getting away from either of them. Time and again he has turned his wrath upon them and rent them, but he has not exorcised them, and even though he regard them both as devils they have provided all that is enduring in his literary work. Without Ireland and without Catholicism it is probable that George Moore would have produced no great work ; he might have been but a thin shadow of Émile Zola, and his work would have been forgotten when the bulky substances of his master's work had outlived its day. Moore's obsessions, the nationality and the religion for which he reserves his sneers and his curses, have in fact proved to be his salvation as a writer and a great literary artist. Without them *Hail and Farewell* could never have been written, and the world would have been the poorer for that masterpiece of indiscretion and imaginative history. He might have outraged the complacency of the good English Mrs. Grundy, but that was an easy task which would never have tried his strength nor extended his powers ; a Noel Coward or a Michael Arlen can do that even in our day. Had George Moore been limited to that he would never have become a great figure in English literature, and from that limited field Ireland and Catholicism saved him. He may not be grateful for his salvation, but at least he must be aware of it.

The Ireland that George Moore would have desired, and in which he might have consented to live permanently, would have been an Ireland which contained all the comforts and amenities of England added to its own intellectual activity and spiritual depth. But it is possible that the addition of the English qualities would kill those that are now peculiarly Irish. That is the fear of many Irishmen who dread the

coming of industrialism. They fear that the mental activity
and spiritual grace will be sacrificed to money-making, and
that personality will be sacrificed to the mechanical efficiency
and monotony which characterise the industrial civilisation
of our day. Better have poverty and imagination, they say,
than wealth, mechanisation, and newspapers with the largest
circulation in the world. It was just that mechanisation and
the debasement of the English language by the national
schools and the newspapers which turned the thoughts of
George Moore towards his native country at the end of last
century. The Boer War had brought to the surface all that
was mean, vulgar, and unpleasant in the English people. In
the vicissitudes of that disastrous war there had been made
plain to everyone who cared to notice the vulgarising effects
of the Industrial Revolution and a century of factory civilisation. The mob became articulate ; its voice was the headline
of the cheap press ; and what it had to say was neither
pleasing nor worthy. ' Mafficking ' and ' jingoism ' had no
place in the England that had won the affectionate regard of
George Moore ; but that England existed no more, it had
passed with the passing of the eighteenth century. The
obtrusion of these unpleasant facts and aspects of the life of
England proved so revolting to the aesthetically utilitarian
soul of George Moore that they made Ireland seem by
comparison a place of ancient peace and intellectual activity.
He had heard of the language movement and the literary
revival from his intimate friend Edward Martyn, and his
disgust at the novel England that was being revealed to him
gave the news more than ordinary significance. He became
impatient to take a part in the new movements in Ireland : he
would create a new literature in a new language. A new
literature could be created in Ireland, and a new language
was there ready to be exploited ! That language had never
been used in world literature, it was virgin and unspoiled by
the soiling contact of the cheap press and the haggling of
hucksters in the market-place ! He would give to Ireland the
great work for which it waited ; and the new centre of the

Arts in Europe would be Dublin ! It seemed as if that great desire of all humanity to have a fresh start with a new life had been offered. George Moore was not the man to resist such an offer, so he shook the dust of England from his feet and came to live in Dublin.

Like most novelists, who try to write plays at some time in their career, George Moore had written plays. His interest in the drama had brought him into intimate association with the founders and supporters of the Independent Theatre, and he was one of the most stalwart champions of the ' new ' drama of the 1890's. His criticism of the conventional play and the commercial theatre (*Impressions and Opinions*, 1891) vigorously supported all that Bernard Shaw was saying at the time. In an essay entitled ' Our Dramatists and their Literature ' he aimed blows all around him with such vigour that a challenge was forthcoming from George R. Sims, who was one of the popular dramatists of the day. Sims challenged Moore to write an ' unconventional ' play, and offered to pay £100 for a stall to witness the first performance when the play would be produced. Moore objected that the word ' unconventional ' would leave any play which he might write entirely to the judgment of Sims, so the offending word was therefore withdrawn. Thus it was that George Moore came to write his first play, *The Strike at Arlingford*, which was produced by the Independent Theatre in 1893. There was little that was ' unconventional ' in the play, but the circumstances under which it came to be written and performed, and the fact that George R. Sims had to pay £100 for his seat in the theatre, combined to give it an air of unusual importance and significance. It cannot be said that Mr. Moore neglected to take full advantage of the interest which those circumstances aroused in London, and in focussing the interest upon himself he proved that arts of the showman were not amongst the least of his gifts. The performance and publication of *The Strike at Arlingford* got very much more than normal attention from the press in criticism, letters, and interviews, and all the fuss that was

made about it may have induced the public to believe that
a new era had dawned for the English theatre. The ' unconventional ' play, the play that would appeal to the intellect
and which would be at the same time literature, was to be the
play of the future in England. In this way, by his criticism,
his publicity work, and his play, George Moore came to be
regarded as something of an authority on drama. He had
secured a place in the English theatre, and he tried to
maintain that place by collaborating with ' John Oliver
Hobbes ' (Mrs. Craigie), who was then at the height of her
popularity as a novelist, in a play that was for some time in
the repertory of Henry Irving and Ellen Terry, and which
was played by them on tour with fair success. So George
Moore could by comparison with the majority of the literary
dramatists, whose works had never been staged, be termed a
successful dramatist.

He was regarded as a successful dramatist by Edward
Martyn and W. B. Yeats, and it was natural that they should
turn to him for assistance in arranging the practical details
when it had been decided to launch the Irish Literary
Theatre. George Moore was the only person then known to
them who had the experience they desired, and who was at
the same time likely to be interested in such a project in
Ireland. Bernard Shaw was one of the pillars of the Independent Theatre, but he was at that time even less interested
in Ireland than he is to-day. His energies were at that period
all concentrated upon converting England to Ibsenism, and
in the propagandist work of the Fabian Society. The
foundation of a literary theatre merely for the sake of literary
drama would have made little appeal to Bernard Shaw then,
though it might appeal to him now. But Shaw was not in
touch with the Irish group in London, and it is doubtful if he
even knew that there was an Irish group in existence outside
the Literary Society. However, George Moore had many of
the qualities of Bernard Shaw, as he had also other qualities
which Shaw lacked, and all would be useful for the promotion
of the new theatrical venture. Moore was a novelist whose

name was prominent and whose prestige was considerable; he had a knowledge of playwriting and some experience in the casting and production of plays. His provocativeness, and his ability to attract attention to himself and his doings, were at least as great as Shaw's, and he was a critic of some power and eminence. He was, in fact, one of the outstanding personalities in the London of his time in literary and theatrical circles, better known and with a larger following than Bernard Shaw. Then he was also George Moore of Moore Hall in the County of Mayo, the son of a man who had been a prominent Nationalist politician, and a member of a family which had done something in the struggle for the political freedom of Ireland. His father had been a generous landlord who had embarrassed himself financially in his efforts to succour the starving people at the time of the Famine. That political connection was of great importance, as none of the other founders of the Theatre were of Nationalist descent, and it was likely to bear more than its just weight in the venture. All these factors were in the minds of Edward Martyn and W. B. Yeats when they sought the assistance of George Moore. The assistance was given readily, even enthusiastically, because Moore had tired of England and desired a change. His friendship, which covered some admiration for excellent qualities in the man, for Edward Martyn ; a great deal of intellectual curiosity and a desire to have some place in the excitement incidental to the birth of a new literature ; and, perhaps, some lingering patriotic feeling, all had their share in influencing George Moore to take a hand in the work. To him fell the work of gathering the company and rehearsing the plays in London, and this gave him material for some of the wittily malicious pages of *Hail and Farewell*. It is doubtful that there was anything very positive in his decision to take a share in the venture. He was never deeply committed to it as were the other three. But then George Moore never belonged to Ireland in the way that the others belonged, he had lived his life away from Ireland, and in his prolonged absence he had become markedly antipathetic to nearly all things Irish. In so far as his work was known in Ireland it was not well thought of, and there were some who regarded him as an evil influence. But he gave of his best to the Irish Literary Theatre, and his assistance in the early formative stages was of the utmost importance. Without that assistance the difficulties of the venture in finding suitable actors in London would have been very considerably increased, and the lime-light that was thrown on the venture by the London press would have been very much less. Without George Moore it is possible that the London press would not have noticed the beginnings of the Theatre at all, and without that valuable publicity in the beginning the Irish dramatic movement would not have become known to the world perhaps for many years. And that would have altered its whole course by lessening its artistic success in the eyes of its own adherents.

CHAPTER IV

DIVERGENCE : DRAMA OF IDEAS OR FOLK-DRAMA ?

The main purpose : Literary Drama—National Theatre only secondary—
' Turn to Norway for inspiration '—Dublin as London and Paris—
Plays on Irish subjects—And on Heroic Legends—' Celtic ' Plays
—Mr. Yeats and the peasant—Standish O'Grady dissents—And
'A.E.' replies—' Immoral ' plays—Edward Martyn criticises—New
Projects—Synge and the ' Peasant Play '—Partial eclipse of Mr.
Yeats—And ultimate triumph of Edward Martyn.

THE ground that was most immediately common to all the
four founders of the Irish Literary Theatre was the desire to
produce plays that were different from, and better than, the
stereotyped drama of the commercial theatre. They were in
reality part of a universal revolt against the conditions of that
theatre, and two of them, as has been noted, were associated
with the practical expression of that revolt in London. It is
somewhat difficult to discover that the creation of a national
drama was at any early stage the main purpose of the enterprise, as it is certain two of the founders, if not three, were
more deeply concerned about the resurgent drama in Europe
than with the nationalistic expression or interpretation. Of
the four pioneers Lady Gregory was the only one who was
openly and avowedly concerned with the expression of the
folk mind in an Irish Theatre and a National Drama. George
Moore was the literary artist without any preoccupation with
nationality in drama or in anything else, and the creation of a
separate Irish drama, as such, made little appeal to him.
Edward Martyn was interested only in the ' drama of ideas '
as that drama was then understood in the plays of Ibsen and
his followers. If he could have that drama in relation to

77

Ireland and Irish conditions written and produced by Irishmen in Ireland so much the better ; but if not then it must be brought to Ireland from other countries. W. B. Yeats was concerned mainly with the poetic drama, and the speaking of verse. In the beginning he was not preoccupied with the creation of a National Drama, but he was interested in the folk mind, and in the old stories of the country people. He was at first willing that his little theatre should be located in London, and it was Lady Gregory who suggested that the theatre should be in Dublin, as it was she also who later brought him to the creation of a National Theatre and concentration upon folk-drama. It will thus be obvious that the four founders of the Theatre were so divergent in ideals, and so different in outlook and sympathy, that the possibilities of disintegration were inherent from the beginning. In effect the three seasons of the Irish Literary Theatre were seasons of silent warfare which ended in a victory for the ideals of Lady Gregory and W. B. Yeats, and the withdrawal from the movement of Edward Martyn and George Moore. From the date of his withdrawal George Moore took no further active part in the work of the Irish Theatre, but Edward Martyn continued the struggle in a series of experimental efforts which ended only when his collaborator, Thomas MacDonagh, was executed for his participation in the Rising in Dublin in Easter 1916.

The first Manifesto of the Irish Literary Theatre in 1898 stated quite definitely in its opening lines that " the Irish Literary Theatre will attempt to do in Dublin something of what has been done in London and Paris ". And *Beltaine*, which was published as the organ of the movement during 1899 and 1900, said in its very first number, " Everywhere critics and writers, who wish for something better than the ordinary play of commerce, turn to Norway for an example and an inspiration ". After a mention of the London and Continental movements the writer refers to inexpensive theatres " which associations of men and letters hire from time to time, that they may see on the stage the plays of

Henrik Ibsen, Maurice Maeterlinck, Gerhart Hauptmann, José Echegaray, or some less famous dramatist who has written, in the only way literature can be written, to express a dream that has taken possession of his mind ". From these statements it seemed that what was intended to be established in Dublin was to be "an association of men of letters" which would hire a theatre and there have produced such plays of the literary, and ' advanced ', dramatists, as the association might desire to see on the stage, such plays in fact as were at the time being produced in the independent theatres of London and Paris. But in the Irish scheme there were some significant reservations and modifications. The Manifesto states that the Irish Literary Theatre " if it has even a small welcome, will produce, somewhere about the old festival of Beltaine, at the beginning of every spring, a play founded upon an Irish subject ". And in the organ of the movement, *Beltaine*, it was stated by the Editor, Mr. Yeats, that " the plays will differ from those produced by men of letters in London and Paris, because times have changed, and because the intellect of Ireland is romantic and spiritual, rather than scientific and analytical ". It is somewhat difficult to understand just what is intended to be conveyed by the announcement that "times have changed", as it was just that point that was being emphasised by the critics and the younger dramatists throughout Europe. Perhaps it was intended to mean that Ireland was not yet ready for the ' advanced ' drama of the Continent. But if so why was it stated that Norway was to be an example and an inspiration ? It seems plain that some compromise had been effected at the beginning and that some difficulty was being experienced in giving it practical effect. Anyhow the issue was clearly knit in the organ of the movement at an early stage of the Theatre's existence. In its general tone the organ of the movement was not definitely national, its dominant note was European and cosmopolitan rather than locally Irish. The nationalist note was struck by the Editor in his plea for plays dealing with Irish mythology and the heroes of classical history, while his collaborators were drawing the attention of Ireland to the new drama of Continental Europe as being most worthy of attempted emulation. They pointed to the rise of the intellectual drama on the Continent, and even quoted as examples some of the plays that had been written and produced in England under the inspiring influence of Ibsen. In support of the drama based upon Irish legend there were published vague announcements of plays that were to be written by Fiona Macleod and Standish O'Grady, but these plays never, in fact, materialised. Superficially all appearances pointed to a clear victory for the Continental advocates because of the default of the nationalist playwrights. The advocates of the intellectual drama were further fortified by the respect paid to the printed play, in Ireland as elsewhere at the time. " In all or almost all cases the plays must be published before they are acted, and no play will be accepted which could not hope to succeed as a book ". However, in the event, Ibsen and Hauptmann, Maeterlinck and Echegaray, no less than unknown foreigners, were all neglected by the Irish Literary Theatre, as not even a single play by any of the dramatists whose names had been mentioned in the Manifesto was ever produced. All the seven plays produced in its three seasons by the Theatre were by Irish authors, and were based upon Irish subjects.

Lady Gregory has quite frankly stated that the word ' Celtic ', which was used in the original Manifesto of the Theatre, conveyed at the time little or nothing to her, and that it was used deliberately in the hope of attracting Fiona Macleod. The word will convey little or nothing to most people because in fact it has little or nothing to convey, only, perhaps, some vague reference to Macpherson or Macleod. But it did convey something to W. B. Yeats, and he gave it a meaning which it probably still carries to people outside Ireland. He managed to put into the meaning of the word all the necromantic ideas with which he had saturated himself, and to connect these ideas in a somewhat peculiar way with the superstitious beliefs and fairy-lore of the Irish country-

side.   The Celticism of W. B. Yeats is not that of Fiona
Macleod, nor is it that of Standish O'Grady, but it has something in common with that of George W. Russell ('A.E.') by
virtue of a common eastern ancestry.   There is more of
India than of Ireland in the so-called Celticism of W. B.
Yeats, only the body is Irish as the spirit is from India, and
that is some part of the reason why the plays of Mr. Yeats
have never achieved popularity in Ireland.   But there is
another, and a much more important, reason for the comparative unpopularity of his plays in Ireland : it is, that Mr.
Yeats has seriously misjudged the Irish character, and has
given to the world a false interpretation of that character by
endowing it with his own ideas and beliefs.   In *Beltaine*
he had said that " the intellect of Ireland is romantic
and spiritual, rather than scientific and analytical ", and no
statement of such a generalised kind could well approximate
less to the actual facts.   It is true that the Irish intellect is not
quite so scientific or analytical as, for example, the intellect
of contemporary France or Germany ; but that is only true
relatively, and because of the absence of scientific training.
It is quite untrue to say, or to suggest, that the Irish intellect
is not exact or logical, because in fact it is so logical and so
exact that it is capable of pushing logic to extremes where it
is mistaken by other peoples for romance.   Anyone who is
familiar with the history of the Irish political struggle during
the past five centuries, or, better still, familiar with the Sinn
Fein movement from its origins in the articles by Arthur
Griffith in *The United Irishman* (1899-1900) to its triumphant
culmination in the creation of the Irish Free State in 1922,
will not need to be told that it was logic and analysis, rather
than romance, that were at work.   It was during these fateful
years that Mr. Yeats lamented in beautiful verse the passing
of romantic Ireland, but that Ireland had not passed because
it existed only in Mr. Yeats himself.   The romantic Ireland
of the Englishman is the creature of fancy created by Englishmen for their own use and amusement.   In fact Ireland is
romantic and spiritual only in the same way, and in about the

same degree, that France is romantic and spiritual. To the Englishman France is romantic as Ireland is romantic, and as France and Ireland have much in common this is easily intelligible. The most important common possession of the two countries is the Catholic faith and tradition with its basic Latin culture. But there are other points in common also between the French and the Irish. France is a nation of peasants as Ireland is also, and though the Irish peasant lacks some of the finer traits of his French brother he has retained all the coarser traits of the French and added a few of his own. The Irish peasant is as brutal and as cruel as the French peasant ; he is a realist in all things, and, despite a surface generosity, there is a meanness which can be discovered without much probing. To discover how wrong Mr. Yeats was when he said that the Irish intellect was romantic and spiritual it is necessary to be familiar only with the repertoire of the Abbey Theatre, with the novels of such writers as Brinsley MacNamara and Liam O'Flaherty, or with the history and social conditions of the country. The mystical strain may, of course, be found in Ireland as in all other countries, particularly in countries where there is a Catholic environment and where the Catholic tradition has not been interrupted or broken, but Ireland has produced no great mystics, no Saint Francis, no Swedenborg, no Blake. As Bernard Shaw has shown in *John Bull's Other Island* there are Peter Keegans but there are far more Matty Haffigans and Larry Doyles. Instead of romance or spirituality there is a deadweight of grasping materialism with a thin veneer of superstition which is quite attractive to all who never try to get beneath it. If the fairies are ' the good people ' that is only because they can be accused of none of the land-grabbing designs of human neighbours. There is nothing romantic, nothing spiritual, nothing mystical, in Ireland that cannot be discovered in equal measure in the rural and more secluded parts of other countries. Ireland is not a freak among the nations of Europe, and the ' Celtic Twilight ' is nothing more than ' the mist that does be on the bog '.

The opening attack on the dramatic movement was not, however, made directly upon this serious misconception of the national psychology. The first attack came from quite an unexpected quarter, and by implication only did it refer to the alleged romantic and spiritual intellect of the Irish people. It was Standish O'Grady, he who had done so much to bring the ancient legends to the notice of the modern world, who made the first attack. He denied the wisdom of staging the legends, and of bringing the gods and the heroes to the level of the crowd. " The Red Branch ought not to be staged. . . . That literature ought not to be produced for popular consumption, for the edification of the crowd. . . . I say to you drop this thing at your peril. . . . You may succeed in degrading Irish ideals, and banishing the soul of the land. . . . Leave the heroic cycles alone and don't bring them down to the crowd " (*All Ireland Review*, 1902). It was the aristocratic politician, the author of *Tory Democracy* (1886), rather than the ' father of the Irish Literary revival ', who believed that uneducated people could not understand nor appreciate heroes who lived in such different times and amid different conditions, who made this attack. The heroes of Irish mythology, for instance, had many wives, and modern commonalty could not be expected to comprehend the reasons for such a departure from its known conditions ! Better, therefore, leave the heroes to the vagueness of legend, and the remote seclusion of scholarly literature ! For some time a lively controversy, in which all the prominent writers of the time joined, raged about the point. The most effective reply was made by 'A.E.' (George W. Russell) in the columns of *The United Irishman* in an essay on ' The Dramatic Treatment of Legend '. " All the heroes and demigods returning ", he said, " will have a wider field than Erin for their deeds, and they will not grow weary warring upon things that die but will be fighters in the spirit against immortal powers, and, as before, the acts will be sometimes noble and sometimes base. They cannot be stayed from their deeds, for they are still in the strength of a youth which is ever renewing itself. Not for

all the wrong which may be done should they be restrained.
. . . They have no special message to the aristocrat more than
to the man of the people. The men who made the literature
of Ireland were by no means nobly born, and it was the bards
who placed the heroes, each in his rank, and crowned them for
after ages, and gave them their famous names. . . . Though
we fall short to-day of the bodily stature of the giants of the
prime, the spirit still remains and can express an equal
greatness. . . . The drama in its mystical beginnings was
the vehicle through which divine ideas, which are beyond the
sphere even of heroic life and passion, were expressed ; and
if the later Irish writers fail of such greatness, it is not for that
reason that the soul of Ireland will depart. I can hardly
believe Mr. O'Grady to be serious when he fears that many
forbidden subjects will be the themes for dramatic art, that
Maeve with her many husbands will walk the stage, and the
lusts of an earlier age be revived to please the lusts of to-day.
The danger of art is not in its subjects, but in the attitude of
the artistic mind " (*Imaginations and Reveries*, pp. 23-25).
The controversy effected nothing, though it ended all hope
of Standish O'Grady ever contributing plays on the heroic
legends, ' Celtic ' or otherwise, to an Irish theatre. The main
issue had not been touched, because to do so would be to
rouse the ire of a very considerable section of the population.
Ireland was then still the ' Island of Saints and Scholars ' to
its own people, and any suggestion to the contrary was certain
to be violently contradicted by self-conscious patriots. So
it was not at all outside the bounds of possibility that the
Theatre would be attacked as ' immoral '. Such an attack
had been hovering and gathering strength since the beginning,
but it only broke in full force when *In the Shadow of the Glen*
was produced in 1903. The charge when it came was met
by Mr. Yeats with his usual courage. " Above all ", he said
in reply, " we must not say that certain incidents which have
been a part of literature in all other lands are forbidden to us.
It may be our duty, as it has been the duty of many dramatic
movements, to bring new kinds of subjects into the theatre,

but it cannot be our duty to make the bounds of drama narrower. For instance, we are told that the English theatre is immoral because it is preoccupied with the husband, the wife, and the lover. It is, perhaps, too exclusively preoccupied with that subject, and it is certain that it has not shed any new light upon it for a considerable time, but a subject that inspired Homer and about half the great literature of the world will, one doubts not, be a necessity to our National Theatre also " (*Plays and Controversies*, p. 57). When a new accusation, that of merely reviving and emphasising the ' stage Irishman ', was brought against the Theatre by a prominent politician none was willing to take it seriously. The *intelligentsia* was busy discussing ideals and ideas for the new drama, while the *proletariat* was being given lurid accounts of the ' paganism ' and the ' immorality ' of the plays which were being produced and written. There can now be little cause to doubt that much of the antipathy of the press was directed against the personality of George Moore, as there is also reason to suppose that the attack from Standish O'Grady was inspired by the production of *Diarmuid and Grania*, in which Moore collaborated with W. B. Yeats. The novels of Moore had made him suspect, and in the play was found much of the ' naturalism ' of which Moore had been the advocate in England and France. Such treatment could not, of course, be expected to appeal to Standish O'Grady, who has no sympathy whatever for the ideas and ideals of the world in which he finds himself.

But the main attack, which was destined to reveal the fundamental divergence of ideals amongst the founders of the Theatre, came in the mildest possible manner from the pen of Edward Martyn. In an article which he contributed to *The United Irishman* in 1902, then a powerful influence under the editorship of Arthur Griffith, he urged that Irish actors should try to train themselves so that they should be able to present competently and adequately the modern intellectual drama of society. The plays based upon the heroic legends, which were being talked about, or plays like

Kathleen ni Houlihan, in which the speech was that of the country people, were not, and could never be, a preparation for such drama. It had always been clear that Edward Martyn and George Moore inclined markedly towards the theatre of Ibsen and the modern drama of intellect, as W. B. Yeats and Lady Gregory inclined towards the folk-drama. The mixed nature of the programmes presented make the divergence between these two groups plain enough. But there was no reason why all kinds of drama should not find places in the repertoire of the Theatre, as none of them was mutually exclusive. As the three years' experimental term of the Irish Literary Theatre neared its end, however, plans for its continuance began to be discussed, and among the suggestions was one that a stock company should be formed under endowment from certain public bodies and from private subscriptions. This company would perform for six weeks every year in Dublin, and for the remainder of the time it would tour the Irish towns and those towns in England where there was any large proportion of Irish people. " It would perform plays in Irish and English, and also, it is proposed, the masterpieces of the world, making a point of performing Spanish, and Scandinavian, and French, and perhaps Greek masterpieces rather more than Shakespeare, for Shakespeare is seen, not well done indeed, but not unendurably ill done, in the theatre of commerce. It would do its best to give Ireland a hardy and shapely national character by opening the doors to the four winds of the world, instead of leaving the door that is towards the east wind open alone " (*Samhain*, 1901). This seemed to be a definite indication that the ideas of Edward Martyn were to be made effective in the future conduct of the enterprise, but that such was not the case in fact was made abundantly clear within a very short time. " I do not know ", wrote Mr. Yeats in *Samhain*, " what Mr. Moore or Lady Gregory thinks of these projects. I am not going to say what I think. I have spent much of my time and more of my thought these last ten years on Irish organisation, and now that the Irish Literary Theatre has completed the plan I had in my head ten years ago, I want to go down again to primary ideas. I want to put old stories into verse, and if I put them into dramatic verse it will matter less to me henceforward who plays them than what they play, and how they play ". There is a slight tinge of petulance in these words which is unusual in anything that Mr. Yeats writes. It will be noted that the name of Edward Martyn is not mentioned, and it may be presumed that the matter had been discussed with him. Perhaps that discussion led to the display of petulance and the somewhat defiant note which the words contain. The words may not have been intended to say what Mr. Yeats thought at the time about the Theatre, nor upon its future, but they do most certainly indicate that Mr. Yeats had made up his mind, as they indicate also the direction of his future work. And when he says a little later in *Samhain*, " The moment we leave even a little the folk tradition of the peasant, as we must in drama, if we do not know the best that has been said and written in the world, we do not even know ourselves. . . . All Irish writers have to choose whether they will write as the upper classes have done, not to express but to exploit this country ; or join the intellectual movement which has raised the cry that was heard in Russia in the seventies, the cry ' To the people ' ".

This was the end of the Irish Literary Theatre. The company which the brothers Frank and William Fay had gathered together could raise that cry which had been heard in Russia, as it could also go down to primary ideas. In the Irish National Dramatic Company Mr. Yeats found all that he needed to make his appeal to the people, with the materials drawn from the lives of the people, and clothed in the speech of the people. So Mr. Yeats joined 'A.E.', and in a short time Lady Gregory also was included, in the work of the Company, but neither George Moore nor Edward Martyn had any part in it. They had just dropped out when the Literary Theatre was allowed to lapse. There was no open breach, no quarrel amongst the four people who had directed the Theatre. The experiment had ended at the end of the

three years for which it had been planned, and when that
experiment ended a new experiment was begun, but the two
men who stood for the Ibsen drama of ideas, for the inspiration which was to come from Norway, were not invited to
take part in it. From the date in 1902 when the Irish
National Dramatic Company gave its first performance until
after the Great War the Irish drama was mainly a folk-drama,
it had gone to the peasant and for more than twenty years
it had remained with him. In reply to Edward Martyn's
article in *The United Irishman* Mr. Yeats wrote : " Our
movement is a return to the people, like the Russian movement of the early seventies, and the drama of society would
but magnify a condition of life which the countryman and the
artisan could but copy to their hurt. The play that is to give
them a quite natural pleasure should tell them either of their
own life, or of that life of poetry where every man can see his
own image, because there alone does human nature escape
from arbitrary conditions. Plays about drawing-rooms are
written for the middle classes of great cities, for the classes
who live in drawing-rooms ; but if you would ennoble the
man of the roads you must write about the roads, or about
the people of romance, or about great historical people. We
should, of course, play every kind of good play about Ireland
that we can get, but romantic and historical plays, and plays
about the life of artisans and country people, are the best
worth getting ". Plays about the country and the country
people came to be written in great abundance, but the
romantic and historical plays were very few indeed. None
of the new playwrights who were encouraged by the movement ventured to touch the heroes of Irish mythology with
the solitary exception of John M. Synge, and he only ventured
upon legend in his last, unfinished play. It would almost
seem that the playwrights were not willing to risk the peril
against which Standish O'Grady had warned those who
would attempt to place the heroic cycles on the stage. The
poets could have the heroic cycles, and to the poets they have
been given ; the dramatists have left them very severely alone.

When the first plays of Synge, Padraic Colum, and Lady Gregory were staged the Theatre settled down definitely to the ' peasant ' play by which, ' being the imitation of nothing English ', it has made itself famous throughout the world. Not only did the ' peasant ' play give to Ireland something that was novel, something which other countries did not have, but it also encouraged dramatists in other countries to utilise the materials lying to their hands amongst their own peoples. That there is now in many parts of the world, notably in England and America, a flourishing folk-drama is due mainly to the work of the Irish Theatre and to the genius of John Millington Synge, from whom all the newer folk-drama takes its rise.

But Edward Martyn clung as tenaciously to his own ideals as did Mr. Yeats, and with the help of amateur organisations like the Players' Club, the Independent Theatre, and the little theatre which he founded himself in 1914, which he called The Irish Theatre, he continued his activities by producing his own plays, and plays by Ibsen, Tchechov, Strindberg, and Galsworthy, together with several new plays by Irish writers who did not specialise in the ' peasant ' play. It may be said, however, that the ideals for which Edward Martyn contended were never realised, and it is certainly true that his art was frustrated by the absence of facilities for its adequate expression and the lack of critical appreciation. He lived long enough to see his ideals realised when after the Great War the Abbey Theatre began to stage the plays of European dramatists, and when the Dublin Drama League was formed to undertake the work that he had tried to do a quarter of a century before. The ideals of Mr. Yeats have never been fully realised either, and in some ways he has suffered a worse fate than Edward Martyn. When the ideal of a small and understanding audience gave place to that of a ' peasant ' drama nearly everything for which Mr. Yeats had contended went overboard. The Theatre took on a narrowness against which he had fought, and as its audiences consisted mainly of city folk it never got anywhere near the attention of the ' man of the roads ' who might have been ennobled had he but known that ennobling influences, especially designed for him, were in his vicinity. As the scope of the Theatre narrowed the influence of Mr. Yeats grew less and less. He is the only dramatist in the movement who has attempted plays in verse, and he is unlikely to have any successor. The models for the newer dramatists who were encouraged to write by the existence of the Theatre were provided by Synge, Padraic Colum and Lady Gregory, and it was Synge who first caught the attention of the world and attracted it to the Irish Theatre. Indeed it might be said that when he lost the support of Edward Martyn and George Moore, who did certainly share his literary ideals, Mr. Yeats lost also his control of the growing Theatre. He has been one of the Directors of the Theatre since its first performance in 1899, but neither his plays nor his ideals have been effective in moulding the plays that reached its stage. His ideals, in fact, would probably have had more influence upon the Irish literary revival had the Irish Literary Theatre been continued, as it so easily might have been, with his assistance. When at length the Abbey Theatre had come back to the ideals of the Irish Literary Theatre, at the end of the Great War, it was too late. Edward Martyn was ill, George Moore had left Ireland for the last time, and Mr. Yeats had ceased to be interested in the people. So the Theatre produced plays by Bernard Shaw, Nicholas Evreinov, Anton Tchechov, Martinez Sierra, and others of the more recent continental dramatists. Another type of ' new ' drama had come to Europe, and this time the Irish Theatre is likely to take full advantage of all that it has to give, and all that it has to teach. So perhaps in the end it is the ideal of Edward Martyn that has triumphed.

CHAPTER V

THE SUBSIDISED THEATRE : 1904-1910

The Irish National Theatre Society formed—Its Acting praised by the London Critics—Some Members go to America—The Title challenged—A Political Attack—' Immoral ' Plays !—The Attack on Synge—Miss Horniman provides a Theatre—Restrictions in the Patent—The Abbey Theatre opened—Gathering an Audience and searching for Playwrights—Lady Gregory's Great Work—*The Playboy* Riots—And a Declaration of Independence—The Cause of the Riots ?—Many New Playwrights—The Departure of the Brothers Fay—Defying the London Censor—The Lord Lieutenant interferes—Miss Horniman withdraws.

In March 1903 a form of prospectus was issued in which it was stated " The Irish National Theatre Society was founded to continue on a more permanent basis the work of the Irish Literary Theatre ", and in this prospectus the name of the organisation appears in its final form. The actual organisation, however, had to be changed at a later date from that of a co-operative society to that of a private limited liability company. This prospectus appeared almost simultaneously with the performance of Lady Gregory's first play, *Twenty-Five*, while the company under the direction of the brothers Fay still rehearsed in the little clubroom in Camden Street and produced its plays at the Molesworth Hall, a small assembly hall owned by a Church of Ireland Society, in Molesworth Street. But a visit to London on the invitation of the Irish Literary Society gave to the company that confidence which only the commendation of the most competent criticism can give. The leading critics of the London press were generous, even enthusiastic, in the praises which they lavished upon the performances given by the company at the Queen's Gate Hall, Mr. A. B. Walkley, usually sparing in his bestowal of praise, being particularly eloquent in *The Times*, as was Mr. C. E. Montague in *The Manchester Guardian*. " It is natural ", commented Mr. Yeats in *Samhain*, " that we should be pleased with this praise, and that we should wish others to know of it, for is it not a chief pleasure of the artist to be commended in subtle and eloquent words ? " It was probably the success of this visit to London, and the generous appreciation which the acting of the Irish company evoked from the London press, that prompted the organisers of the Irish Section of the Saint Louis Exposition to invite the company to visit the United States and give performances of Irish plays at the Exposition and elsewhere. The company as a whole, or as an Irish organisation, found itself unable to accept the invitation, because it was " thought that our work should be in Ireland for the present ". Some members of the company, including Dudley Digges, P. J. Kelly, and Miss Quinn, accepted the invitation, and have never since returned to Ireland. It was, perhaps, the recognition of this danger which induced the organisation to decline the invitation. Those members of the company who went to America were a very great loss indeed to the Irish Theatre at the time, but everyone who has taken any interest in the American theatre and drama during the past twenty years would be ready to testify to the great work which they have done in America. Dudley Digges in particular has been one of the greatest forces in the contemporary theatre, and it is not too much to say that without his aid the American drama would not have achieved the very distinguished position which it holds to-day. The prestige of the native American drama has been gained largely by and through the work of such organisations as the Theatre Guild and the Provincetown Players, with similar groups scattered throughout the United States, and in the formation and training of these groups the influence of the Irish actor has been very marked and often decisive. But Ireland lost what the United States gained. The departure of these three players was the first break in the personnel of the little company, and it emphasised a danger against which the Irish Theatre must always be prepared to contend, the greater financial inducements which can be offered by theatres in England and America to actors and actresses who have achieved some fame at home. By going to America these early migrants from the Irish National Theatre Society did good work for the American theatre and achieved a secure fame for themselves, and they also escaped the stormy period through which their colleagues who remained in Dublin had to pass within a few years. But the approval of the leading dramatic critics of England and America was something well worth while, and it was probably that approval which, more than any other single factor, emboldened the Directors and enheartened the players during their years of struggle. Irish criticism was often of the most bitter kind, and it rarely had any connection whatever with the merits or demerits of the plays as drama ; it was usually the expression of prejudices, patriotic or religious, uttered in the raucous tones of the bigot and the fanatic. Mr. Yeats has spoken of critics defending their " articles of belief among a wild people, and thinking mournfully of distant cities, where nobody puts a raw potato into his pocket when he is going to hear a musical comedy ". Not many months were destined to pass before Mr. Yeats would discover that raw potatoes would be carried in the pockets of the critics of his own theatre so that they could be hurled at the players on the stage.

The right of the new organisation to use the title it had chosen, The Irish National Theatre Society, was challenged from the start. It was held by the more extreme section of the Gaelic League that only a theatre using the Irish language solely in its plays could legitimately use the title ; and the organ of what was then beginning to be known as the Sinn Fein movement seemed to suggest that only a theatre staging political plays could be Irish and National. At the time there were several theatrical bodies using the drama as a vehicle for political propagandist purposes, and it was one of these bodies, The Daughters of Ireland, which first produced Mr. Yeats's *Kathleen ni Houlihan*, with Miss Maud Gonne in the title-role. Miss Gonne was then a very prominent leader in the militant political movement and she brought to her acting all the intensity of her political beliefs. " It was a fine thing ", says Mr. Yeats, " for so beautiful a woman to consent to play my poor old Cathleen, and she played with nobility and tragic power. . . . The most beautiful woman of her time, when she played my Cathleen, ' made up ' centuries old, and never should the part be played but with a like sincerity." Despite this tribute it must be said that these bodies had no real interest in the drama as such, they only used the stage and the drama to engender political enthusiasm and passion for specific purposes and at fitting times. For some time their work threatened to eclipse the work of the National Theatre Society, and to take from it such popular support as it then had ; and had it not been for the courageous and continuous propagandist work of Mr. Yeats the Society might have been crushed in its very first year by the malicious misrepresentation of the press and the sectional activities of the political and linguistic societies. Political passion had been aroused in the mass of the people by the agitation against the Boer War, and they had been kept at white heat in a considerable section of the population of Dublin by the organisation of a protest against the visit of Queen Victoria just prior to her death. Attempts were being made to utilise these passions for a new orientation of Irish politics. At the time the attempts failed ; there was but a small response from the people in general, but a large section of the intelligentsia became, and remained, associated with the new Sinn Fein movement.

When the political flank-attack failed to smash the National Theatre Society a new attack was launched based upon a charge of ' immorality '. This attack became narrowed, and focussed upon a definite object, when Synge's *In the Shadow of the Glen* was produced in October 1903. This new attack upon the Theatre was opened in the daily press, but soon the organ of Sinn Fein, *The United Irishman*, which had once supported the dramatic movement, joined in the attack, and from this time onward criticised adversely almost every play produced by the Theatre. It was especially hostile to Synge, who was accused of being ' a French decadent ', and to this consistently hostile propaganda in an influential periodical can be traced the beginnings of the riot which greeted the first production of *The Playboy of the Western World* four years later. Synge's first play, *In the Shadow of the Glen*, was attacked on the ground that no Irishwoman could be so base as to encourage a lover as did his Nora Burke ; and Nora Burke was simply a Nora Helmer in terms of Irish life. But it has to be borne in mind that the relations of the sexes is very straitly guarded in Ireland. The attitude towards sexual morality is somewhat hypocritical, so that Irish people are smugly complacent in the belief that they are not as other peoples in this respect. Other peoples may be lax and promiscuous, but not the Irish ! This puritanical attitude is due to the very tight grip which the Catholic clergy keeps upon all intercourse between the sexes, and it was at this grip that Synge was alleged to have struck in his play. In reply to the attacks in the press Mr. Yeats mentioned an English play, *Mice and Men*, which had run for five hundred nights in London, and had been played in Dublin with the approbation of the press. In this play the turning point is the caddish dismissal of a mistress so that a man may marry another girl. " If a man of intellect had written of such an incident ", said Mr. Yeats, " he would have made his audience feel for the mistress that sympathy one feels for all that have suffered insult, and for that young man an ironical emotion that might have marred the marriage bells, and who knows what the curate and the journalist would have said of the man of intellect ? Even Ireland would have cried out : Catholic Ireland that should remember the gracious tolerance of the Church when all nations were its children, and how Wolfram of Eisenbach sang from castle to castle of the courtesy of Parzival, the good husband, and of Gawain, the light lover, in that very Thuringia where a generation later the lap of Saint Elizabeth was full of roses. A Connacht Bishop told his people a while since that they ' should never read stories about the degrading passion of love ', and one can only suppose that, being ignorant of the chief glory of his Church, he has never understood that this new puritanism is but an English cuckoo " (*Essays and Controversies*, p. 53).

This alleged ' immorality ' of the Irish Theatre has never been effectively and finally disposed of, so that it is as strongly stressed to-day as it was in 1903, and attacks are still being made upon the alleged ' paganism ' of the Theatre. It was one of the strongest arguments brought in opposition to the grant of a Patent to the Abbey Theatre in 1904, and it is the main point made against the plays of Sean O'Casey to-day. Miss A. E. F. Horniman, who was to become famous a few years later for her work at the Gaiety Theatre in Manchester, had been so favourably impressed by the company which she saw in London, and because she had ' great sympathy with the Irish National Theatre Company as explained by Mr. Yeats ', that she offered to provide and equip a small theatre in Dublin and maintain it free of all charge to the company for a period of years. An old theatre in Abbey Street, ' The Mechanics', which had fallen from high estate to be the home of variety of a low class, and part of the city Morgue in Marlborough Street, were selected as being suitable for adaptation to the requirements of the Society. The work of reconstruction was entrusted to a Dublin architect, Mr. Joseph Holloway, the decorations and embellishments were done by Irish artists, and so far as was practicable all the necessary work was done by Irish people. The necessary reconstruction work and equipment of the building for use as a theatre is said to have cost Miss Horniman £13,000, a sum which could not have been secured in Ireland for any theatrical enterprise at that time. The very fact that the necessary financial support could not be secured in Ireland at the time makes the debt of gratitude which all lovers of the Irish drama owe to the generosity and the sympathy of Miss Horniman one which should always be kept in mind. Miss Horniman herself probably feels, as a great lover and benefactor of the theatre, that the success and fame which has attended the Abbey Theatre has more than justified and rewarded her sacrifice on its behalf. But the grateful thanks of all Irish drama-lovers is also hers, and her portrait which hangs in the vestibule of the Abbey Theatre is a continuous reminder of her generous aid. The generosity of an English-woman could provide the Theatre but it could not prevent Irish opposition to the grant of a Patent. The theatrical law of Ireland was made by the Irish Parliament of 1782-1800, and if that law made no Censor it provided for the grant of a Patent from the Crown before a new theatre could be opened to the public. The grant of this Patent to the Abbey Theatre was opposed by the other Dublin theatres, most vigorously by the two theatres which were owned and controlled by a London syndicate. When the application for a Patent for the Abbey Theatre came before the Irish Privy Council the opposition relied greatly upon the alleged ' immorality ' of the plays which the company had produced, and the names of Ibsen and Maeterlinck were mentioned as being those of notoriously ' immoral ' dramatists. It was also suggested that the Society had produced a play ' which had attacked the sanctity of marriage ', a charge obviously directed against *In the Shadow of the Glen*. But despite all the opposition the Patent was granted to ' Dame Augusta Gregory ' authorising her to open a theatre for the amusement and instruction of the public, with the restriction that only plays by Irish authors, and foreign masterpieces other than English, might be produced. This restriction has since been removed and the Theatre can now produce any play which it may desire. But the Patent also deprived the Abbey Theatre of what is considered to be one of the most important adjuncts of the commercial theatre—there should be no bar where intoxi-cating liquors were sold. So alcoholic liquors have never been sold, and probably never will be sold, within the pre-mises of the Abbey Theatre. There are, of course, people who regard this as a deprivation which should be resented, but it is probable that the Directors will never make any attempt to have things otherwise. So in that respect the terms of the original Patent are still observed.

With such slight, and comparatively unimportant, restrictions in the original Patent the Abbey Theatre gave its first public performance on the evening of the 27th December, 1904, and remained open for a wcck. During that first week four plays were performed, all being in one act, *On Baile's Strand*, and *Kathleen ni Houlihan*, by W. B. Yeats, *Spreading the News*, by Lady Gregory, and *In the Shadow of the Glen*, by J. M. Synge. Two of the plays, *On Baile's Strand* and *Spreading the News*, were performed for the first time, and Lady Gregory's *Spreading the News* is probably the most popular one-act play in the Theatre's repertoire. Thus in the first programme which the Abbey Theatre submitted appeared the names, and the work, of the three people who were to dominate it for many years. It may be of some interest to note that it was on the same evening that the Abbey Theatre opened its doors to the public for the first time that Sir James Barrie's *Peter Pan* was performed for the first time at the Duke of York's Theatre in London. Since that memorable evening in December 1904 almost the entire world, and certainly that part of the world which takes an interest in the theatre and the drama, has become familiarised with both the Abbey Theatre and Sir James Barrie's play. In making her offer of a theatre Miss Horniman had said, " I can only offer to make a very little theatre, and it must be quite simple. You all must do the rest to make a powerful and prosperous theatre with a high artistic ideal ". That the Abbey Theatre has become powerful there are few who will doubt, but financial prosperity lingered though that prosperity which consists in appreciation came in abundance. It can hardly be claimed, however, that the high artistic ideal has been consistently maintained ; as indeed the high artistic ideal could not hope to be maintained when the nationalist restriction and the folk drama had once been accepted as alternatives. But as Mr. Yeats wrote in *Samhain*, " It is better to fumble our way as children. We may grow

up, for we have as good hopes as any other sturdy ragamuffin".
In one sense it may be said that the Theatre did grow up : it
grew steadily in popularity and influence.   But in another,
and perhaps a more important, sense the Abbey Theatre has
been as Peter Pan who shared its birthday. The quality of
its plays did not consistently improve, and many competent
judges have given it as their opinion that the best plays which the
Theatre has produced were those of its early years. But when
Mr. St. John Ervine wrote in 1924 that the Irish dramatic
movement " speedily perished from lack of staying power "
(*These Eventful Years*, p. 406), he made a statement that is so
obviously contrary to the facts that he seemed to have merged
his critical faculty in personal pique. A Theatre that has
discovered scores of new dramatists, good, bad, and indifferent, as is the custom of all theatres, and has performed
hundreds of new plays, most certainly did not lack staying
power. It has now been opened to the public for twenty-
four years, and it has made for itself a place quite distinctive
and very conspicuous in the dramatic history of this century.
It has gathered an audience which can at all times fill its six
hundred seats, and it can rely upon popular support for its
efforts, even if in the process of securing that popular support
it has had to make some small sacrifices of artistic ideal.
During its early years plays were performed only on three
evenings a week, but for many years now there are seven
performances a week, six evenings and one matinee.

William Boyle was the first of the new dramatists to be
discovered by the Abbey Theatre, and his comedies were for
some years the most popular, as they were the first full-length,
comedies which appeared on the programme of the Theatre.
Boyle's first comedy, *The Building Fund*, had its first production in April 1905, and for the two succeeding seasons he with
Lady Gregory, Yeats, and Colum provided the plays. In
these two years Lady Gregory alone provided six of the
thirteen plays which were produced. The industry and
versatility of Lady Gregory during these early years of the
Abbey Theatre are simply amazing. She had been prevented

by illness from being present at the opening performance of
the Theatre, but she had taken her full share in the important
work of preparation and rehearsal. So inspiring was her very
presence to the members of the company that Mr. Yeats had
to tell her, " The company are very disappointed that you
will not be up for the first night. Fay says they would all act
better if you were here " (*Our Irish Theatre*, p. 43). Not
only did she inspire and encourage the company, she took
her part in the management and direction of the Theatre, did
a vast amount of publicity and propagandist work, encouraged
and assisted others to write plays, and herself wrote and
translated more than twenty of the plays produced by the
Theatre during the first five years of its existence. Nowadays
when people express their amazement at the industry and
versatility of a Benevente, a Sierra, or a Pirandello they
might also pause to pay tribute to Lady Gregory, who kept
steadily working at her collections of folk-tales and her
translations of the heroic cycles throughout her theatrical
activities. She is truly an amazing woman, a woman of whom
Ireland and the Irish Theatre have every reason to feel proud.

The great testing-time for the Abbey Theatre and its
Directors came with the first production of *The Playboy of the
Western World* in January 1907. The plays of Synge had
already excited suspicion and hostility, and it was not,
therefore, very surprising that the production of this play
should have led to riotous scenes such as are rarely witnessed
in a theatre, and a vehemence of opinion such as is rarely
excited in any country by a play. The critics came with their
' raw potatoes in their pockets ' which, instead of eating, as
the austerity of Mr. Yeats might have induced him to
suppose, they proceeded to throw at the actors on the stage.
Early in the second act the disturbances began, and then the
booing, yelling, catcalling, and noisy clattering of boots
upon the floor, converted the play into little better than dumb
show. Missiles of many kinds were hurled at the stage, so
that finally the assistance of the police had to be requisitioned
to quell the disturbance. The press unanimously demanded

the withdrawal of the play as demoralising to the community
and damaging to the national prestige abroad, but the
Directors very courageously persisted in keeping it on for the
seven performances which had been announced. At every
performance organised interruptions by gangs which had
come especially for that purpose made the play inaudible.
Some of the gangs had come from Trinity College in support
of the play, which they too regarded as damaging to nationalist
hopes, but their noisy support drowned the voices of the
company just as effectively as the noisy opposition of the
hostile groups. Every night there were fights in the theatre,
and when the police removed the belligerents the fights were
continued in the neighbouring streets. There was what
amounted to a riot, and by the end of the week nearly five
hundred police were required to keep order in the theatre
and its precincts. When the curtain fell on the Saturday
night amidst ' thunders of applause ' the play had never been
heard in the theatre, it had only been heard *of* in the columns
of the newspapers or the gossip of the streets, so the applause
was that of political faction not that of artistic appreciation.
Nevertheless *The Playboy* did achieve a triumph at the time,
a triumphant vindication by the Directors of their claim for
freedom in the theatre. The play was the subject of a debate
in the Abbey Theatre on the evening of 4th February, 1907,
which gave to Mr. Yeats an opportunity to counter-attack his
opponents and to express definitely the principles for which
he contended. " Gentlemen of the little clubs and societies ",
he said on that occasion, " do not mistake the meaning of our
victory ; it means something for us, but more for you. When
the curtain of *The Playboy* fell on Saturday night in the midst
of what *The Sunday Independent*—no friendly witness—
described as ' thunders of applause ', I am confident that I
saw the rise in this country of a new thought, a new opinion,
that we had long needed. It was not all approval of Mr.
Synge's play that sent the receipts of the Abbey Theatre this
last week to twice the height they had ever touched before.
The generation of young men and girls who are now leaving

schools and colleges are weary of the tyranny of the clubs and leagues. They wish again for individual sincerity, the eternal quest of youth, all that has been given up for so long that all might crouch upon the one roost or cry in the one flock. We are beginning once again to ask what a man is, and to be content to wait a little before we go on to the further question : What is a good Irishman ? " The prophecy contained in that statement was never realised in fact, and Mr. Yeats now knows that it was only the names of the little clubs and leagues that were changed, and that the tyranny remained. The tendency to ' crouch on one branch ' and ' cry in the flock ' still remains, and there are yet no signs of change, except perhaps that Mr. Yeats is now more willing to give heed to the cry of the flock than he was twenty years ago. Where there has been change at all it has been in the attitude of Mr. Yeats himself, who now seems to demand less ; there has been little or no change in Irish opinion on the vital matter of freedom of the arts and the artists.

The week's rioting drew the attention of the world to the Abbey Theatre, to *The Playboy*, and to J. M. Synge, and did more to establish all three in the attention of the world than any other single event of the time. But it had a very unsettling effect upon Synge himself. " He was always nervous at a first production", says Lady Gregory, "and the unusual excitement attending this one upset him. . . . I think the week's rioting helped to break down his health. . . . He took a chill and was kept to his bed for a while " (*Our Irish Theatre*, p. 134).

What was it that caused the rioting ? This is a question that has exercised the minds of others than Irishmen since that day, and the opinion expressed outside Ireland tended always to the suggestion that Irishmen were too thin-skinned, and could not tolerate a joke at their own expense. Lady Gregory and Mr. Yeats seemed to think that it was the unusual amount of ' bad language ' which Synge introduced into the play. " There were far too many violent oaths ", says Lady Gregory, " I took out many phrases which, though in the printed book, have never since that first production been spoken on our stage " (*Our Irish Theatre*, p. 134). Others there were who thought it was the mention of feminine underclothing that caused the tumult : " Audience broke up in disorder at the word shift ", Lady Gregory telegraphed to Mr. Yeats. And there were still others who thought it was the reference to ' khaki cut-throats ' which had aroused the suspicious interference of Dublin Castle. Some, or even all, of these may have contributed to the cause of the disturbances, but behind and beyond all these there was the tender self-consciousness of an Irish audience in a period of political tension. Everything that could be used as an argument for or against Home Rule was eagerly sought and carefully gathered by one party or the other, and *The Playboy* seemed to be an argument against Ireland, as it seemed also to be a particularly atrocious attempt to revive the ' stage Irishman ' which all sections were combined to drive from the stage. Nationalist Irishmen were trying to keep up the best possible appearance of virtue before the world. Synge's plays seemed to them to thwart that laudable design, and as a consequence he was regarded, and treated, as one who tried to belittle his Motherland, and give gratuitous arguments to the enemies of his country. This, of course, was an entire misunderstanding of Synge's design and purpose, but the realistic manner in which the play was staged, and the general stage realism of the time, gave such an interpretation of the play some justification. There was then observable little of the fantastic comedy spirit in which the play is now performed, and it was judged not as art, but simply as a Unionist attempt to malign the country. But there can be no doubt that Synge did intend to convey a warning to his countrymen, and events have since proved that the warning was as needed as it was ignored. Readers of a recent novel by Con O'Leary, *Break o' Day*, will discover that even those who disliked *The Playboy* lived to become playboys themselves. Curley Bogue in that novel is a greater scoundrel than was Christy Mahon, but he posed as a patriot, and for that much was forgiven him. A demoralised community does not feel capable of distinguishing scoundrels from heroes, that seemed to be Synge's warning, and it was unheeded.

That it was the alleged political slur that caused the protest against *The Playboy* was amply proven a year later when *The Piper*, by Conal O'Riordan, was produced on 13th February, 1908. This play deals with the Rising in Wexford in 1798, and its chief character, Black Mike, has some very unpalatable things to say about the Irish character. The play is a rather obvious satire upon Irish political tactics of the then recent past, and upon Irish mentality generally, and it has some affinity with *John Bull's Other Island*, which was written as a contribution to the Abbey Theatre's repertoire but which could not be played there because the necessary cast was not available. *The Piper* at its first performance also evoked protest from the audience, but the disturbances were neither so violent nor so prolonged as they had been at *The Playboy*. This may have been only because *The Piper* being a one-act play presented less scope for hostile demonstrations. The recurrence of the disturbances at such a play, however, proved conclusively the political basis of the riots of 1907. As Conal O'Riordan was a new playwright the hostile reception given to his first play might have prevented him trying again ; fortunately it did not, and he has since written many excellent plays for the theatres of Ireland and England.

The first plays of George Fitzmaurice, Lennox Robinson, Lord Dunsany, R. J. Ray, T. C. Murray, and Seumas O'Kelly were all produced by the Abbey Theatre in the years from 1907 to 1910. Seumas O'Kelly had been connected with some of the other theatrical groups, but he came to the Abbey Theatre when Padraic Colum returned in 1910. Colum had been one of those who protested against *The Playboy*, and demonstrated his disgust by withdrawing his plays from the Theatre. In consequence his play, *The Fiddler's House*, was first staged by another company, The Theatre of Ireland, and was not staged at the Abbey Theatre until 1919, more than twelve years after its first production in Dublin.

In January 1908 the company again suffered severe loss by
the departure of the brothers Fay and Miss Bridget O'Dempsey from the Theatre. This second break in the company
was due to disagreement amongst its leading members,
probably because it was thought that the Fays were mono-
polising the credit which was due to the entire company.
They had given the company its training, and its distinctive
style of acting ; and in their methods there was no place for
the 'star'. But this 'star' system was to make its appearance
in the years immediately following their departure from the
Theatre. Since they left the Abbey Theatre they have never
found adequate scope for their peculiar talents ; they have
tried the commercial theatre in England and America, but
even their greatest admirers cannot claim that they have done
themselves justice there or that they have achieved any
success. It is surely a pity that personal antagonism and
petty differences should have caused the loss to the Abbey
Theatre of the two men who had done most to make it
distinctive in acting and staging, and all lovers of the Theatre
will share Lady Gregory's expressed regret that they did not
remain to take their share in the success of the Theatre they
had done so much to serve.

The Abbey Theatre found itself inadequately equipped to
stage Mr. Shaw's *John Bull's Other Island* in 1905, but it
could take *The Showing-up of Blanco Posnet* when that play
was banned by the English censor in 1909. There was, and
still is, no censorship of the theatre in Ireland. A Censor of
Films was appointed under statute in 1923, so that it is
possible a censorship of the theatre may be established in due
time, as there is considerable agitation for such an appointment by vigilance committees and such bodies. In the
absence of a censor in 1909, however, the Abbey Theatre
could stage *Blanco Posnet*, and it did. But the staging was
not achieved without some difficulty, as the authorities at
Dublin Castle endeavoured to prevent the performance at the
instigation of the Censor of Plays in London. The Theatre
was threatened that its Patent would be revoked, but as

the performance of the play had been announced before the
Castle took action a fight had once more to be made for the
freedom of the Theatre. This time the threat came not from
a mob but from the Lord Lieutenant, the representative of
the King in Ireland. Lady Gregory, who conducted the
negotiations in her capacity of Patentee of the Theatre, stood
firm, and she had the very effective backing of Mr. Bernard
Shaw, who had old scores against the Censor of Stage Plays
in London dating back to 1892 when *Mrs. Warren's Profession*
had been banned. This ' fight against the Castle ' did much
to restore the Abbey Theatre to the good opinion of advanced
Nationalists, and of those who had withdrawn from active
support of the Theatre in 1907. The banning of the play in
London, and the attempt to prevent its performance in
Dublin, gave to *Blanco Posnet* a degree of publicity in the
press which it probably would not have secured on its own
merits. It was staged with great success in Dublin, where it
was the special attraction at the Abbey Theatre for Horse
Show Week, 1909. Horse Show Week is the great social
week in Dublin, and the Theatre was packed at every performance for the week. Success seemed to have come to the
Theatre at last after a bitter struggle. An audience had been
secured, and it had grown steadily in numbers and influence,
and there were hundreds of people to whom ' The Abbey '
was very much more than a mere theatre. To these it was
something of a symbol and something of a creed. The
Theatre had indeed become part of the life of Dublin, if not
exactly of Ireland. It had been caught in the ' folk ' current,
and it was that current, as Lady Gregory says, " that brought
it on its triumphant way. It is chiefly known now as a folk-
theatre. It has not only the great mass of primitive material
and legend to draw on, but it has been made a living thing by
that discovery ". Such was the position of the Irish National
Theatre when Miss Horniman withdrew from its support in
1910, after a period of six years.

CHAPTER VI

THE IRISH NATIONAL THEATRE : 1911-1928

A New Organisation—Self-supporting—Tour in the United States—The Riots about *The Playboy*—The Company is 'Arrested' in Philadelphia—Formation of a School of Acting—Mr. Nugent Monck as Director—The Season at the Court Theatre, London—Dublin Criticism—Mr. St. John Ervine retorts—Mr. Ervine as Manager—The Dublin 'Rising', 1916—Losses to the Theatre—A Shaw Boom —A State Subsidy and a new Outlook—Back to the Irish Literary Theatre.

WHEN Miss Horniman decided to withdraw her support from the Irish National Theatre she surrendered all her rights in the building to the Directors for the trifling sum of £1,000. A private Limited Liability Company was formed to take over the ownership and control of the organisation, which was slowly but certainly assuming the complexity of any ordinary commercial theatre. For some years the members of the company had been receiving salaries, and amateur acting was no longer relied upon as one of the main contributions to the support of an artistic and patriotic enterprise. But up to this time the playwrights had received no royalties from the Theatre, and of course they could neither be expected nor depended upon to continue such altruistic conduct. For these and other more ordinary business reasons the Society was compelled to conform with the usual commercial organisation of the theatre, and accept the business methods of its rivals and competitors. But these changes in form did not change in any way the spirit in which the Abbey Theatre was conducted. Not the playwrights only went unremunerated for their services : scenes were designed by Mr. Robert Gregory and Mr. Gordon Craig ; costumes were designed and made ; and necessary services of many kinds were rendered by many people without either hope of or demand for financial reward. The Directors, too, performed their often very arduous work without fee : in fact it might be said that almost all the services given to the theatre in its early years were entirely voluntary and unremunerated. For about four years there had been three Directors : Lady Gregory, W. B. Yeats, and J. M. Synge ; but when Synge died in 1909 his place was left vacant, and the remaining two Directors controlled the affairs of the Theatre until 1922, when Mr. Lennox Robinson was selected for a seat on the Board. When the Private Company which took over the Theatre from Miss Horniman was formed in 1911 only the two Directors in control at the time were named, but power was taken to add to the number as changing circumstances might require. The capital of the Company was fixed at £1,000, divided into £1 shares, and 390 of these shares have been issued. Of the shares issued the Directors hold 376 amongst them, and no invitation has ever been given to the public to subscribe for the shares, because one of the Articles of Association expressly prohibits any such invitation. So the Irish National Theatre is, from a legal or commercial point of view, the private property of the Directors who hold its capital. But they derive no profit whatever from that owner-ship beyond such royalties as they, in common with all other playwrights whose plays are performed in the Theatre, may receive from the performance of their plays, or any fees which may be paid to Mr. Lennox Robinson for his services as Producer. Instead of financing the Theatre by an invitation to all interested to take shares in the Company, as is the method adopted by commercial and repertory theatres alike in other countries, the Directors of the Abbey Theatre asked for an Endowment Fund of £5,000 to be constituted by voluntary gifts from admirers of, and sympathisers with, the work of the Theatre. As part of the propaganda necessary to raise this sum an extended tour of the principal cities and towns of Great Britain and the United States was undertaken during 1911 and 1912. It is probable that at this time

Edward Martyn might have been induced to rejoin the Theatre, and to provide at least a part of the Endowment Fund. Whether any serious effort was made to bring him back is doubtful, so his interest was never regained and he founded his own little Irish Theatre in 1914.

The tour of the company in Great Britain was an artistic triumph, and a great financial success. In London as in the provincial cities the plays and the players were received with an enthusiasm that could not be surpassed. The praise of the critics, and the chorus of approval in the press, was even more lavish than they had been on earlier visits. But the visit to the United States, though it, too, was a great success artistically and financially, provided thrills in abundance for the Directors and the Players. The trouble began with the production of *The Playboy* in Boston, and a storm of hostile criticism was directed against the whole Irish dramatic movement, and upon the separate items in the Theatre's repertory.

This American tour had been for several years in contemplation by the Directors, but when it was actually undertaken it was not either arranged or controlled by them. It was to a considerable extent due to the pronounced success of the London season, at the Court Theatre, as an outcome of which an offer was made by a well-known firm of theatrical agents, Liebler & Co., for a tour lasting three or four months in the United States during the winter of 1911-12. Among the plays mentioned by the Agents as essential to the success of the tour was *The Playboy*, and the inclusion of this play aroused the hostility of the Irish population of the United States from the beginning ; propaganda against the Players began when the tour was first announced. Within the company there was some little difficulty about this play also ; it was necessary to secure a new actress to play Pegeen Mike, as Miss Maire O'Neill, who had created the role, had married and retired temporarily from the stage. But an admirable substitute was soon found in the person of Miss Eithne Magee, a young actress who afterwards did excellent work for the Theatre. The entire company under the direction of Mr. Yeats, and including Miss Sara Allgood, Miss Eithne Magee, Messrs. Arthur Sinclair, J. M. Kerrigan, Fred O'Donovan, J. A. O'Rourke, and Sydney Morgan, sailed from Queenstown (Cobh) on 12th September, 1911, arriving at Boston, Massachusetts, about a week later. Lady Gregory followed from Ireland on 19th September, and arrived at Boston on 29th September to find that hostile demonstrations were being very actively organised against the plays and the players. One critic wrote to the *Boston Post* to say he " never saw anything so vulgar, vile, beastly, and unnatural, so calculated to calumniate, degrade, and defame a people and all they hold sacred and dear " (*Our Irish Theatre*, p. 179). This language was used to describe two plays which had been received with enthusiasm by audiences in Ireland and in England, Lady Gregory's *Hyacinth Halvey* and T. C. Murray's *Birthright*. So the storm gathered force, and when *The Playboy* was announced for production on the evening of 16th October it broke. *The Gaelic American*, organ of the Clann na Gael, led the hostility in the press, and it gave prominence to the resolve of the United Irish Societies of New York ' to drive the vile thing from the stage '. The Police Commissioners of Boston sent their Censor, and the Mayor sent his Secretary, to report upon the play. Both reported very favourably and there was no further trouble in Boston, where the company had a very successful season lasting for six weeks at the Plymouth Theatre. The company left Boston on 30th October, 1911, and from that date until its departure from the United States on 5th March, 1912, it was pursued by a press campaign of malignant vilification, punctuated by riots in the theatres, and molestation by the police. At New Haven, Connecticut, where the company played mainly for the students of Yale University, there occurred one of the few humorous incidents of the tour. The Police Commissioner, acting for the Mayor, had been deputed to censor *The Playboy*, had attended the theatre for that purpose and had seen what he thought was a rehearsal

of the play.   What he actually attended was a matinee
performance of Mr. Shaw's *Shewing-up of Blanco Posnet* and
Lady Gregory's *The Image*.   However, that did not prevent
the newspapers from stating that several phrases had been
objected to, and that these phrases had been suppressed at
the evening performance.   No wonder that Yale laughed
when it became aware of the facts !   But the laughter of Yale
did not prevent *The Gaelic American* from stating that there
had been ' careful excision of obscene passages ' (*Our Irish
Theatre*, p. 188).   The people of Washington were informed
that the company had left Dublin " followed by the hisses
and indignation of an outraged populace ".   " The Dublin
people never accepted the plays.   They virtually kicked them
from the stage.   England gave them no reception ".   Such
were some of the statements in a leaflet handed out in the
streets by members of an Irish political, and alleged patriotic,
society.   Washington took no heed of such propagandist
efforts ; instead it gave the plays an enthusiastic reception,
the President and Mrs. Taft being amongst those who went
out of their way to do honour to the company.   In New York,
where the season at the Maxine Elliott Theatre opened on
19th November, 1911, the adverse propaganda began to show
its finest effects.   The large Irish population of the city had
been exhorted to make a protest, and make a protest it did.
" *The Playboy* must be squelched ", commanded *The Gaelic
American*, " and a lesson taught to Mr. Yeats and his fellow-
agents of England " (*Gaelic American*, 18th November, 1911).
The Playboy was performed on the evening of 27th November, and immediately the curtain rose the disturbances
began.   " A good many potatoes were thrown on the stage
and an old watch, and a tin box with a cigar in it and a
cigarette box " (*Our Irish Theatre*, p. 204).   Ten men were
arrested by the police and were subsequently fined sums
ranging from three to ten dollars each.   In the theatre many
missiles were found after the performance, including bottles
containing noxious fumes, which the owners were evidently
either unwilling or unable to use.   Theodore Roosevelt came

to this performance and afterwards published a glowing appreciation of the plays and the players in his paper (*Outlook*, 16th December, 1911).   In Philadelphia the players were ' arrested ', but fortunately only technically, that is arrest-warrants were issued but were suspended by the signature of bail-bonds, and *The Playboy* was actually performed while the company was under bail.   The arrest was made under the terms of a municipal bye-law forbidding ' immoral and indecent plays ', and was originally aimed at Sarah Bern-hardt, being passed just prior to her visit to the city in 1910. The ' arrest ' of the players caused great excitement through-out the United States, and also in England and Ireland, but it did not prevent the production of the play as its instigators had hoped and believed that it would.   In the end, after a week's delay, the case against the company was dismissed. Chicago prepared to receive the company by the formation of an Anti-Irish Players' League from amongst its large Irish population.   A petition demanding the suppression of *The Playboy* was drafted, and was signed by thousands of people who probably had never even heard of the play.   At its meeting on 29th January, 1912, the City Council of Chicago directed its Mayor to prohibit performance of the play in the city, and Lady Gregory received an anonymous letter, complete with drawings of a revolver, coffin, hammer, and nails, in which she was informed " never again shall you gaze on the barren hill-tops of Connemara.   *Your doom is sealed* ".   Afterwards it was discovered that the City Council had no authority to prohibit the play except the Mayor decided that it was immoral or against public policy.   " I read three pages of the book", said Mayor Harrison (*Chicago Record-Herald*, 1st February, 1912), "and instead of finding anything immoral I found that the whole thing was wonderfully stupid ".   So *The Playboy* was performed for a week in Chicago, and the theatre was crowded at every performance, with ' never a boo or a hiss '.

The American tour was a financial no less than an artistic success.   Before the tour was undertaken some of the plays were known, and Synge's fame was secure, in the United States, but seeing the actual company from the Abbey Theatre made a tremendous difference. The Irish Drama was placed in a very prominent position before the immense audience of the United States, and in the time that has since passed that position has been more than maintained, as the impression was deepened by the subsequent tour of a somewhat different company in 1913. Since that time Ireland has been one of the outstanding ' drama ' countries for vast numbers of Americans.

While the company was absent in America a School of Acting was formed in the Theatre in Dublin under the direction of Mr. Nugent Monck. The primary reason for the formation of this School was to provide a second acting company to relieve the principal company of some of the strain incidental to continuous repertory work. It was also projected that the second company would undertake the necessary tours in the Irish provinces. Lady Gregory had expressed the hope that her history plays would be performed in cycles in different parts of the country, and that schools and colleges would do some of their teaching of history through the medium of these plays. And the declared ambition of Mr. Yeats was to reach ' the man working on the road and in the fields '. Neither the hope nor the ambition had been realisable because the theatre had only one company, and that company had been playing in Dublin almost continuously since the opening of the Theatre. There had been occasional visits to provincial towns, but they had never been sufficiently numerous or prolonged to make any deep impression. The formation of a second company, even had there never been an American tour, was a necessity if the hopes and ambitions of the Directors were to be realised. A School of Acting was, therefore, decided upon, and Mr. Nugent Monck was chosen to direct it because he seemed to possess in the greatest degree those qualities which the Abbey Theatre desired in its actors. He had been favourably known in England as a disciple of Mr. William Poel, was known to favour simplicity in staging, and to emphasise clarity of diction in his theatrical work. He has since achieved considerable fame as Director of the Maddermarket Theatre at Norwich, but it cannot be said that his work in Dublin made either a profound or a lasting impression. Very few members of the School have since achieved a reputation on the stage, Miss Una O'Connor in London, Mr. H. E. Hutchinson with Mr. Arthur Sinclair's ' Irish Players ', and Mr. A. P. Wilson, who was for a time manager of the Theatre, has written some plays, and is now the moving spirit of the Scottish National Players. The choice of plays for the training of this company was characteristic rather of Mr. Nugent Monck than of the Irish National Theatre. A series of old morality and mystery plays, including *The Interlude of Youth*, *The Second Shepherd's Play*, *The Annunciation*, *The Flight into Egypt*, and *The Worlde and the Chylde*, was presented by members of the School, in addition to revivals of some of the best known plays of the Theatre, and first productions of three new plays. *Red Turf*, Rutherford Mayne's only contribution to the Abbey Theatre, was first staged by the pupils of Mr. Nugent Monck, with the assistance of Miss Maire O'Neill ; as was also *Macdarragh's Wife*, written by Lady Gregory on her voyage across the Atlantic in September 1911, and Dr. Douglas Hyde's *The Tinker and the Fairy*, which was written and played in the Irish language. Thus the basis was broad enough, as the bias was towards the ' peasant ' policy of the Theatre, in the course of training which Mr. Monck adopted. But for some reason that second company never prospered, and with the return of the principal company from America it gradually faded into oblivion. In January 1912, when the ' arrest ' of the company at Philadelphia had been announced, Mr. Yeats wrote to Lady Gregory, " We have done very well this week with the school. I am rather anxious that the school, or No. 2 Company, as it will be, should have in its repertory some of our most popular pieces. . . . The great thing achieved is that if Philadelphia had permanently imprisoned the whole Company, our new Company would in twelve months have taken their place here in Dublin. We have now a fine general effect, though we have no big personalities " (*Our Irish Theatre*, p. 236). The performances given by members of the school were generally good, but, with the exception of Mr. Nugent Monck himself, no individual gave any memorable performance. As Aleel, in Mr. Yeats' *Countess Cathleen*, Mr. Monck gave a performance that made a permanent impression on the minds of all who witnessed it. Another performance of that time that has remained in the memory was given by Miss Cathleen Nesbitt, a newcomer to the Theatre, in a very mediocre play by William Boyle called *Family Failing*. As that second company of 1911-12 failed to realise expectations so have the several other second companies that have since been attempted, and the Theatre has never really had at its disposal the two companies which are needed for its work. Many attempts have been made by the Directors, and much energy and time have been expended, to secure two companies, but always when the efforts seemed to have been crowned with success something happened which dispersed the principal company, and the Directors were left to make the best use they could of the acting material at their disposal. But always, in time, the company that remained has proven that it was at least as good as the company that had gone. For a time, during and after the Great War and the little wars in Ireland, the standard of acting declined, but to-day the Theatre has at its service a company equal to any that it had in the past. The present-day company, however, is not the product of any School of Acting ; it has just come into being through the inclination and natural ability of its members, combined with continuous experience on the stage. Some of its members have been with the Theatre from its early years, and they have had to wait long for opportunity to distinguish themselves. Evidently artists such as the brothers Fay, Arthur Sinclair, J. M. Kerrigan, Fred O'Donovan, F. J. MacCormick, M. J. Dolan, or Barry Fitzgerald, cannot be produced by a School of Acting any more easily or certainly than a Sara Allgood, a Maire O'Neill, an Eileen

O'Doherty, a Maire NicSuibhlaigh, an Eithne Magee, or an Eileen Crowe.

On its return from the American tour the company again went to London in the early summer of 1912. Once again this season at the Court Theatre was a triumphant success, made doubly memorable by the fact that two new plays were then staged for the first time. The two new plays which then received their first production in London were *Maurice Harte*, by T. C. Murray, and *The Bogie Man*, by Lady Gregory. This departure from the usual procedure of giving the first production at the Abbey Theatre was fully justified by the efforts which were being made at the time by London friends and supporters of the Theatre to raise money for the Guarantee Fund, efforts which were ably supported by the members of the company, and which achieved very considerable success. There were tea-parties and special matinees, lectures and discussions, 'at homes', receptions, sales of souvenirs, and many other devices for the collection of money; and all brought in their quota, so that for a time the finances of the Theatre were not a critical matter for the Directors. At this time it was London and America which saved the Theatre financially, as at an earlier date it was an Englishwoman who had made its existence possible. But this London season was also an artistic triumph the memory of which is still sufficient to secure attention for any company calling itself 'The Irish Players' in the English capital. The critics of the London press surpassed themselves in their praise of the company and the plays, many of them using the company as an exemplar to the actors and dramatists of Britain. That these repeated lectures from the press critics had some effect is borne out by the growth of a folk-drama in England and Scotland, and by the spread of the Repertory Theatre movement at the time.

The first play by Mr. St. John G. Ervine was produced at the Abbey Theatre on 30th January, 1911, without having any particular attention paid to it. It was entitled *Mixed Marriage*, and treated a theme very much in the public mind

of Ireland at the time. Dublin criticism was not enthusiastically favourable to the play, and when *The Magnanimous
Lover* was produced on 17th October, 1912, it became quite
definitely hostile. The critic of one Dublin newspaper
dismissed the play in a few sentences, with the comment that
he was ' not a sanitary inspector '. This play, which is
simply a Belfast variant of the late Stanley Houghton's well
known play, *Hindle Wakes*, was also attacked in the American
press as a part of the effort to disparage the entire Irish drama.
" *The Magnanimous Lover* presents the nasty ' problem play '.
Of course our humiliation would not be complete without the
' problem play '. And the words that this play puts into the
mouth of an Irish peasant girl." This was the comment of a
Miss Mary MacWhorter in *The National Hibernian* of New
York. Mr. St. John Ervine was not the man to take such
criticism lightly ; he knew the newspaper critics of Dublin,
and he made no effort to hide the fact that he despised them.
But his way of countering this particular attack was somewhat
novel ; he wrote a play having its scene in the vestibule of the
Abbey Theatre, and in it he ridiculed them to his heart's
content. This play, *The Critics*, was produced on 20th November, 1914, and gave much amusement to Dublin for a time,
but it did nothing to change the newspaper critics nor their
standards of criticism. So when Mr. Ervine shortly afterwards assumed the management of the Theatre he was not
very popular, and in fact he never achieved popularity in
Dublin. He lectured actors, dramatists, and audiences in the
pontifical manner which has since become so widely known
to large numbers of people outside Ireland ; he deplored the
poor quality of the plays submitted to the Theatre, and
announced his intention of producing 'world masterpieces',
including *Samson Agonistes* and *The Knight of the Burning
Pestle*, so that Irish dramatists might learn their business. The
aim of Mr. Ervine was not that of Edward Martyn, nor was
it that of the Directors of the Theatre. The Abbey Theatre
was, and is, something more than a mere theatre as Mr.
Ervine comprehended the theatre; it was, and is, an expression

of Irish national culture in terms of dramatic art. This aspect of the Abbey Theatre, that it was in fact as well as in name, the Irish National Theatre, was either not understood or was ignored by Mr. Ervine, and he would have had the Theatre, as he has since suggested in one of his books (*The Organised Theatre*, 1924), merely one in a chain of Repertory Theatres in the British Isles. He stood alone for this ideal, as few people in Dublin or in Ireland take even a passing interest in the development of the English Drama or the English theatre, and the aggressive methods of Mr. Ervine alienated even those few. Had he been more interested in Irish drama, or even in world drama, and less interested in organising a chain of Repertory Theatres in the British Isles he might have effected a change, but as it was he effected nothing. It was possible that Mr. Ervine might have brought the ideals of Edward Martyn and those of Mr. Yeats and Lady Gregory into harmony in the Theatre, but he never seemed to grasp that possibility, and certainly he did nothing to realise it. In the end the company revolted, the majority of the players left the Theatre and never returned ; and Mr. Ervine left Ireland to write *The Island of Saints, and the Way to get out of it.*

The first production of a new play by a new author had been announced for Easter Monday, 25th April, 1916, but that date has gone into history with much more significant events. The new play, *The Spancel of Death*, was never acted because the Abbey Theatre was in the centre of a battle zone, and the population of Dublin was under all the rigorous restrictions of Martial Law. No one connected with the Theatre had any foreknowledge that there was a military rising planned for that Easter Monday, and the Theatre, in common with the bulk of the population, was taken by surprise. While the fighting lasted the Theatre was always in danger of destruction. From one side it was threatened by fire and from the other by shells from a gunboat in the river Liffey. The Theatre is situated just behind Liberty Hall, and Liberty Hall as the Headquarters of James Connolly was subjected to a violent bombardment which completely wrecked it. Fire raged in the vicinity of the Theatre, destroying whole blocks of buildings in the surrounding streets. But while both ends of the street in which the Theatre stands were destroyed, including the buildings of the Royal Hibernian Academy, the Abbey Theatre itself escaped almost miraculously. Its Directors and its devoted patrons had many anxious days ; no one knew from hour to hour how it fared in the inferno that raged about it. The Theatre itself escaped, but many of its staunchest champions and strongest defenders perished. Padraic Pearse had been its friend in stormy days, and James Connolly had defended it against the prejudices of mobs. Thomas MacDonagh had written plays, one of which had been staged in the Theatre, and had been the constant colleague of Edward Martyn in his effort to found an intelligent theatre. Sean Connolly, shot dead on the steps of Liberty Hall, had been an actor of considerable ability in the Abbey and other companies. These are but a few of the more prominent supporters of the Abbey Theatre and the Irish Drama who perished in that gallant demonstration of Easter 1916. And yet it was sought to bring the General Maxwell who had sanctioned the execution of these men to the stage of the Theatre to be introduced to the members of the company ! But Mr. Ervine did not understand, and for his lack of understanding he may be forgiven. The finest acting company that the Theatre has known, a company which included Sara Allgood, J. M. Kerrigan, Fred O'Donovan, Arthur Sinclair, J. A. O'Rourke, and Sydney Morgan, was scattered to the ends of the earth by this lack of understanding and sympathy.

When the Theatre opened for the new season in September 1916 it had a new manager and a new company. The new manager, Mr. J. Augustus Keogh, had a considerable reputation as an actor in the plays of Bernard Shaw, and he opened the season with three Shaw plays in succession, followed on 13th December, 1916, with Mr. Lennox Robinson's very successful comedy, *The Whiteheaded Boy*. The

new manager and the new company had to gather a new
audience in the face of difficulties of every kind. But the
audience was successfully gathered, and there was something
of a boom in the plays of Bernard Shaw. Up to this time only
The Shewing-up of Blanco Posnet, of all Mr. Shaw's plays, had
been performed at the Abbey Theatre, and then in a single
season came *John Bull's Other Island*, *Widowers' Houses*, *Arms
and the Man*, *The Inca of Perusalem*, *Man and Superman*,
and *The Doctor's Dilemma*, but when Mr. Keogh left the
Theatre in 1917 the Shaw boom subsided, and two years
had to elapse before *Androcles and the Lion* was produced
in November 1919. For a time Mr. Fred O'Donovan
undertook the management, but it was obvious to everyone
that the Theatre had reached the most critical period of its
history. Dublin was in a state of nervous tension, and for
the time politics had assumed the dominating place in the
national life and consciousness. Ireland had entered upon
what proved to be the final phase of its political struggle.
National drama had deserted the theatre and was being
enacted upon the wider stage of the country itself. For
nearly five years this state of tension persisted, and during
that troubled period there were few who would have dared to
predict what the future of the Abbey Theatre was likely to be,
or indeed to predict that it had any future at all. But with
that dauntless courage which has never deserted them, even
in the darkest hour, Lady Gregory and Mr. Years held on.
New plays continued to be presented at intervals, and the old
plays were revived, and at any cost the Theatre was kept open.
A small but faithful audience continued to patronise the
performances, but the financial position was a cause of grave
concern. Despite all this another new company was slowly
and laboriously gathered together and trained. Some who
had been for years connected with the company were now
given their chance to prove their worth, and some who had
been away from the Theatre, such as Mr. M. J. Dolan, the
present Manager, returned, and some new members were
recruited. The country was undergoing a process of change,

and the Theatre could not be expected to escape. The acting
of the company of which the brothers Fay were the outstanding members had achieved artistic success, the company
which included Arthur Sinclair had achieved popularity, it
remained for the new company to endeavour to combine both.

For some years during this troubled period from 1916 to
1923 the tendency of the Theatre was quite definitely towards
melodrama and farce, and few plays of any distinction were
produced. Of this tendency George W. Russell ('A.E.')
remarked : " We have developed a new and clever school of
Irish dramatists who say they are holding up the mirror to
Irish nature, but they reflect nothing but decadence. They
delight in the broken light of insanity, the ruffian who beats
his wife, the weakling who is unfortunate in love, and who
goes and drinks himself to death ". And Ernest Boyd
pointed out (*Contemporary Drama of Ireland*, p. 165) : " By
an irony of fate, this violent reaction has merely resulted in
very often substituting these plays with cheap effects for the
restrained and careful work of the genuine realists ". The
Irish Theatre seemed to be in its declining stages and the
Irish Drama to have worked itself out. Those who had made
the reputation of the Theatre all seemed to have gone, actors
and dramatists alike. Of the dramatists Synge and Seumas
O'Kelly were dead, and would write no more. Mr. Yeats
seemed to be interested only in plays for drawing-rooms, but
not of course about the folk who live in drawing-rooms, or
plays that did not require actors. Lady Gregory is still
writing plays, but she has evidently passed her zenith, and
her recent plays are hardly above the level of others acted by
the Theatre. Padraic Colum has lived in America for many
years and seems to have become part of the literary life of that
country, though it is said that he has now completed a new
play which will enhance his already high reputation. But new
dramatists and a new drama may be expected ; indeed they
have both already begun to make their appearance. It is to
be hoped that the worst days are over, and during these bad
days it must be said that neither the plays or acting were of

the quality which are usually associated with the name of the
Abbey Theatre.   The Irish Literary Movement began with
poetry, developed into drama, and has now, apparently,
settled down to novels.   The novel is now the accepted
medium for Irish writers, as the play was ten or fifteen years
ago, and the Abbey Theatre has suffered in consequence.
There are already a few signs that this is but a passing phase,
and that when the political toil and trouble have ceased the
drama will take on a new life.   The ten years' strife through
which Ireland passed from the great Dublin strike in 1913 to
the end of the Civil War in 1923 will provide material in
plenty for the potential dramatist ; as will also the efforts at
national reconstruction in process.   It is probable that many
who have hitherto written only trivial plays, and many others
who have never written plays at all, will be urged to place
their thoughts in dramatic form, and that something of the
world-disgust which is the aftermath of the Great War in
Europe will not be without its effect in Ireland.

When the Irish Free State came into being in 1921 Mr.
Yeats began to see the possibility for the realisation of a life
ambition.   " In a little while ", he wrote (*Plays and Controversies*, Preface), " Dail Eireann and our Dublin newspapers
will consider, as I hope, the foundation of an Irish State
Theatre ".   Five years have elapsed since this hope was
published, but neither Dail Eireann nor the newspapers of
Dublin have given the slightest attention to any such project.
What Dail Eireann actually did, in 1924, was to vote the sum
of £1,500 for the encouragement of the drama.   Of this
money the Abbey Theatre was to receive £850 and the Gaelic
Drama League, which produces plays in the Irish language,
£650.   The subsidy to the Abbey Theatre has since been
increased to £1,000 per annum.   One of the conditions upon
which this subsidy was granted was that an additional
Director should be appointed.   This Director is not appointed
to represent the Government, but as he is nominated by the
Minister of Finance it is generally understood that in fact he
does represent the Government.   Fortunately the present

Minister of Finance, Mr. Ernest Blythe, had been an admirer of, and a constant attendant at, the Abbey Theatre for many years before there was any prospect of his Ministerial office, and consequently his two nominations have been made from outside the circles of the politicians. The first Director nominated in this way was Dr. George O'Brien, a Professor of the National University and the author of several works on the economic history of Ireland. When Dr. O'Brien resigned in 1926 his place was filled by the nomination of Dr. Walter Starkie, a Fellow of Trinity College, Vice-President of the Dublin Drama League, and author of works on Benevente and Pirandello. Whether this nominated Director has any veto on the plays to be produced is not yet as clear as it might be, but it is plain to all who have been familiar with the Theatre for a prolonged period that there is some new restraining influence at work, and that the policy of the Directorate is now much more conservative than it had been for the twenty years before there was any governmental subsidisation.

In fact the policy of the Directorate would seem to be set towards the attainment of the status and dignity of a State Theatre, as that title is understood throughout Europe, and the tendency is causing some uneasiness amongst the younger dramatists and potential dramatists. And no less marked is the tendency to accept the ideal of Edward Martyn rather than that of Mr. Yeats and Lady Gregory, by placing less emphasis on the 'peasant' play and giving more attention to the work of European and American dramatists in the selection of the repertory. But the younger dramatists have some fear of a State Theatre ; they know how rigid a State Theatre may be, and how easily it may be influenced by the dominant politicians of the time. The State Theatre is almost invariably conservative and averse from experiment in form or technique, and it usually tries to avoid ' shocking the bourgeoise '. There has never been any censorship of the theatre in Ireland and the fear is entertained that one of the signs of the new order will be the establishment of such

a censorship, as there has been already established a censorship of films, and a censorship of publications is now extremely
likely. In the course of a lecture which he delivered in the
Rathmines Town Hall, Dublin, early in 1927, Mr. Lennox
Robinson stated quite boldly that speculative or experimental
productions of the plays of new and unknown dramatists need
not be hoped for in the immediate future. New dramatists
will have placed at their disposal, for a small rental, an
intimate theatre to seat 100 persons, in the Abbey Theatre
buildings, and in this theatre they can try experiments at their
own expense. In fact, the alternatives before the new Irish
dramatists are that they should keep their plays in their desks
or produce them in this little theatre at their own cost, in
competition with the Abbey Theatre around the corner.
"It is not", said Mr. Robinson in announcing the construction of this Peacock Theatre, as it is named, " the intention
of the Abbey company to produce plays in this theatre. The
new theatre is intended for the convenience of the general
public interested in the writing or production of plays ".
The resentment of the younger dramatists has been voiced
in some pointedly personal criticism of the Directorate in the
Dublin press, and an organisation called the Irish Dramatists'
Association has made a demand that the Theatre should be
placed definitely under public control, and that a Reading
Committee other than the present Directorate should be
appointed. The resentment may be organised into a boycott
of the new little theatre.

   More significant of the new tendencies of the Theatre was
the statement made by Mr. Robinson in the course of the
same lecture that plays are rejected because, being the work
of inexperienced writers, they show faults in technique which
render them unsuitable for the stage of the Theatre ; and
other plays are rejected because of the narrowness of their
appeal. In its earlier days the Theatre did not reject plays
of promise simply because of technical faults : " If a play
shows real promise and a mind behind it, we write personally
to the author, making criticisms and suggestions " (*Our Irish*

Theatre, p. 103). And Mr. Yeats has recorded (*Plays and Controversies*, p. 203), " When the Abbey Manager sends us a play for our opinion and it is my turn to read it, if the handwriting of the MSS. or of the author's accompanying letter suggests a leisured life I start prejudiced. There will be no fresh observation of character, I think, no sense of dialogue, all will be literary second-hand. . . . On the other hand, until the Abbey plays began themselves to be copied, a handwriting learned in a national school always made me expect dialogue, written out by some man who had admired good dialogue before he had seen it upon paper. The construction would probably be bad, for there the student of plays has the better luck, but plays made impossible by rambling and redundance have often contained some character or some dialogue that has stayed in my memory for years. . . . At first, . . . I used to recommend some reading of Ibsen or Galsworthy, but no one has benefited by that reading or by anything but the Abbey audience ". Should the policy announced by Mr. Robinson be followed it is probable that new dramatists will not come forward in any number, and it must be considered fortunate that many of those who had plays produced in the Theatre began to write in a more generous time. It might have been expected that the grant of a subsidy by the State would have induced the Directors to experiment more freely, and to use the subsidy, at least to some extent, in encouraging new dramatists and training new companies of actors. But that, evidently, is just what the Directors are not prepared to do.

There is indeed some suggestion that the Directorate of the Theatre is hardening into something resembling the type of management against which the Irish Literary Theatre was formed in protest nearly thirty years ago. Certainly the great adventure of an Irish National Theatre might never have been embarked upon if the controllers of the commercial theatre of that day had not banned plays ' because of the narrowness of their appeal '. Such an explanation for the suppression of any plays suggests that the box-office is becoming the test of

merit. But even to-day, after nearly thirty years of propagandist effort, a play like *The Countess Cathleen* appeals to
' only a few people ', so that it appears in the programme of
the Theatre at but rare intervals. If that play were offered
to the Directors of the Theatre to-day it is possible that it
would be rejected because of 'the narrowness of its appeal'.
It is said that the authors of to-day should do for themselves
what the authors of a previous generation did, they should
start a new theatre for themselves. That, however, is not
quite in harmony with the declared objects of a National
Theatre, which should certainly find room for all types of
plays and all ages of authors.

There is some reason, however, for timidity on the part of
the Directors, as within recent years the audience at the
Theatre have changed almost as much, and possibly even
more than, the plays. The typical audience of the Theatre
is radically different from the audiences which gave a first
welcome to the plays of Synge, Yeats, Lady Gregory, Lennox
Robinson, T. C. Murray, and others of the older school. To
some extent the advent of this newer audience coincides with
the emergence of Sean O'Casey, and the grant of a subsidy by
the State, and that it is a less discriminating and less critical
audience than those of the past there can be no doubt. Sean
O'Casey is the great discovery of recent years, and after a very
lean period the welcome and the praise which he has received
are somewhat extravagant. He uses the disillusionment of
the post-war period in such a way as to attract the kindly
attention of all the anti-Irish elements in the country, and to
attract at the same time an audience which sees only humour
in his grim irony. But on the whole it would seem that the
days of pioneering experiments at the Abbey Theatre have
gone for ever, and the days when the Directors were prepared
to stake their all against screaming partisans are now definitely
buried with the dead past. The pioneers have grown weary
of pioneering, and it seems that the Abbey Theatre is to
settle down to the repertory work of a State Theatre, where
the ' great plays ' of the Masters will be presented at suitable

intervals, and the works of expatriate Irishmen, from Farquhar to Shaw, O'Neill, and Munro, will be claimed for the greater glory of Ireland. The plays of leading continental dramatists would also be presented, as they are being presented in growing numbers even now. This is, of course, very useful and very necessary work, but it is not quite the work for which the Irish National Theatre was founded : it is the work of the Irish Literary Theatre revived after thirty years, and a triumph for Edward Martyn long after his death. As late as 1908, while Miss A. E. F. Horniman still subsidised the Theatre, Mr. Yeats boasted of a Theatre "that is free for a certain number of years to play what it thinks worth playing, and to whistle at the timid ". The Directors do not now whistle at the timid ; they must now keep in mind organised timidity which calls itself the Vigilance Committee, which they treated with contempt many times in the past, and the non-literary timidity of Dail Eireann, of which they have already had some little experience. It is probable that a censorship may be set up, but perhaps the Government nominee on the Board of the Theatre is the most effective censorship that could be established. There is really only one serious theatre in Ireland, generally the theatres are music-halls or branches of English syndicates.

The greatest days of the Abbey Theatre would seem to lie in the past. The enthusiasm of its founders has been spent, and they have no longer the creative glow which makes for renown. Lady Gregory has grown old, and Mr. Yeats has tired of his creature. " You and I and Synge ", he wrote in an open letter to Lady Gregory in 1919 (*Plays and Controversies*, pp. 209-212), " not understanding the clock, set out to bring again the Theatre of Shakespeare or rather perhaps of Sophocles. I had told you how at Young Ireland Societies and the like, young men when I was twenty had read papers to one another about Irish legend and history, and you yourself soon discovered the Gaelic League, then but a new weak thing, and taught yourself Irish . . . but the modern world is more powerful than any propaganda or even than any special circumstance, and our success has been that we have made a theatre of the head, and persuaded Dublin playgoers to think about their own trade or profession or class and their life within it, so long as the stage curtain is up, in relation to Ireland as a whole. . . . I want to create for myself an unpopular theatre and an audience like a secret society where admission is by favour and never to many. Perhaps I shall never create it for you and I and Synge have had to dig the stone for our statue and I am aghast at the sight of a new quarry ". Others can now go to the men of the roads and the fields should they so desire, and if the Abbey Theatre is to become as other theatres Mr. Yeats will still try to collect his audience like a secret society. For many years the Abbey Theatre had an audience of that kind, and these were the years of its greatness. Its actors, dramatists and audiences have all changed with the passing years, and there are few to maintain that popularity has done nothing to spoil it. But still it is vital ; new dramatists there are, a school of acting and a school of the ballet are both being conducted, a large audience has been collected which is fairly constant in its attendance, and the acting is up to the best that the Theatre has had in the past.

CHAPTER VII

THE POET IN THE THEATRE : W. B. YEATS

The Attraction of the Theatre—Not Primarily a Dramatist—The
Unpreoccupied Mind—Belief in Magic—' Beauty Like a Tightened
Bow '—Character in Drama—Legend and Symbolism—Influences
—The Conflict of the Material and the Spiritual—Devastating
Criticism—The Plays Examined—Disappointment with the Popular
Theatre—The Poet in the Theatre—Not a Great Dramatist—No
School and no Successor.

FROM his earliest years Mr. Yeats was interested in the
theatre and the drama, but his interest was always that of a
poet. His interest was in the words and the ideas rather than
in that ' business ' which makes up so much of what is
mistaken for drama. " What attracts me to drama ", he said
in 1904, " is that it is, in the most obvious way, what all the
arts are upon a last analysis. A farce or a tragedy are alike in
this, that they are a moment of intense life. An action is
taken out of all other actions ; it is reduced to its simplest
form, or at any rate to as simple a form as it can be brought to
without losing our sense of its place in the world. The
characters that are involved in it are freed from everything
that is not a part of that action ; and whether it is, as in the
less important kinds of drama, a mere bodily activity, a hair-
breadth escape or the like, or as it is in the more important
kinds, an activity of the souls of the characters, it is an energy,
an eddy of life purified from everything but itself. The
dramatist must picture life in action, with an unpreoccupied
mind, as the musician pictures her in sound and the sculptor
in form ". And in the *Advice to Playwrights* which he sent
out from the Abbey Theatre he stated, " We do not desire
propagandist plays, nor plays written mainly to serve some

129

obvious moral purpose ; for art seldom concerns itself with these interests or opinions that can be defended by argument, but with realities of emotion and character that become self-evident when made vivid to the imagination ". These statements indicate plainly enough that the theatre which interested Mr. Yeats, and for which he has laboured incessantly throughout his life, had nothing in common with the ordinary theatre of commercialised amusement. He wanted plays that would be 'remote, spiritual, and ideal', and hoped to hear fine speakers make great poems greater.

There is little doubt that the dramatist who can 'picture life in action with an unpreoccupied mind' is likely to produce great drama. But it cannot be said that Mr. Yeats has been in a position to do that. As early as 1901 he could say, " I believe in the practice and philosophy of what we have agreed to call magic, in what I must call the evocation of spirits, though I do not know what they are, in the power of creating magical illusions, in the visions of truth in the depths of the mind when the eyes are closed ; and I believe in three doctrines, which have, as I think, been handed down from early times, and been the foundations of nearly all magical practices. These doctrines are :

" (1) That the borders of our mind are ever shifting, and that many minds can flow into one another, as it were, and create or reveal a single mind, a single energy. (2) That the borders of our memories are as shifting, and that our memories are a part of one great memory, the memory of Nature herself. (3) That this great mind and great memory can be evoked by symbols " (*Essays*, p. 33). There is nothing very novel in this preoccupation by which Mr. Yeats tried to suggest the inexpressible by symbols, and to make all his auditors merge in the single mind. There is something of Blake in it, and something also of Maeterlinck, and in its execution there will be found a trace of William Morris and a little of Coleridge. None of the plays has a thesis : there is nothing to be argued, nothing to be demonstrated, nothing to be proved. It is only necessary that we ' go from the theatre with our eyes dim for an old love's sake '. It is only during the last five years that Mr. Yeats has forsaken poetry for argument. He has ceased to write for the theatre because the theatre cannot give him the effects he sought, and his plays are now written for select audiences in drawing-rooms, as his argument is directed to his fellow-Senators of the Irish Free State.

All his plays are a quest for Beauty—' Beauty like a tightened bow '—and all have the quality of dream rather than reality of everyday. He has pointed out in reply to the suggestion that " the dramatic moment is always the contest of character with character " that " character is continuously present in comedy alone, and that there is much tragedy, that of Corneille, that of Racine, that of Greece and Rome, where its place is taken by passions and motives, one person being jealous, another full of love or remorse or pride or anger " (*Essays*, p. 297). In none of his plays is there any real attempt to create character, but rather is there an attempt to express the emotions and elemental passions through the persons of figures which are but symbols. A play by Mr. Yeats is as full of symbolical persons as is *The Pilgrim's Progress*, but the symbols are not labelled as plainly as if John Bunyan had been at work. The protagonists of his plays are neither full-bodied nor red-blooded, they do not emerge as personalities, but always there is conflict. Not, perhaps, the conflict of will with will, but certainly the conflict of the material and the spiritual worlds. Such a conflict can be shown by created personalities as Ibsen has made plain with others in our day, but Mr. Yeats has chosen to show it through fairies, demons, and visions. There are those who contend that because of this preoccupation Mr. Yeats has shown himself to be Irish and Celtic, but there is more of Asia than of Europe in it, and more of India than of Ireland ; they present Irish legend in a setting of Oriental mysticism. The outlines of his plays, the bare bones of his plots, are Irish, taken invariably from Irish legend or folklore, but the philosophy with which they are filled is neither of pre-Christian nor Christian Ireland. It is Ireland by the light of Asia.

There are other critics who contend that the plays of Mr.
Yeats represent just the words in which they are written.
" To search for a meaning behind his babblings of the little
people, or his visions of blue-gowned figures is to court
madness. For *Where there is Nothing*, there is—W.B.Yeats ",
says Storm Jameson in *Modern Drama in Europe* (p. 207).
The poet himself had said, " Where there is Nothing, there
is God ", but Miss Jameson will have none of that, so she sees
just nothing. To her Mr. Yeats represents " the last state
in symbolic imbecility " (*Modern Drama in Europe*, p. 207).
This opinion was published in 1920, and three years later Mr.
Yeats was awarded the Nobel Prize for Literature, so that
neither the Royal Academy of Stockholm nor the Irish
people agree with Miss Jameson. The Irish people never for
a single moment thought of Mr. Yeats' plays as the last
' state of symbolic imbecility '. To them he was always very
much in earnest, a man whose every word was intended to
mean something, and whose sincerity was at no time open to
doubt. They did not necessarily believe that what they
understood him to say was true, in fact they violently resented
it as false on at least one occasion, and he has always been
labelled a Pagan. A rural nation, with a population mainly
peasant, like Ireland, is elemental in its beliefs, so that fairies
still survive and life is permeated with a philosophy which is
other than material. So Miss Jameson overstates her case,
and her effort to be clever by a play upon words brings her
close to absurdity. To say that there is nothing in the plays
of Mr. Yeats is as foolish as to say that he is one of the world's
great dramatists. It is probable that he wrote plays for the
stage rather from a desire to give Ireland a national drama
than from that overwhelming urge to dramatic expression
which gives the world its Ibsens, Strindbergs, Tchechovs, and
Shaws. He was first and always a lyric poet, who was
attracted to the theatre by patriotism rather than drama, but
who had certainly a desire to hear noble verse nobly spoken.
It is unfair to dismiss his plays with a sniff of contempt, and
to make fun of the title of a play which he has withdrawn and

disowned. The better way is to try to discover what Mr.
Yeats endeavoured to do, and to measure his achievements
by the standards of his desire. It happens that the very play
which Miss Jameson dismisses with a jest is the play which
first expressed that conflict of the material and the spiritual
which is the burden of all Mr. Yeats' dramatic work.

Where there is Nothing was written in collaboration with
Lady Gregory. It was written in a fortnight, " to save from
a plagiarist a subject that seemed worth the keeping till
greater knowledge of the stage made an adequate treatment
possible ". Although it was published in 1903 as the first
volume of the *Plays for an Irish Theatre* it was never produced
at the Abbey Theatre, but by the Stage Society in London in
1904. The theme was again used in *The Unicorn from the
Stars*, which was first produced at the Abbey Theatre on
21st November, 1907, but this second play has little of the
glamour of the original. In *Where there is Nothing* a young
landowner, Paul Ruttledge, gives up his wealth and his easy
life to join a group of wanderers. After many adventures his
delicate constitution is undermined and he falls ill, and in a
monastery to which he is brought for treatment his latent
mysticism is awakened by the close proximity of religion.
He recovers, and decides to join the religious brotherhood in
the hope of finding peace. By his preaching he brings the
brethren to share his belief that " where there is nothing
that is anything and nobody that is anybody " they will find
God. In a great sermon he advocates widespread destruction
in which even the Church itself will not be spared. He and
his disciples are ejected from the Order, and in an effort to
convert the peasantry, whose fury is excited by something
they cannot comprehend, they fall victims to the mob.

The play as a whole has something of the Russian spirit in
it, something of Dostoevsky, as it has also the only note of
social protest to be found in Mr. Yeats' plays. Its first three
acts have the everyday life of the people for material, while
the two remaining acts contrast the life of the monastery
centring upon spiritual ecstasy. In reading the play one is

struck by this marked contrast between the monastic spiritual life and the ordinary life of the market-place, and this contrast would, doubtless, be equally marked upon the stage. Paul Ruttledge somewhat resembles Prince Myshkin, in *The Idiot*, and his philosophy is in striking accord with that of Padraic Pearse, the Irish Revolutionary Leader who was executed in 1916 for his part in the Rising of that year.

In *The Unicorn from the Stars* there is obviously more of Lady Gregory than of Mr. Yeats. It is simply a three-act 'peasant' play from which all traces of satire, as of intellectual and spiritual revolt, have been carefully removed. The protagonist is no longer an aristocratic landlord, he is now a coach-builder named Martin Hearne, who is thrown into a trance by a flash of light on the golden unicorn which he had carved to ornament one of his carriages. Hearne also undertakes a campaign of destruction, and the details are almost exactly those of the original play. But *The Unicorn* has none of the glamour of *Where there is Nothing*, it is coarser in writing, superficial in its appeal, and somewhat chaotic in its construction. When it was presented at the Abbey Theatre it bewildered the audience, and the press critics for once found themselves in agreement with the audience by failing to discover what the play was all about.

The Countess Cathleen, Mr. Yeats' first play, was published in 1892 and staged in 1899, but since then it has undergone prolonged and extensive revision. Originally it was a lyrical play in which the lyrical content far surpassed the dramatic. For plot it has as basis a simple folktale familiar in all the literatures of the world, but with its scene laid in Ireland. In a time of famine two demons assume human shape and in the guise of merchants go about bartering food for souls. Moved by their terrible plight the Countess Cathleen offers all her wealth in an effort to save her people, but the demons have stolen her money and delayed her grain ships because it is their supreme ambition to secure this truly noble soul. They very nearly succeed. The Countess Cathleen agrees to sell her soul to the demons on condition that they release the souls already bartered to them, and provide the food necessary to support the starving people until relief comes.   When she realises the enormity of the sacrifice she has made she dies of grief, and in a final scene she is carried to heaven, because " the Light of Lights looks always on the motive, not the deed ".

The Countess Cathleen provoked violent opposition from many directions in Ireland when it was first produced, but despite that it cannot be said that the play is entirely effective or convincing on the stage.   The theme is not robust enough for the theatre, and the materialisation of the demons verges upon melodrama.   The whole play, however, is written in language of such exquisite charm that it is certainly one of the most beautiful poetic dramas of modern times.   Beautiful lines abound, as in Cathleen's dying words :

> Bend down your faces, Oona and Aleel :
> I gaze upon them as the swallow gazes
> Upon the nest under the eave, before
> He wander the loud waters. . . .

Or the song of Aleel, the lover of Cathleen :

> Impetuous heart, be still, be still :
> Your sorrowful love may never be told.
> Cover it up with a lonely tune.
> He who could bend all things to His will
> Has covered the door of the infinite fold
> With the pale stars and the wandering moon.

The play which Mr. Yeats wrote in collaboration with Mr. Moore, *Diarmuid and Grania*, has never been published, although it was acted by the Irish Literary Theatre in 1901. An extract from the play, in French, may be found in *Hail and Farewell* (*Ave*, p. 355), but beyond that neither of its authors has acknowledged it by inclusion in his collected work.   The play as acted by Sir Frank Benson's Company achieved an artistic success, but it was held by critics to be too naturalistic in treatment.

In 1902 Mr. Yeats had two plays produced which are

sharply differentiated from the body of his work. Both are in prose ; one a patriotic tragedy, and the other a farcical comedy. *Kathleen ni Houlihan*, the patriotic tragedy, is the most popular, and the most dramatically effective, of Mr. Yeats' plays. It has been said against it that it is ' stupid and trifling ', without an intimate knowledge of Irish political conditions, " and a play that depends for its effect entirely upon the assumption of a secret understanding between authors and audience is not a play, but an acrostic " (*Modern Drama in Europe*, p. 208). The popularity of the play in countries other than Ireland is proof that it is something more than an acrostic. Patriotic ardour is not the monopoly of Ireland, and as patriotism is the theme of the play it is easily intelligible to any audience; English and American audiences, at any rate, never had the slightest difficulty in understanding its message. The scene of the play is laid in Killala, on the eve of the French landing, in 1798, and the plot consists of a straightforward story told quickly. Michael Gillane is about to marry Delia Cahel, and thereby solve some of the domestic problems of his parents, when a haggard old woman enters the cottage. She is questioned as to the reason for her woebegone condition, and in reply attributes her sufferings to the presence of ' strangers in the house ', who had robbed her of her ' four beautiful green fields '. The story of her sufferings fires Michael, who offers to assist her in recovering her home. " It is a hard service they take that help me ", she tells him, and as she goes out of the cottage she sings :

> They shall be remembered for ever,
> They shall be alive for ever,
> They shall be speaking for ever,
> The people shall hear them for ever.

Michael stands entranced, while his brother returns with the news that the French have landed. Michael breaks away to leave the cottage, and as he does so Peter, the father, asks Patrick, " Did you see an old woman going down the path ? " And Patrick replies : " I did not, but I saw a young girl, and she had the walk of a queen ". *Kathleen ni Houlihan* is probably the most dramatically effective one-act play in Irish drama, as it is also one of the greatest one-act plays of the modern theatre.

The Pot of Broth, a one-act farcical comedy, is a slight thing resembling Lady Gregory's short plays rather than any of Mr. Yeats' other work. It illustrates the simplicity of country folk by showing how a voluble tramp pretends to make broth by magic from a stone, while in reality he uses a chicken supplied by the befooled cottagers. On the stage it is effective and is very popular with Abbey Theatre audiences.

In *The Hour Glass*, a prose version of which was first produced in 1903 and revised in a mixed prose and verse form in 1912, Mr. Yeats has written the greatest morality play of the contemporary theatre. We are told that the early version of the play converted " a music-hall singer and sending him to mass for six weeks" (*Plays*, p. 422), but it did not satisfy its author. The characters are those of the mediaeval morality : the Wise Man symbolising Reason ; the Fool, Instinct ; and the Pupils those who will accept what they are told. The Wise Man had denied the existence of the Invisible World, and had taught his pupils to deny ; but when they come to ask for refutation of a contrary passage in their reading the Wise Man is troubled, and his assurance is shaken. It is further shaken when the Invisible World materialises in the form of an Angel, who warns him that he will die when the sands of the hour-glass have run out, but if he can find but one soul

> Before the sands have fallen, that still believes,
> One fish to lie and spawn among the stones
> Till the great fisher's net is full again,
> You may, the purgatorial fire being passed,
> Spring to your peace.

Vainly he sought belief in those about him, the Fool alone had escaped his negative teaching. But the Fool is too intent upon trivial things to affirm his faith until it is too late. The

Wise Man submits and is humble, he bows to the will of
God :

> For all that we have done's undone,
> Our speculation but as the wind.

In the earlier version the Wise Man was saved by the con-
fession of the Fool, following exactly the text of the folk-tale
of which the play is an elaboration, but the revised version is
much more convincing. The play is now no ' platitude of the
stage ', as the poet had complained, but a faithful projection
of thought in language that is unaffectedly simple and beautiful. When staged in the settings designed for it by Gordon
Craig the emotion it arouses is unlikely to be forgotten by any
audience. In technique, in style, and in dramatic effective-
ness it is Mr. Yeats' finest play.

The King's Threshold, staged in October 1903, in striking
contrast with all Mr. Yeats' other plays, might be said to be
almost topical in its appeal. He had been conducting a
strenuous agitation in favour of the artist in the national life,
but no change had been effected in public opinion. The claims
of the artist were challenged by the politicians and the
moralists, and in this play no room was left for doubt as to
the place which Mr. Yeats demanded for the artist in the life
of the nation. That the topicality was deliberate is indicated
by a note which the poet appended to the play in 1911. The
play, he says, "was written when our Society was beginning
its fight for the recognition of pure art in a community of
which one half is buried in the practical affairs of life, and
the other half in politics and a propagandist patriotism".
King Guaire had commanded that the poet Seanchan should
be seated at a table lower than his counsellors:

> Three days ago
> I yielded to the outcry of my courtiers—
> Bishops, Soldiers, and Makers of the Law—
> Who long had thought it against their dignity
> For a mere man of words to sit amongst them.

Seanchan had refused to take the lower seat assigned to him, and had gone to lie upon 'the King's threshold', refusing to touch food of any kind,

> for there is a custom,
> An old and foolish custom, that if a man
> Be wronged, or think that he is wronged, and starve
> Upon another's threshold till he die,
> The common people, for all time to come.
> Will raise a heavy cry against that threshold,
> Even though it be the King's.

The King sends food to Seanchan, and finally comes with food himself. But he will not admit the claim of the poets to equality, and the pupils of Seanchan are led upon the stage with halters about their necks. So Seanchan dies in protest, and as they carry the litter from the stage the Youngest Pupil says :

> O silver trumpets be you lifted up
> And cry to the great race that is to come.
> Long-throated swans upon the waves of time,
> Sing loudly for beyond the wall of the world
> The race may hear our music and awake.

In common with almost all Mr. Yeats' plays *The King's Threshold* has been subjected to drastic revision, and the ending is now entirely different from that of the original production. When the play was first staged it ended with the surrender of the King, who offered his crown to Seanchan in token of his control of public opinion, and Seanchan bowing to the will of the King, satisfied that he has vindicated his race. In the newer version the poet is permitted to die, and none but his fellow poets take any heed. An interesting note is appended to the play by Mr. Yeats in 1922 : "When I wrote this play neither suffragette nor patriot had adopted the hunger strike, nor had the hunger strike been used anywhere, so far as I know, as a political weapon" (*Plays*, p. 423). Since that time the hunger strike has played a very important part in the politics of Great Britain and Ireland, but in the end it defeated itself, and the strikers were, like Seanchan at the court of King Guaire of Gort, left to die. The plot of the play is taken from an old Irish story, which is followed closely, and on the stage the play is one of great interest. Nowhere does the verse impede the story, which progresses with gathering impetus to its tragic end. At the Abbey Theatre it is always sure of a welcome, but it is now rarely presented.

The next play to be presented on the stage was one upon which Mr. Yeats has laboured for the greater part of his life, and with which he is even now not quite satisfied. *The Shadowy Waters*, staged in January 1904, is a tapestry of dreams and visions and symbols woven in the most delicate verse. A stage success it can never be, nor is it ever likely to be popular in the theatre, although Mr. Yeats has revised and altered it many times in an effort to make it suitable to the theatre. But its fabric is too delicate, and its symbolism too refined, to survive the ordeal of presentation, and the effect produced in the theatre is one of a vague beauty which is never entirely realised. Forgael has sailed the shadowy waters for three moons in search of his ideal, with only the birds for his guides. In despair that the chance of plunder will ever be presented to them the members of the crew rebel, and ask Aibric to be captain instead of Forgael. Aibric's faith is almost gone, but his loyalty prevents him joining the plot. He goes with his doubts to Forgael, who is thus presented with an opportunity to voice the poet's idealism. He describes the impulse which led him to seek ' some strange love the world knows nothing of ', and while he is in the very act of describing his longings a ship is sighted. The spirits of the crew are revived at the prospect of booty, and soon they have taken the strange vessel and its occupants into their keeping. One of the prisoners is Queen Dectora, who demands satisfaction from those who have killed her husband. Forgael is disappointed that fate should thus bring him but a mortal woman ; and his mysterious speech is incomprehensible to Dectora, who in an angry rage calls upon the sailors to kill him. But the magic of Forgael's harp casts a spell upon them all, and when Dectora recovers from her trance she finds herself in love with Forgael. Dectora pleads that they should return together, but Forgael cannot disregard his ideal, and he prepares to abandon Dectora rather than his vision. Dectora perceives the nobility of his choice, and in a flash she cuts the rope connecting the galleys, thus permitting her friends to depart. She is with Forgael on his immortal quest.

> The World drifts away,
> And I am left alone with my beloved,
> Who cannot put me from his sight for ever.

It is doubtful if *The Shadowy Waters* can ever be made into a poem sufficiently objective to be a stage success. Better, perhaps, that it should be read as a poem, because it is one of the most beautiful poems of modern days. But the poet desires to have it on the stage, and to that end he has changed and revised it many times, even to the extent of preparing a special 'stage version' which differs materially from the poem. But Forgael and Dectora never become recognisably human, and that in itself is enough to prevent the success of the poem on the modern stage.

While *The Shadowy Waters* is composed of the material of 'such things as dreams', the play which followed it was based directly upon Irish legend. *On Baile's Strand*, which was first staged on 27th December, 1904, as the opening performance of the Abbey Theatre, is a dramatic arrangement of the story which tells of the duel between Finmol and his unrecognised father, Cuchulain. The play is written in mixed verse and prose, and it reaches a very high level of tragic intensity as the story develops. A Blind Man and a Fool, who seem to be aware of the identity of the antagonists, play parts akin to that of the chorus in a Greek tragedy, and it is from their casual remarks that Cuchulain learns that he has killed his own son. On the verge of madness he rushes away to the sea, wishing that he may drown, while the gossips continue to talk of trivial things. The ironic symbolism which makes a Fool and a Blind Man precipitate a tragedy is characteristic of the poet's attitude, as it is obvious that fools and blind people cause most of the unhappiness in the world through their aimless chatter. This play has, of course, been revised, and it has been improved. Technically it succeeds as a play though audiences have few chances of witnessing it nowadays. A definite story, with poignantly tragic effects, *On Baile's Strand* is one of Mr. Yeats' most successful efforts in drama.

For the plot of his next play, *Deirdre*, staged for the first time on 24th November, 1906, he again went to old Irish literature, and selecting a theme that has appealed to almost every Irish poet, and to many dramatists. Both George Russell ('A.E.') and J. M. Synge have selected this 'sorrow of story-telling' for dramatic performance, but unlike them Mr. Yeats confined himself to the last act of the tragedy, and has concentrated its essence into a single act of great dramatic intensity. The play opens with the arrival of Naisi and Deirdre at the palace of King Conchubar. Fergus has guaranteed the good faith of the King, but Naisi and Deirdre suspect that the desire of revenge is behind the invitation to return. The conversation of the King with his musicians enables an audience to know of the events that have preceded the home-coming of the lovers, while the rapidity of the narrative produces the necessary tension and expectancy. The forebodings of the musicians prepare the audience for the treachery of the King, who has made use of the friendship of Fergus and Naisi to get the lovers into his power. Apparently insignificant happenings assume significance as the intentions of the King are made plain. Suspicion and hate are in the very air, and sinister figures move in the background ready to do the King's bidding. Naisi is doomed, and only his renunciation by Deirdre can save his life. Deirdre is willing to make the sacrifice to save him, but Naisi forbids it, and he is murdered by the King's ruffians. Deirdre in passionate delirium feigns affection for the old King so that she may be permitted to go to the body of Naisi. When she is allowed to go she kills herself so that she may be with him in death. By the beauty of its language and the intensity of its tragedy *Deirdre* must be given a very high place amongst the poet's plays. In the theatre its success is undoubted, its characters possessing all the human qualities that are usually absent from Mr. Yeats' plays. But, perhaps, as has been noted by critics, this is due more to the inherent qualities of the old Irish storytellers than to Mr. Yeats. Whatever the reason it may be said that *Deirdre* proves conclusively that human beings are not quite outside the range of Mr. Yeats' creative powers, and demonstrates that he is a master of high tragedy.

A prose version of his next play was called *The Golden Helmet*, staged in March 1908, and a revised version in ballad verse called *The Green Helmet* was staged in February 1910. It is described as 'heroic farce', and is founded upon an old Irish story called *Bricriu's Feast*. The Red Man, a sea-spirit, has by supernatural powers made Conall and Laegaire appear to be cowardly, and only Cuchulain among the Champions is strong enough to withstand him. Cuchulain thus becomes entitled to wear the Helmet, the possession of which gives him the supremacy among the Champions. In this play the Champions are stripped of their semi-divine attributes, much as Mr. Shaw has stripped Cæsar or Napoleon, and much satirical fun is extracted from the vanity of the heroes, and the quarrels of their wives for precedence. The play is interesting in thus modernising the heroes of Irish epic, but it cannot be said to be altogether a success on the stage.

The Land of Heart's Desire, which was staged in London in 1894, was not produced at the Abbey Theatre until 26th February, 1911. But since that date it shares with *Kathleen ni Houlihan* the distinction of being most frequently revived. Both England and America saw this play on the stage before Ireland had that opportunity, yet its theme is a simple Irish fairy story which might be held to have little interest for these countries. Shawn Bruin has just brought home his newly-wedded bride, Mary, to the kitchen of his father's house. Mary Bruin is a delicate, dreamy girl who is more attracted by fairy lore than by mundane housewifery. Shawn's mother appeals to the priest to break Mary from her reading ; but Mary has been fascinated by the story of the Princess Edain who had followed a voice one May Eve until she came to a land

> Where nobody gets old and godly and grave,
> Where nobody gets old and crafty and wise,
> Where nobody gets old and bitter of tongue.

She is warned of the dangers that threaten her on this May Eve through such belief, but she ignores the warning and cries to the fairies to take her. She has placed herself in their power by giving food and fire to callers who were of 'the good people', and is ensnared by the singing of a child. This child enters the kitchen, and, after persuading the priest to remove the crucifix, with song and dance lures away the soul of Mary Bruin. Without the crucifix the beholders are helpless, and Shawn is left with the lifeless body of his wife in his arms. Mary Bruin had gone to that ' Land of Heart's Desire ' where

> The wind blows out of the gates of the day,
> The wind blows over the lonely heart,
> And the lonely heart is withered away,
> While the fairies dance in a place apart.

Despite the beauty of its language *The Land of Heart's Desire* cannot be accounted a success. The symbolism is plain enough, but the execution deserves at least some of the scorn with which Storm Jameson has treated the play (*Modern Drama in Europe*, p. 208). It is the music of the language which, alone, saves the play in the theatre.

For several years, from 1911 to 1919, only revised versions of his plays came from Mr. Yeats until *The Player Queen* was staged in London by the Stage Society. This play was also revised and produced at the Abbey Theatre on 9th December, 1919. Of the play Mr. Yeats says : " I wasted the best working months of several years in an attempt to write a poetical play where every character became an example of the finding or not finding of what I have called the Antithetical Self ; and because passion and not thought makes tragedy, what I made had neither simplicity nor life. . . . At last it came into my head all of a sudden that I could get rid of the play if I turned it into a farce. . . . It is the only play of mine which has not its scene laid in Ireland " (*Plays*, p. 429). The play is not distinguished in any way, and there is little in it to suggest that it is the work of the greatest of contemporary poets.

The theatre is now almost spurned by Mr. Yeats ; he has turned to select audiences in drawing-rooms, and for such audiences he has written his *Four Plays for Dancers*, published in 1920. But he has also translated and adapted *Oedipus the King* and *Oedipus at Colonnus*, of Sophocles, and both have been produced at the Abbey Theatre. In these adaptations there was little scope for anything but verbal beauty, and this Mr. Yeats has given them in full measure. Their success in the Theatre, however, owed much to the very fine acting which they received, particularly from Mr. F. J. MacCormick as Oedipus. It is probable that the versions of Professor Gilbert Murray will still be preferred by the majority of people.

On the whole, though Mr. Yeats has enriched the theatre of our time with much that is memorable, and much that is beautiful, it cannot be maintained that he is entirely at home on the stage. Two or three of his plays are dramatic in the ordinary meaning of the word, but all the others depend upon something which is strictly not necessary to the theatre. In few of his plays is there any action, and in one only is there any attempt made at individual characterisation. Of course, Mr. Yeats has stated that characterisation is the attribute of comedy only, and comedy he has resigned to others. He has made few experiments in form, but in the verse treatment of his subject-matter he has been a pioneer in the modern theatre. He is not the greatest of the symbolists, in fact it is doubtful if he be a profound thinker at all. Surfaces and emotions have attracted him more than logic and thought, and always he has held that reality is in the mind only. No one will ever remember the names of his characters after they leave the theatre, they will not go home with audiences as Nora Helmer goes with them, or Christy Mahon, but audiences will want to read the plays when they have seen them so that the beauty of their lyrical content may be enjoyed more fully and more frequently. In every sense he is the poet in the theatre rather than the poet-dramatist, and it is remarkable that he has no successor in the Abbey Theatre. The verse plays of younger poets have been rejected and have been left for little theatres in England to put upon their stages. So Mr. Yeats stands alone as the only poet-dramatist of the Irish theatre, not so much because he is the only one as because the work of the others has never been produced. That his contribution to the modern theatre has been remarkable will be admitted, but it cannot be contended that he is a great dramatist.

CHAPTER VIII

THE FOLK DRAMATISTS

John Millington Synge—Lady Augusta Gregory—Padraic Colum—
George Fitzmaurice.

IT was one of the most fortunate of accidents that brought
John Millington Synge back to Ireland, and attracted his
interest to the theatre. He had been born in the County
Dublin, at the foot of the Dublin Mountains, in 1871 ; had
graduated in the University of Dublin, and had then gone to
wander on the Continent, to study French literature, and to
settle in Paris. It was in Paris that W. B. Yeats encountered
him. " Six years ago ", wrote Mr. Yeats in 1905, " I was
staying in a students' hotel in the Latin Quarter, and somebody, whose name I cannot recollect, introduced me to an
Irishman, who, even poorer than myself, had taken a room
at the top of the house. It was J. M. Synge, and I, who
thought I knew the name of every Irishman who was working
at literature, had never heard of him " (*Essays*, p. 370). Synge
had been writing articles, mainly reviews, on French literature
for the English and French press, and he was also reading
those authors, Villon, Petrarch, Ronsard, Rabelais, Cervantes,
Nash, Greene, and Herrick, who figure so frequently in his
intensely personal poems. It is sufficient to name those
authors to indicate not only Synge's literary tastes, but also
something of his view of life. In physique he was frail and
delicate, he died before he had reached his thirty-ninth year,
but he lived mainly in the open, tramping the Dublin Mountains and indulging his inclination for natural history. It did
not take Mr. Yeats long to discover the type of man with
which he had made contact, quickly he divined the streak of

wildness and the love of picturesque and highly-coloured language. So he advised Synge to get away from Paris, " You will never create anything by reading Racine, and Arthur Symons will always be a better critic of French literature. Go to the Aran Islands. Live there as if you were one of the people themselves ; express a life that has never found expression " (*Essays*, p. 370).

So Synge went to Aran, the stony group of islands at the entrance to Galway Bay on the west coast of Ireland, ' where men reap with knives because of the stones '. There he lived the ordinary life of the islanders, conversing with them in Irish, entertaining them with his fiddle and noting the beauty of their English speech, Elizabethan in texture and Gaelic in idiom. He has left a record of his life on the islands in that delightful book, *The Aran Islands*, which has sent so many people there since its publication. It was on the islands that he first heard many of the anecdotes which afterwards became the germs of his plays. His stay on the islands was not always complete happiness, his restless nature demanded change, and his taciturn, brooding, temperament was a hindrance to the completest intercourse. " On some days ", he wrote in a personal letter, " I feel this island as a perfect home and resting-place ; on other days I feel that I am a waif among the people. I can feel more with them than they can feel with me ". Like the inhabitants of other small islands the folk of the Aran group are reserved in their manner with strangers, and Synge also was shy and reserved, but a strong friendship was quickly made with an island boy ; and it was this boy who made Synge intimate with the island folk. From this intimacy derives nearly all of Synge's work, but more particularly that rhythmic speech which was destined to attract so much notice abroad and to dominate the Irish drama for twenty years.

Despite the fame which he afterwards achieved Synge's entry to the Irish Theatre was not by any means triumphant. His first play, *In the Shadow of the Glen*, met with a very hostile reception when it was produced in October 1903,

because it was alleged to be a libel upon the peasant women
of Ireland. The hostility had nothing to do with the artistic
merits of the play, but solely upon grounds which were at the
time held to be moral. Since then the play has been many
times revived without the slightest trace of hostility, but
on the contrary every indication of enjoyment, in its Irish
audiences. In that first play Synge showed that he had
nothing to learn as a dramatist, the entire action went with
amazing precision from beginning to end. Nora Burke, like
Nora Helmer, slams the door upon her husband, but Nora
Burke was accompanied by a wanderer of the roads who had
caught her fancy by his fine speech. It is the old story of the
young woman married to the old man which has done such
prolonged service to the novel and the drama in all countries.
Daniel Burke, old and ailing, is jealous that his wife speaks
with all who pass the door of their lonely cabin 'on the back
hills' of Wicklow. So he feigns death in the hope that he will
catch his wife in the act of betrayal. A tramp arrives and asks
for shelter, and he is informed of what has happened. He
agrees to stay in the house while Nora goes in search of some
neighbourly aid. While she is absent the 'corpse' sits up in
his bed, to the astonishment of the tramp and usually to the
amusement of the audiences, and tells the tramp that he has
'a bad wife' and that he intends to chastise her. He is just
settled again in bed with his stick when Nora returns with
Michael Dara, a neighbouring small farmer. They settle
down to refreshment and discussion, counting the money left
by Burke, and then Dara suggests that they "wait now till
himself will be quiet awhile in the Seven Churches" and then
they should marry. Daniel Burke jumps from the bed with
his stick in his hand and bars the way to the door. " You'll
walk out now from that door, Nora Burke; and it's not
to-morrow or the next day, or any day of your life that you'll
put in your foot through it again ". Nora goes with the
tramp, and Daniel sits down to a friendly drink with Michael
Dara. Nora demanded human sympathy, and intercourse
with her kind, and there was more likelihood that she would

find them on the roads as a tramp than as the wife of Daniel Burke ' in the shadow of the glen '. There is nothing to suggest the prentice hand in the play, and there is all in it which characterised Synge's later work.

Riders to the Sea, produced in February 1904, is generally regarded as the finest one-act play of the modern theatre. " The play in a few moments thrills whole theatres to the kind of hush that comes when Othello approaches Desdemona. Synge, from the first, is as terse, as exacting, as strange as he likes ; yet everyone sees what he means, and all of his people have always the tragic importance ." Synge, again says the same critic (C. E. Montague, *Dramatic Values*, p. 2), " takes you straight into black tragedy ; you step through one door into darkness ". George Moore, however, found it " an experiment in language rather than a work of art ", " a painful rather than a dramatic story ". A painful story it certainly is, but related as Synge relates it the story is also dramatic. It is dramatic in language rather than incident, and tragic in the current journalistic sense rather than in the Aristotelian. In the play is vividly depicted the life of all seafaring communities ; every time a member puts to sea he places his life in the hands of Providence : the story is of little significance as it is upon the language that the effects depend. Atmosphere and action are both implicit in the words used, and it is by contrasting the homely life of everyday with the grim struggle upon which that life depends that the tragic effect is produced. There is no doubt that, whether the play be strictly a tragedy or not, it is theatrically effective and true to life.

In *The Well of the Saints*, produced in February 1905, is contrasted the vivid life of the imagination and the comparatively sordid life of every day. The play is unique in Synge's work in having an element of the supernatural, and perhaps for this reason it is the least popular of the plays. Two blind beggars are told by their neighbours that they are the most beautiful woman and the handsomest man that were ever seen. Their imagination plays about this until their own conception of themselves surpasses all reason. A wandering Saint restores their sight with water from a holy well, and they view each other with earthly eyes for the first time. Their disillusionment is heartrending, and the display of their wrath gives Synge's language full scope. They ask to be made blind again, and in the end their blindness returns, but they have lost their illusions. In this play Synge's laughter is bitter at the expense of those of his countrymen who would prefer the dream to the reality. Since he wrote those countryman have had their blindness cured, and there are some, no doubt, who would cry with Martin Doul to be blind again.

Preference for dream rather than reality is also the theme of *The Playboy of the Western World*, which was first produced in a gathering storm of hostility on the evening of January 26th, 1907. *The Playboy* is the most widely known of all Synge's plays, and it has won approval from the world's most exacting critics. It is the fullest and most elaborated of all his plays, the plot is more complex and the characterisation more detailed than any he had previously attempted. The play is really Elizabethan, presenting a little world of vigorous men and women in the lives of whom tragedy and comedy are inextricably mingled. " In it ", says Maxim Gorki (*English Review*, April 1924), " the comical side passes quite naturally into the terrible, while the terrible becomes comical just as easily. J. M. Synge, like a truly wise artist, does not inject his own point of view ; he just exhibits the people : they are half gods and half beasts, and are possessed of the childish desire to find a ' hero ' among themselves ". That is not all, however : there is little reason to doubt that Synge's own point of view was expressed in the play. Does the title symbolise Ireland ? Whether it does or not the play does satirise the country in merciless fashion. Ireland loves ' heroes ' and if it cannot find them in one walk of life it will find them in another. The more primitive the community the less likely is it to discriminate. It was not Synge's satire, however, that outraged his compatriots ; it was the realism

with which the play was written and presented. It was
thought that Synge implied that the peasantry of Mayo
believed it to be a heroic thing to kill one's father. The play
had sociological implications, but they were not those which
the earlier audiences fancied. These audiences did not see
that the acceptance of appearances was just the thing Synge
satirised.

Christy Mahon comes to the village public-house with a
vivid tale of how he killed his father. The peasants are only
old men, women, and fools, all the others evidently had
emigrated. Christy finds himself a hero in this degenerate
company, which takes his unnatural crime as a mark of
unusual strength. Higher and higher, as he rises in the esteem
of the company, his fancy takes him while he woos Pegeen
Mike, the daughter of Flaherty the owner of the public-house.

PEGEEN. I'm thinking you're an odd man, Christy Mahon.
The oddest walking fellow I ever set my eyes on to this hour
to-day.

CHRISTY. What would any be but odd men and they living
lonesome in the world.

PEGEEN. I'm not odd, and I'm my whole life with my father
only.

CHRISTY. (*With infinite admiration.*) How would a lovely
handsome woman the like of you be lonesome when all men
should be thronging around to hear the sweetness of your voice,
and the little infant children should be pestering your steps, I'm
thinking, and you walking the roads.

PEGEEN. I'm hard set to know what way a coaxing fellow the
like of yourself should be lonesome either.

CHRISTY. Coaxing.

And so it goes on in what is probably the most beautiful
love-scene in all Irish drama. The end is pitiful. Old
Mahon appears in his bloody bandages and the hero is thrown
from his pedestal. Synge does not spare that last touch of
scorn. The humour is so bitter that laughter is impossible to
a discerning audience. Synge is sometimes called a romantic
dramatist on the basis of *The Playboy*, but there is nothing

romantic in his work save his fantastic plots and exotic language. All else is the highest realism, not a mere adherence to facts but adherence to a conception of life. The play must be judged as satire rather than as the comedy it is usually accepted to be. As fantastic as *Gulliver's Travels* and as bitter in its purpose *The Playboy* is Synge's masterpiece and the greatest single play of the Irish Theatre. In it there is " the rich joy found only in what is superb and wild in reality " expressed in language that is a fitting vehicle for such exuberant vitality.

" Of the things which nourish the imagination ", wrote Synge in the preface to *The Tinker's Wedding*, " humour is one of the most needful, and it is dangerous to limit or destroy it ". In the play he did not hamper his own humour, and the absence of limitation gives an impression of farce rather than comedy. *The Tinker's Wedding* has never been staged at the Theatre for which it was written because it is held that the indignities inflicted upon a priest by the rollicking vagabonds would give offence to a large section of the population. It was probably Synge's first effort at drama, having been written about 1902, but it was not published until *The Playboy* had made his name throughout the world. Sarah Casey had lived with Michael Byrne for years of vagrant wandering, but she suddenly craved for the blessing of the Church upon their union. Arrangements were accordingly made with a priest to perform the marriage ceremony for a fee of ten shillings and a new can, " a little sum wouldn't marry a child ". When the priest came to inspect the can he found only three empty bottles ; Michael Byrne, with that lack of scruple for which tinkers are notorious in Ireland had bartered the new can for drink. The priest is outraged ; he rounds upon the tinkers, and refuses to perform the wedding ceremony. He is overwhelmed with a flood of vituperative abuse, bundled into a sack and thrown into the ditch. To read this play will produce laughter almost without restraint, and in the theatre it should be one of the most hilarious plays of modern times. " In the greater part of Ireland, however, the whole people from the tinkers to the clergy, have still a life, and a view of life, that are rich and genial and humorous. I do not think that these country people, who have so much humour themselves, will mind being laughed at without malice, as the people in every country have been laughed at in their own comedics ". So Synge thought, but the Directors of the Irish Theatre still think differently, and so to this day *The Tinker's Wedding* remains unstaged by the Abbey Theatre.

> Adieu, sweet Angus, Maeve and Fand,
> Ye plumed yet skinny Shee,

Synge wrote in one of his poems, but the hearty contempt which is there expressed for the denizens of the Celtic Twilight did not in any way prevent him accepting the very human story of Deirdre for what was to be his last play. Synge's *Deirdre of the Sorrows*, left unrevised at his death and produced on 13th January, 1910, is as humanly vital as *The Playboy*, and more in accord with the frank materialism of the original story than any other modern re-telling. Death and old age are the leading ideas of the play, as they are of so many of Synge's intensely personal poems. Deirdre laments the passing of life as much as the passing of Alban when she says pathetically : " Woods of Cuan, woods of Cuan, dear country of the east ! It's seven years we've had a life was joy only, and this day we're going west, this day we're facing death, maybe, and death should be a poor untidy thing, though it's a queen that dies ". " Queens get old, Deirdre ", says Owen, " with their white and long arms going from them, and their backs hooping. I tell you it's a poor thing to see a queen's nose reaching down to scrape her chin ". Synge's view of that humanity which has its feet in the mire and its head among the stars is nowhere better exemplified than in *Deirdre*, and the final scene, when Deirdre kills herself on the body of Naisi, shows Synge at his highest as a tragic artist.

> I've thirty months, and that's my pride,
> Before my age's a double score,

he wrote in September 1908, but he was destined never to reach that double score, for he died six months after the poem was written, on 24th March, 1909. He had never been robust, and so, like Stevenson and Henley, he was attracted by everything ' that was fiery and magnificent ' in life, and certainly he exaggerated his desire to

> Search in Red Dan Sally's ditch,
> And drink in Tubber fair,
> Or poach with Red Dan Philly's bitch,
> The badger and the hare.

He thought that Ibsen and Zola treated the reality of life in joyless and ' pallid words '. " On the stage one must have reality, and one must have joy ; and that is why the intellectual modern drama has failed, and people have grown sick of the false joy of the musical comedy, that has been given them in place of the rich joy found only in what is superb and wild in reality ". The meaning of vital zest, which he attached to the word ' joy ' is made clear when he says (*Poems*, Preface), " before verse can be human again it must learn to be brutal". He fashioned his artistic conceptions and theories from the reality of the life around him. At the time of his death he had in contemplation a play dealing with the slum life of the Irish cities, but the utilisation of that exceedingly vital material was left for Sean O'Casey.

In his short artistic life Synge wrote six plays ; three in three acts, one in two acts, and two in one act. His dramatic work is not large in bulk, but when it is remembered that it was all produced in about six years it will be seen that something even greater might have been confidently hoped for had his life been prolonged. Small as is his dramatic work in quantity, however, its quality is so high that it cannot be ignored in any estimate of the great drama of modern times. He will not take rank with the greatest, perhaps, but he is in no danger of being ranked with the mediocre. He has been a dominating and a formative influence in the Irish theatre for twenty-five years, and that his influence has been equally formative outside Ireland may be noted in the plays of dramatists so widely different as John Masefield and Eugene O'Neill. In his plays there are no ' joyless and pallid words ' ; instead there is a language which, if not indeed the ordinary language of the average Irish peasant, is in idiom and diction that of English-speaking Ireland selected and arranged by an artist in speech. In the library as in the theatre Synge's plays will continue to give pleasure wherever vital language is valued for its colour and its exuberance. Synge is the greatest dramatist that Ireland has yet had, as he is Ireland's contribution to the great drama of the contemporary world.

The plays of Lady Gregory have had an even greater formative influence on the lesser Irish dramatists than those of Synge. They have been much simpler in theme and structure, less selective in their language, and therefore much easier to copy. Lady Gregory's plays have also been the most popular plays in the Abbey Theatre repertoire, being revived again and again without any evident waning in their appeal. Comedy is the path of popularity, if it be not always the path to great art. Audiences want to laugh, and invariably go to the theatre for that very purpose. They do not go to the theatre to be preached at, to be derided, or to be bored. In Ireland Lady Gregory has produced the greatest laugh of the greatest number.

The popular conception of an Irishman, in Ireland as elsewhere, is still largely composed of a blend of Lever, Lover, and Boucicault, and neither Larry Doyle nor Broadbent, by the simple process of reversing the characteristics of tradition, can change that popular misconception. The clowning of Handy Andy remains to delight audiences and benefit box-offices. In the Ireland of to-day the caubeen has been displaced by the peaked cap worn over the left eye, and the twirling shillelagh by a hitching of the trousers. But the essentials remain ; only the superficialities have been changed, and even they have not been improved. ' Erin, the tear and the smile in thine eyes ' is what is desired because it is what the people believe. Rollicking farce followed by a

copious tear-flow is still held to be ' true to life ', and anything
which confirms that view is certain of success.   Christy
Mahon or Larry Doyle could not be true to Irish life when
there was Myles-na-Coppaleen or Paddy-the-next-best-
Thing available to testify to the contrary.   The old stage
Irishman is dead, surely, but his son has succeeded to his
place.   He still plays the fool for the amusement of the
nations, including his own, and for the profit of the theatre.
Synge's *Playboy* is now played in Dublin as a farce, and the
most popular of Abbey Theatre plays get their effects with
cynical plasterers or quay-labourers.

Comedy is the humour of character ; farce is the humour
of situation. *John Bull's Other Island* is comedy because its
humour springs directly from the contact of the personalities
of Doyle and Broadbent with Ireland.   Lady Gregory's
Spreading the News, produced on 27th December, 1904, and
typical of much of her work, is farce because its whole
structure depends upon the deafness of Mrs. Tarpey.   Had
Mrs. Tarpey heard correctly the whole series of ludicrous
incidents which constitute the play would have been obviated,
and Bartley Fallon could never have figured as the typical
Irishman upon whom " all the troubles of the world are sure
to come ".   Fallon and Haffigan are brothers in affliction
from the lips out ; they are both easily recognisable as that
whining Irishman who is more common than national
prestige can afford to tolerate.   They are both figures of fun,
but while the laugh is at Haffigan's shrewdness it is at Fallon's
cringing imbecility.   It is possible to pity Bartley Fallon, but
he simply must be laughed at.   He is a figure of farce not of
comedy.   Lady Gregory's humour in her early plays of this
type is the humour of situation ; her comic figures have
' characters ' not character, they have mouths but it is
impossible to believe that they also have brains.   Lady
Gregory herself says of this play, her first has never been
published, " I let laughter have its way with the little play.
I could only think of Bartley Fallon as dull-witted or silly or
ignorant ".   It is easier to laugh at a fool than to laugh with

the wise, and Lady Gregory chose the easier way. Bartley Fallon, Davideen, Hyacinth Halvey, and the other inhabitants of Cloon, are direct descendants of Handy Andy, observed with the same objective detachment yet born about the same year as Shaw's Larry Doyle and George Meredith's O'Donnell. At a time when pure comedy was being written about Ireland and Irishmen, Lady Gregory chose to confound comedy with farce, and to play to the level of the stage Irishman. When compared with Bartley Fallon or Hyacinth Halvey, Synge's Christy Mahon is a hero indeed ; yet Fallon and Halvey were laughed at and Mahon was execrated.

There is nothing in literature quite like her bewildered peasantry, a friendly critic has said, but neither is there anything in life. They are the product of a rich humanity, a keen sense of the ridiculous, and an unconscious snobbery, served with a garnishing of dialect speech which is magnificently effective for use on the stage. How really effective that dialect is Lady Gregory has demonstrated in her translations from Molière and Goldoni. The comedies of Molière she has naturalised in the dialect of her Kiltartan peasantry, thus giving those comedies their finest setting in English. That Lady Gregory has some kinship with Molière there can be little doubt. It is, however, a kinship of outlook only, which brings nothing of the wide mentality of Molière to her original plays. The fine subtlety of Molière will be sought in vain in Lady Gregory's plays; she loves broad situations, and characters sketched in bold lines, each embodying some simple fundamental human quality. Her creatures are all extravagantly simple—there is no Haffigan guile in them—and they are exquisitely helpless. They have none of that shrewd cunning which marks the peasant in Ireland as elsewhere. They are simple to the verge of imbecility.

Lady Gregory has written thirty-one original plays, of which all but two have been produced at the Abbey Theatre. She has been writing plays for twenty-five years, in addition to her splendid work as a Director of the Theatre, a biographer, historian, and folk-lorist. Her industry and enthusiasm are amazing, resembling somewhat those Spanish dramatists at whose versatility Northern Europe stands aghast. Most of her work can be studied on the printed page as it has nearly all been published. Her first volume of plays, *Seven Short Plays*, 1909, contains her most popular and much of her typical work. Some of these plays have been referred to already, they are farcical comedies with a strong undercurrent of satire. In *The Workhouse Ward*, 1908, is satirised that tendency to quarrel about nothing which is marked in (though not peculiar to) Irish people. It is possible that a political satire was intended, and perhaps the play says more about Irish politics than the politicians have yet learned. The political interest is stronger in *The Rising of the Moon*, 1907, in which those who appear to be against the Irish struggle for political liberty are shown not to be so in fact. A conflict between sympathy and duty rages about the police sergeant who is the central figure in the play. The sergeant's choice is difficult, and the artistry by which Lady Gregory enables the ballad-singer to arouse his latent patriotism is a masterpiece of dramatic technique. Another of these short plays, *The Gaol Gate*, 1906, has all the tragic intensity of *Riders to the Sea*, reaching a climax in the triumphant *caoin* of grief and joy with which the mother greets the news of her son's fidelity till death. All the elements of doubt and uncertainty, pity and helplessness, are combined in this little play to make it one of the great tragic experiences of the modern theatre.

Some of the most interesting, and the most successful, of Lady Gregory's plays will be found in the volumes of *Irish Folk-History Plays*, 1912. The plays are an attempt to translate the subjects of mythology and history into terms of folk-drama, and in the Kiltartan dialect Lady Gregory found a medium of expression excellently adapted to that purpose. Five of these plays have been produced at the Abbey Theatre, the first being *Kincora*, produced in 1905 and revived after revision in 1909. It was made more coherent by the revision, but it remains more close to melodrama than tragedy. " I had had from the beginning ", Lady Gregory says of these plays, " a vision of historical plays being sent by us through all the counties of Ireland. For to have a real success and to come into the life of the country one must touch a real and eternal emotion, and history comes only next to religion in our country ". *Kincora* was her first attempt to make this vision a reality, but neither this play nor its successors have yet become part of the life of the country. They have been staged only rarely, and at long intervals. This is to be regretted because her best ' comedies ' are those based upon folk history. More astonishing is the fact that her finest tragedy, *Grania*, based upon the famous folk-tale of Diarmuid and Grania, has never been produced at all.

Next to *Grania* the tragedy of *Dervorgilla*, 1907, is the best of the tragic folk-history plays. Its single act is devoted to the " swift, unflinching, terrible judgment of the young ". No audience could remain unmoved as the tragedy of the unhappy Queen unfolds itself ; there is strength, power, and nobility in it which will bear comparison with similar plays by Ibsen, Strindberg, or Hauptmann.

Grania is Lady Gregory's highest achievement in historical tragedy, and here she is superior to the Ibsen of *The Vikings at Helgeland*, the Strindberg of *Gustavus Vasa*, or the Hauptmann of *Florian Geyer*. In emotional content and poetic intensity *Grania* can bear the comparison with Synge's *Deirdre* to which it has been subjected. Deirdre has had her admirers in plenty, almost every Irish poet is included in the number, but Grania has had, if the result of the Moore-Yeats collaboration be ignored, only Lady Gregory. Grania is to marry Finn, but she prefers the youthful Diarmuid, with whom she flees and wanders for seven years. Diarmuid refuses to become her lover, remaining faithful in his allegiance to Finn, until circumstances compel them to live together for a week. When Diarmuid has surrendered Grania turns from him, having discovered charm evidently only in his resistance. They are about to quarrel when Finn arrives, disguised as a beggar, to accuse Diarmuid of treachery.

Touched by remorse Diarmuid rushes away to prove his constancy and is slain in battle. Finn regains the wayward affections of Grania, who heals her wounded pride by becoming ' an old man's darling '. " I think ", says Lady Gregory, " I turned to Grania because so many have written about sad, lovely Deirdre, who when overtaken by sorrow made no good battle to the last. Grania had more power of will, and for good or evil twice took the shaping of her life into her own hands." In this three-act tragedy of love and jealousy there are only three persons, but in falling under the spell and ' fascination of things difficult ', Lady Gregory achieved her masterpiece in tragedy. It is generally considered that she is at her best in the one-act play, and it is true that she has failed more often in her long than in her short pieces, but the success of this three-act play in characterisation, dialogue, and construction is a standing refutation of the statement. Why *Grania* has never been staged in Ireland is something of a mystery, and it is certainly time that the play had a chance of demonstrating its tragic power on the stage.

In political satire Lady Gregory is especially strong. Her best comic effects are satirical, and the majority of her plays are capable of political interpretation. Indeed her work might almost be used as a continuous commentary upon the Irish political scene during her lifetime. Her best three-act comedy, *The Image*, 1909, is based upon a story related by the poet 'A.E.', which has also been used by George A. Birmingham for his popular play, *General John Regan*. It is announced that the carcases of two whales have been cast up on the shore of a West Irish village, and a heated argument follows as to the best use the village could make of the money that their oil will bring. While the wrangling continues it is discovered that the oil has been taken from one of the whales by men from a neighbouring village, and that the other has been washed back into the sea. The satirical content of the comedy is as obvious as it is successful.

In *The Canavans*, 1906, is satirised an aspect of Irish character that is too rarely subjected to such treatment.

There are large numbers of Irish people who will be on the winning side at any cost, as there are, no doubt, numbers of people in all other countries. The play differs only in its historical setting from William Boyle's comedy on the same theme, *The Eloquent Dempsey*. It is possible to laugh at the whining obsequiousness of Peter Canavan. Peter tries very hard to be on the winning side in the warring factions, and in the end he falls badly between the two. Laughter vanishes when Lady Gregory satirises the popular treatment of Parnell, as she does under a very transparent disguise in *The Deliverer*, 1911. In this play will be found a bitterness which rarely obtrudes itself in Lady Gregory's work, but that the bitterness is justified few will be found to deny. *The White Cockade*, 1905, deals with another historical subject, and one which is still the basis of acute controversy in Ireland—the Battle of the Boyne. As a laughter-maker the craven run-away King James as he appears in this play would be difficult to equal, and *The White Cockade* must be ranked as a high achievement. Though its satire is sharp, it is deserved, and its humour is spontaneous and unfettered.

In addition to satire a strain of mysticism has been evident in Lady Gregory's work from the beginning, and in some of her recent plays it comes close to triumphant expression. *The Golden Apple*, 1920, challenges comparison with the fantasy of Barrie or Maeterlinck. This is a fairy play surpassing in its magnificent simplicity the sophisticated *Peter Pan*, and is worthy of rank with *The Blue Bird*. All the best qualities of Lady Gregory's work are exhibited in *The Golden Apple*, humour, naïveté, humanity, and that sincere faith in the fairy world which Barrie seems to lack and which Maeterlinck possesses. "A play for Kiltartan children", Lady Gregory has called it; but a play for all peoples it certainly is.

Lady Gregory is one of the very few Irish dramatists who have not been afraid to handle directly religious themes. In *The Travelling Man*, 1910, she treated an Irish belief that Christ himself might be in the person of any tramp of the roads, and in one of her most recent plays, *The Story brought by Brigit*, 1924, she has dramatised the story of the Passion from an Irish folk version of the Biblical narrative. The play is based upon a West Irish tale which credits Saint Brigit with presence at the Crucifixion. As a stage piece it has not proved very convincing, and it has not been revived. There is too much *caoining*, too monotonous to be dramatically effective, and the presence of Saint Brigit shows as an anachronism in the theatre. As a piece of literature, however, the play is a delight to read, as in it Lady Gregory comes closer to poetry than in her other work.

Neither of her last two plays has been at all successful or convincing in the Theatre. In *Sancho's Master*, produced in March 1927, there is an attempt to put Don Quixote and Sancho Panza on the stage as if they were inhabitants of the Barony of Kiltartan. The result is rather like reviving Handy Andy and dressing him in Spanish costume. The Don himself is just one of the ' cracked ' inhabitants of Cloon, exhibiting none of that ' quixotic ' glamour with which his creator endowed him. *Sancho's Master* is certainly not one of Lady Gregory's successes, nor is *Dave*, produced in May 1927. Here there seems to be an effort to deal with the effects of ' giving a dog a bad name ', or, conversely, an attempt to prove that humanity will live up to the opinion its neighbours hold of it. The play is in one act, and too much is crammed into the time and space allotted. It is possible that if *Dave* were re-written as a longer play it might be a great success as it has within it all the elements of a great play.

Even the most superficial examination of Lady Gregory's plays must draw attention to a very obvious limitation, which is the lack of imaginative power. Where she has been able to draw from life she has been invariably successful ; even the fairy and wonder plays are drawn from life. It is, however, impossible to deny that her dialogue is always interesting and often masterly. If it has very little of the high poetic quality of Synge's more imaginative selection and variation of Irish peasant speech, it has a rhythm of its own which is as pleasing as it is distinctive, and it keeps close to the level of the actual talk to which she has listened in the cottages of County Galway. It is the custom in Ireland nowadays to laugh at ' Kiltartanese ', but that is only because people who have no qualification of any kind have succumbed to the temptation to write ' peasant plays ' and to imitate Lady Gregory's speech. Lady Gregory's dialogue is crisp, idiomatic, pleasant, rich, and real. It is her strongest point ; but talk alone will not make a great play, seldom even a good play, and the bulk of Lady Gregory's dramatic work is talk only. It can be as tedious and as dull as the worst in the Abbey Theatre's repertoire, but it has also reached the heights of the highest. Lady Gregory, however, has not the strength to remain long on the heights ; her material is too thin and anaemic for the rarefied atmosphere. In time Hartley Fallon and the rest of the ' cracked ' inhabitants of Cloon will share with Handy Andy a small space reserved for variations from the normal. National pathology will deal with them and the stage will know them no more. Then *Grania*, *The Canavans*, *The White Cockade*, *The Golden Apple*, *The Gaol Gate*, *The Workhouse Ward*, and *The Rising of the Moon* will ensure for Lady Gregory a leading place among Irish dramatists, and an enduring, if not an immortal, place among the chief dramatists of her day.

She has been one of the Directors of the Abbey Theatre from its beginning, and in that capacity has exercised a great part of the control of the development of the Irish drama. She showed how apparently easy it was to write ' peasant plays ', and she more than any other of the leading dramatists of the Theatre has been the victim of imitation. There is a long list of silly, senseless, useless plays which probably would never have been written had there not been the example of Lady Gregory to goad their authors. These will for a time continue to make audiences laugh, but that can only be for as long as the audiences remain faithful to the Boucicaultian conception of Irish character. Thus Lady Gregory has had more influence than Synge.

If the influence of Padraic Colum is now seen to have been

less than that of Lady Gregory or Synge it seemed twenty-five years ago that he was destined to be the most influential and important dramatist in the Irish Theatre. He was the youngest dramatist connected with the movement in its early days, and he seemed at the same time to come to the theatre instinctively and fully equipped. He was only nineteen years old when he submitted two short plays for performance by the ' Daughters of Eireann ', an organisation which produced many plays with a definitely political bias, and he was only twenty-two when he had his first stage success with *Broken Soil* in 1903. Even then he was familiar with the works of Ibsen and Maeterlinck, and these two dramatists had considerable bearing upon his plays. He began by writing plays based upon Irish mythology and history, dealing with such subjects as *The Children of Lir* and *Brian Boru*, and later wrote a propagandist play against enlistment of Irishmen in the British Army called *The Saxon Shillin'*. This play and another staged in 1902, *The Kingdom of the Young*, were published in *The United Irishman* newspaper, but none of the earlier plays have been published. In *The Kingdom of the Young* Colum treated a theme which is at the back of all his dramatic work, no matter what other theme may be dominant. It is the hard selfishness of youth when driven into revolt by its elders. In this play a daughter turns against her father with the determination that she will not be deprived of the joy of life as he and his generation had been cheated. In *The Foleys*, 1902, the intolerance and self-righteousness is portrayed ; and in *Eoghan's Wife*, a monologue of the same year, there is a foreshadowing of Synge's *Shadow of the Glen*. In this little sketch a woman feels her home lonely and depressing because she had married the wrong man, and she ponders a way of escape from it all. It was with *Broken Soil*, however, that Colum came into the limelight as a dramatist of some importance. This play was produced in December 1903 and achieved instantaneous recognition : it was afterwards revised and renamed *The Fiddler's House*, and it is under that title that the play is best known.

Padraic Colum belongs to the rich midlands of Ireland, that pasture country which supplies much of the ' roast beef of old England ', and which was a part of 'the English reservation called ' The Pale '. He was born in the County of Longford in 1881, but at an early age he migrated to Dublin to take a position as a clerk in the Irish Railway Clearing-House. It was while in that office that he began his career as a poet and a dramatist, becoming intimate with the leaders of the Irish Literary Revival, and also with the leaders of the new militant political movement. He was one of those who so resented *The Playboy* that he withdrew from the Irish National Theatre Society, and was for a time connected with an organisation named The Theatre of Ireland, but in time he was reconciled and rejoined the Theatre. During the Great War he left Ireland and settled in the United States, and there he has since resided and worked, with only occasional visits to Ireland. Since the production of *Thomas Muskerry* at the Abbey Theatre on 12th May, 1910, he has written only one play, and that was an adaptation from the German. His whole energy in the United States was given to journalism, folk-lore, and books for children.

It cannot be denied that Colum failed to live up to the great promise of his youth, but neither can it be denied that in his three plays there is an achievement that marks him as one of the formative dramatists of the Irish theatre, and one of the considerable dramatists of his time. In *The Land* is dramatised the conflict between the older generation which fought for its little bit of Irish earth and the younger generation which hearkens to the call of the world. Murtagh Cosgar and Martin Douras had fought for the land they tilled, and at last Cosgar was about to become an owner. In the struggle he had sacrificed his family until only one son, Matt, and a daughter, Sally, remain. The others were scattered about the world, and the remaining two were listening to the call. They did not feel the great love for the land that was the very life of their father. The dull-witted Sally Cosgar, and the verbose fool Cornelius Douras will stay if they are allowed to marry ; but the strong Matt Cosgar and the vivacious Ellen Douras cannot be held. Ellen cannot live in the country, she longs for the bright lights, the glittering shops, and the crowded streets, of American cities. Even when Murtagh Cosgar withdraws his opposition to her marriage with Matt she still stands firm against being a farmer's wife. So the land that Martin Douras had gone to jail for, and for which Murtagh Cosgar had sacrificed his life, must go to Cornelius and Sally. The older generation had won the land, but the young and strong fly from it and only the weaklings remain. Such is the actual position in Ireland, and from such sociological material only bitter comedy can be made. *The Land* is a bitter comedy, all the more bitter because its author then deplored the facts upon which it was based ; but since then, he, too, like Ellen Douras, succumbed to the lure of America. The characters in the play are all living and actual, drawn with the fidelity of Ibsen and with Ibsen's technical novelty.

The Fiddler's House is in every respect Colum's best play. The material is sordid enough, and the actuality of its characters so indubitable, that it might in other hands have degenerated into sombre tragedy. But Colum is a poet first and he infused his crude material with the glow of poetry. It is intensely Irish in its scene, but the yearnings of Conn Hourican for the open road and the appreciation of his kind is common to all humanity. Conn was an artist by instinct and a wanderer by inclination. He and his fiddle had been in strange places, and he could not be content with the humdrum life of a small farmer. So he frequented the local tavern, seeking the applause of those whom he despised, and he stooped to petty mean tricks when the occasion demanded. His elder daughter Maire had been the prop of the little family since her mother's death, and had acted as a mother to her sister Anne. Anne was loved by James Moynihan, son of a neighbouring farmer, and Maire loved Brian MacConnell. James wrote verses for Anne, but Brian went to the public-house, quarrelled with his brothers, and lured Conn to play

in the bar. Maire is hard with her father, she remembers the
life of the roads and regards his fiddling as mere vanity, but
sorrow softens her. She has played a losing game, and so
comes to comprehend the old man and to sympathise with
him. When he desires to go to the Feis at Ardagh she fetches
his famous 'Longford' fiddle and declares that she will
accompany him. Anne and James Moynihan will be
married at Ardagh and she and her father will share the
wandering life of the roads. *The Fiddler's House* is a great
play, or at least it is, as its author seems to agree, two acts of
a great play. The third act is weak, and the end is not equal
to the strong effects of the first two acts. The weakening
of Maire is not quite fully explained, and the magnificent
psychology of the earlier acts seems to dwindle into pettiness.
The play really ends when Maire says, " It's no matter at all
now ", to her beloved Brian in the second act. For all that
the play is equal to the greatest in the Irish theatre, and it
deserves a wider appreciation than it has yet had in Ireland
or elsewhere. Although the play was first produced by the
Theatre of Ireland in 1907 twelve years had to elapse before
it received its first staging in the Abbey Theatre.

Thomas Muskerry was first staged at the Abbey Theatre on
12th May, 1910. It is Colum's third long play, and it is in
almost in every respect inferior to *The Land* and *The Fiddler's
House*. It is a study in the Ibsen manner of a man being
brought to ruin by the pressure of his family. From being
the Master of the Workhouse Muskerry is brought by stages
to his death in a pauper's bed in the institution over which he
ruled. It is the blind piper Myles Gorman who gives the
play its significance, and when the skirl of the pipes is heard
on the road in joyous celebration of Gorman's freedom one
feels that Thomas Muskerry, too, has only been set free to
live the life that he would have chosen. The play is true to
life in rural Ireland, sparing nothing of the drab existence in
an Irish country town. As a picture of the ' *petty bourgeois* '
of Ireland the play is memorable.

Of his outlook and his method Colum himself has said all

there need be said in the Preface of *Thomas Muskerry*. " Life, in terms of Catholic philosophy, is means to the individualization of the spirit . . . the dramatist is unable to conceive of one life being less significant than another. . . . We are in a studio and painted canvasses are lying about. The artist puts a frame before one of the canvasses and at once the picture is a mark for our attention. . . . The dramatist is concerned not primarily with the creation of character, but with the creation of situations ". Thus is Colum divided from Synge and brought close to the position held by Lady Gregory.

In the speech which he uses in his plays Colum is far removed from either. It is without the rhythm of the Western peasant, but it is a poet's selection of the more pedestrian speech of the Irish Midlands. In point of fact the speech used by Colum is a very close approximation to the actual speech of the greater part of Ireland. His dialogue seldom suggests the poet, and it is his characterisation rather than his speech that indicates the poet behind the play. The speech and the situations given to the stage by Colum led to the flood of ready-made ' peasant ' plays which every one in Ireland seemed capable of writing.

" Some years ago I thought of a grandiose task, the writing of the comedy of Irish life through all the social stages. I had thought of this work (perhaps after discovering Balzac) as a piece of social history." In these words Colum brings himself into the Ibsen circle, and therein he discovers his master. That grandiose task was soon given up, much to the regret of his admirers who saw in him the potential master-dramatist of Ireland. It must be regretted by everyone who knows his work that Colum so quickly tired of that task which was as necessary as it certainly was grandiose, as it is to be regretted also that he ceased to write plays at a time when his best work was confidently expected.

George Fitzmaurice is the one important Irish folk-dramatist whose work has been almost consistently ignored in Ireland, and yet remains unknown abroad. His first play,

The Country Dressmaker, was produced by the Irish Theatre
in the same year as *The Playboy of the Western World*, and
since that date he has written six other plays of which only
three have been staged. He has written comedy, tragedy,
and fantasy without in any way suggesting that he has been
influenced by any other dramatist ; his peasantry is true to
life and his dialogue is rich and copious. At one time it
seemed that popularity was within his reach, but instead of
following *The Country Dressmaker* with another, and similar,
comedy of rural character as many other dramatists have done
he chose to write a little one-act tragedy which aroused
considerable mirth, while at the same time causing some
bewilderment. That the total of his work is small may in
some way be accounted for by the neglect which he has had
in the theatre, a neglect which is not in accord with the
undoubted merit nor with lack of popular esteem. His
development in theme and in technique has been consistent,
he has not remained at the point from which he started as so
many of the popular playwrights of the Irish Theatre have
done.

The Country Dressmaker, produced on 3rd October, 1907,
extracts comedy from the very ordinary character of Julia
Shea. Her mind had been formed upon that peculiar form
of romance which is the speciality of the novelette. She had
given her love to Pats Connor, and had endowed him with
all the qualities of the novelette-hero, and had cherished the
illusion that Pats was pining for her in America. When he
returned to Ireland it was obvious that he had never once
thought of Julia Shea. Julia in her hero-worshipping way
had ignored the attentions of Edmund Normyle, and it is his
marriage which brings about the crisis between Pats and
Julia. Of course, everything comes all right in the end, but
in the three acts of the play there is more pure comedy than
is to be found in the vast majority of Irish plays. The people
are all carefully drawn, with a scrupulous fidelity to Irish
peasant nature. Their language is in every case a fitting
expression of their characters, and in this first play George

Fitzmaurice showed that he, too, had a mastery of the Anglo-Irish idiom as used in rural Ireland. In many respects *The Country Dressmaker* is the most perfect comedy in the Irish Theatre. The central character, moulded by her reading of cheap fiction, might very easily have degenerated into a figure of farce or caricature had the object of the dramatist been merely to raise a laugh. That temptation was resisted, and instead of a buffoon there is a perfect study of the character of a shallow silly woman, whose simplicity can evoke nothing but the tenderest laughter. She is not a fool to be laughed at for her antics, but rather a simple thing to be pitied because of the glamorous effect of her reading. This is a comedy which deserves to be known wherever human nature is like unto Julia Shea ; and that must mean everywhere in this world of Elinor Glyn.

The Pie-dish, produced in March 1908, is apt to be dismissed as a trifle because it is in one act, but in that one act is summarised the tragedy of an artistic soul. Leum Donoghue, a Kerry peasant, had given his whole life to the moulding and elaboration of a wonderful pie-dish, but infirmity and death came upon him before this masterpiece, this expresson of the artist within him, could be completed. In his dying agony he implores God for time, and then, finding no immediate response to his prayer, he invokes the aid of the Devil. That, too, fails, and as he dies the precious pie-dish falls from his hand and is smashed upon the earthen floor. For some reason which cannot be explained this play was always received with hilarity in the Abbey Theatre. Obviously it is a parable, but perhaps because the old man used the artistic forces of his nature to make a pie-dish rather than a statue he was regarded as something to laugh at. In no other Irish play is there elaborated the theme of the frustration of the artist in Ireland, and the struggle between the Paganism of the artist and his Christian environment. It is probable that the complete misinterpretation of this little play did much to retard the growth of appreciation which its author deserved.

The Magic Glasses, produced in April 1913, is fantasy pure

and simple. Its location is in some region subject to the laws
of time and space, but all else is beyond any recognisable laws.
The Dandy Dolls is a fantasmagoria in which all senses and
dimensions fade away. This play and *The Moonlighter* have
never been staged, but were published in 1914 in a volume
entitled *Five Plays*. The title of *The Moonlighter*, which is a
four-act play, indicates its theme. Peter Guerin had been a
Fenian but his ardour had cooled. His son Eugene would be
a fiery patriot also, but in words only ; when danger threatened he was a coward. The old Fenian was contemptuous of
this verbose younger generation of Irish patriots, and when
his old-time spirit was aroused it was he who translated their
words into deeds. In the play there are all the materials for
splendid drama, as there is also something of the savage
irony of the remnants of Fenianism at the expense of the
Parliamentary Nationalists which was a feature of Irish
politics. Why this play should never have been staged when
so many that were in every way inferior were produced at the
Abbey Theatre is inexplicable to everyone who knows it in
the printed version. Perhaps some day it will be staged.

In 1923, after a silence of ten years, there was produced a
comedy which did nothing to enhance George Fitzmaurice's
reputation. It may be that in disgust at the treatment that
had been given to his finer efforts he had decided to tickle the
groundlings with *'Twixt the Giltenans and the Carmodys*.
But even in this tangle of families there is keen characterisation with no descent to the farcical. Since then only a short
play has been published in *The Dublin Magazine* (January
1926). The little play, *The Green Stone*, is in the fantastic
manner of *The Magic Glasses* and *The Dandy Dolls*. These
plays indicate that George Fitzmaurice may some day give to
Ireland a romantic drama such as Ibsen gave to Norway in
Peer Gynt.

In every play that George Fitzmaurice has written there is
displayed the perfection of dialogue that delights the artist in
words. The wealth of effect which can be gained from a close
fidelity to Irish peasant speech is magnificently exemplified.

In his work there is nothing of the poetry of Synge, nothing of the farcical buffoonery of Lady Gregory, but there is something of the poetic insight of Colum. There is little in common among these four folk-dramatists except that they all demonstrated the perfect dramatic medium there was ready to hand in the speech of the peasant. In the plays of all four there is used the speech of at least four separate parts of Ireland, and that speech has in all cases a dramatic intensity and a savour for which Synge yearned when he threw over drama in ' pallid and joyless words '. Only in Synge's plays is that speech exuberant and fiery ; in the plays of the other three there is a closer connection with the actual speech of the peasant, as there is also a closer fidelity to peasant character.

In the plays of these four dramatists is the foundations of Irish peasant drama, as in their plays the Irish peasant will be found at his truest and best. They made the way easy for many dramatists whose work is comparable with theirs, but they made the way easy also for a mass of melodrama and farce which has little or nothing to commend it. In the plays of these four dramatists will be found much of that which makes the Irish drama interesting, and all that which gave it its distinction and its formative influence upon folk-drama throughout the English-speaking world.

CHAPTER IX

THE REALISTIC DRAMATISTS

Lennox Robinson—T. C. Murray—Seumas O'Kelly—St. John G. Ervine—Brinsley MacNamara—Sean O'Casey.

COMMENTING upon the foundation of the Irish Literary Theatre George Moore says (Preface, *The Untilled Field*, 1914), " We all did something, but none did what he set out to do. Yeats founded a realistic theatre ". Not one of the founders desired a realistic theatre, or a realistic drama, but only a few years were destined to pass ere the Irish Theatre had ceased to be definitely, and defiantly, literary, and had passed into the hands of the realists. It was not that the younger dramatists desired to work in a new medium, it is certain in fact that no such idea occurred to them at the time, but simply that they followed in the path already marked out for them by Synge, Colum, Fitzmaurice, and Lady Gregory. The realism of these dramatists, rather than their selection of language, it was that most strongly attracted the young men who got their first impulse towards drama from the Abbey Theatre. It is somewhat interesting to note that the more important of these younger dramatists all come from the County of Cork, and in consequence the group is sometimes referred to as ' The Cork Realists '. That is not intended to suggest that these dramatists were bound together by any theory of the drama, or by any other bond which would constitute a ' school '. They were all different, and the majority were but poor writers of melodrama. So far from the realistic method in Irish drama being a monopoly of the young men from Cork it was quickly demonstrated that its most expert practitioners were to come from Galway and

174

Belfast, from the Midlands and the slums of Dublin. The Realistic Dramatists have not had their little day, and then ceased to write. Rather has it been in Ireland that the realists have conquered the Theatre and held it as their own. From 1908, when the first play by Lennox Robinson was produced, until the present day the realists have dominated the Theatre through a line of dramatists including T. C. Murray, St. John G. Ervine, Seumas O'Kelly, Brinsley MacNamara, and Sean O'Casey. So there is clear justification for the opinion expressed by Mr. Moore.

Lennox Robinson is certainly the most important of the younger Irish dramatists. He is the senior in point of time, having had his first play staged at the Abbey Theatre on 8th October, 1908, and he has also had the greatest number of plays produced. Thirteen of his plays have been staged at the Abbey Theatre, two or three of which have also met with considerable success in London and New York. He is an actor of distinction, appearing in the productions of the Dublin Drama League, has been Manager of the Theatre for many years, and he is now the Producer and a Director of the Theatre. He has written extensively on the drama, being for some time a critic on the staff of a leading London newspaper. His interest in the drama of other countries led him to be one of the founders of the Dublin Drama League, which produces the plays of the leading European and American dramatists in Dublin. It is somewhat interesting to note that the Dublin Drama League has given the people of Dublin opportunities for becoming acquainted with some of the leading contemporary dramatists before any of their plays had been produced in London. The centre of Lennox Robinson's interest is in Ireland but his circumference is the world.

Lennox Robinson is the son of a Church of Ireland clergyman, born in 1886 at Douglas, a village just outside the city of Cork. Of his boyhood he has written (*T.P.'s and Cassell's Weekly*, 6th February, 1926), " I regret now that I did not idle to better purpose ; my reading should not have been so haphazard. It led at any rate to the establishment, with the help of a cousin, of a monthly magazine which ran for three years. At first many relatives and friends contributed ; later they fell away, and my cousin and I had to write it all ourselves under a bewildering variety of *noms-de-plume* ". He was sixteen, he says, before he first visited a theatre, but later he went to the theatre whenever he could, and "equally adored Martin Harvey and Bernard Shaw ". Then " one hot summer afternoon I saw a performance by the Abbey Theatre Company. A little later I turned a story of my sister's into a one-act play and sent it to that theatre ; amazingly it was accepted. . . . Wonder followed wonder. A longer play was written and played six months later ; and, being the first realistic Irish peasant play, made a small stir. A few months later I was sent by Mr. W. B. Yeats straight from West Cork to St. Martin's Lane, where at the Duke of York's Theatre a repertory season was about to start. I watched Mr. Bernard Shaw produce *Misalliance*, and Mr. Granville Barker produce *Justice*, *The Madras House*, and *The Sentimentalists*, and Mr. Dion Boucicault produce *The Twelve Pound Look*. Two months of watching and I was in Dublin, walking into the Abbey Theatre as its manager and producer". Surely a perfect training for a young dramatist ; a training which has had a very marked effect upon all his plays.

The little one-act play, made out of a story written by his sister, was *The Clancy Name*, produced at the Abbey Theatre on the 8th October, 1908. It is a grim little melodrama, showing how the Clancy name was saved the dishonour of covering a murderer by the accidental death of the culprit in an effort to save the life of a child from a runaway horse. This little play, which presents a careful study of the mother dominated by pride of race, was in many ways superior to the plays which immediately followed it. The first long play, *The Cross Roads*, which was produced in April 1909, is a study in marriage somewhat in the manner of the English repertory dramatists of the time. An educated country girl, because of her patriotic desire to help in the improvement of rural conditions in Ireland, contracts a loveless marriage with a brutal farmer after rejecting her city lover. Everything goes wrong with the farm from the beginning ; the cattle die, hens refuse to lay eggs, crops fail, and the household slowly deteriorates until it becomes little better than a Hell upon earth. The farmer becomes a drunken sot who illtreats his wife upon every possible occasion. Into this scene of misery wanders the discarded lover in a last effort to persuade the woman to come with him. She refuses, and after a highly melodramatic scene, with the husband, wife, and rejected suitor all taking part, her husband goes out announcing that he is " going down the road for a sup of drink " and " God help you when I come back ". When first presented the play had a prologue in the room of the Erin Debating Society in which ardent patriots discussed plans for the regeneration of Ireland. This was subsequently omitted, but despite revision the play could never be made convincing. *The Cross Roads* was the old ' problem play ' in its worst form, made even worse in Ireland by its suggestion that a marriage for patriotic reasons blighted the lives of people. *Harvest*, produced in 1910, is also a thesis play bearing some traces of its author's stay in London. It is typical of Robinson's earlier plays, showing the evil consequences of applying to a rural population a type of education which unfits them for any but an urban life. All the members of the Hurley family have been educated at great expense, except the one who is destined to run the family farm. One has become private secretary to a British Cabinet Minister and no longer acknowledges his family. Another is a solicitor with too many expenses of his own to be able to give any assistance to his home. A third is nominally a typist, but in reality a prostitute, in London. Maurice and his aged father run the farm, and Jack, who is a chemist's assistant in Dublin, arrives with his wife to spend their honeymoon at his home when the play opens. The cost of educating the various members of the family had been so great that the farm had been starved, and old Hurley is in serious financial difficulties. Jack is willing

to assist in the farm work, but the nature of his experience
had rendered him unfit for it.   Driven to desperation by the
unwillingness, or the inability, of his children to help him the
old man commits arson for the sake of the insurance money
which he thinks he can secure.   The play bears all the marks
of the English repertory movement, but the thesis breaks
down, as it is difficult to believe that educational systems can
fairly be blamed for the snobbery, ingratitude, immorality,
and physical weakness of the members of the Hurley family.
It was probably the agitation against the Irish educational
system rather than the human qualities of the Hurleys that
attracted the author to this theme.   The play was social
propaganda rather than drama ; none of the people in it live,
except Maurice who has been unspoilt by education.

In his next play, *Patriots*, produced in April 1912, Mr.
Robinson showed that he could deal with a high theme of
Irish political conditions in a truly tragic manner.   In this
play is dramatised the thought which Mr. Yeats expressed
when he wrote

> Romantic Ireland's dead and gone
> It's with O'Leary in the grave.

That the romantic conception of Irish patriotism had passed
while he had suffered in jail for it is the tragedy of James
Nugent.   In Nugent's day deeds not words were the accepted
weapons of Irish politicians, but the new generation had
accepted the constitutional method of parliamentary agitation.
Professional politicians made speeches at Westminster while
patriots "fumbled in their greasy tills" making money in
their shops.   In vain Nugent strives to revive the patriotic
fervour ; his auditors are insensible to his appeal, being
immersed in profit or pleasure.   The climax of Nugent's
tragedy is reached when no one can be found to attend his
meeting, and the irony of the play is crushed home when the
old hall-keeper remarks as he closes the hall, " Time to go
to the pictures after all ".   The play is a vivid presentation of
a turning-point in Irish politics, emphasising a condition
which was even then near its end.   In thought, in dialogue,

and in construction *Patriots* is one of Lennox Robinson's best plays. All the people in it are alive and real, and the disillusionment of James Nugent is a tragedy of the most poignant kind. It is possible that later events make the play entirely unreal to-day, but it must survive as a tragic moment in Irish history. It has not been staged for some time, so it is impossible to judge how much it has lost in the passing years.

Three years later, and just one year before the Irish Rising of Easter 1916, a play dealing with a different aspect of the same theme was produced. *The Dreamers*, staged 2nd February, 1915, is a historical play in which the author says, "There is fact and there is fancy". It deals with the abortive rebellion of Robert Emmet in 1803, showing the young and enthusiastic Emmet as the tragic victim of the shiftless futility of his following. In a foreword to the published version of the play the author summarises its purpose. After noting that someone may fine fault with an Emmet play which ignores certain well-known characters he continues : " He will also, probably, quarrel with the title of the play and say that Robert Emmet was practical in all his qualities, a soldier, a tactician, a most able organiser. I agree. But all these things were fused together for one purpose by the most practical quality of all—his dream. Dreams are the only permanent things in life, the only heritage that can be hoarded or spent and yet handed down intact from generation to generation. Robert Emmet's dream came down to him through—how many ?—generations. He passed it on un-dimmed. It is being dreamed to-day, as vivid as ever and—they say—as unpractical ". Some of those who read these words died for Emmet's dream within a year.

In December 1916 was produced the play which is generally regarded as Lennox Robinson's masterpiece, *The Whiteheaded Boy*. It is by this play he is known throughout the English-speaking world. It is certainly a comedy of the finest kind, droll in speech, natural in its situations, entirely human in its characters. In Aunt Ellen Mr. Robinson gave the modern stage one of its most delightful comedy characters.

Like all Irish comedy it is essentially satirical, illustrating many of the weaknesses of the Irish character, but at the foibles at which he once scoffed Lennox Robinson here laughs good-humouredly. The play is filled with foolish and delightful people with whom one may laugh without restraint. No one will stop to think that the things done by these people are wrong ; they are wrong, but they are done with such happy inconsequence that condemnation is frozen in the thought. *The Whiteheaded Boy* is certainly the finest comedy written by any Irish dramatist since the death of Synge. It is perfect in its combination of form and content, there is nothing forced in its language or its situations, and its humour derives entirely from the nature of its people. " *The Whiteheaded Boy* is political from beginning to end, though I don't suppose six people have recognised the fact ". So says the author, and he is very probably right in suggesting that few have stopped laughing at the play to see the political satire. That is as it should be. There is little enough to laugh at in Ireland nowadays, and for that which Mr. Robinson has given all are truly grateful.

The political intention which was overlooked in *The Whiteheaded Boy* could not be ignored in the next play, *The Lost Leader*, produced on 19th February, 1918. It is a common form of conundrum in Ireland to enquire, ' What would Emmet do were he here now?' and parties are divided upon conjectural opinions of dead leaders. In *The Lost Leader* Parnell is set to solve the problem of Ireland in 1918. The play uses as its basis the popular belief that Parnell did not die in 1891, but continued to live in retirement. In Lucius Lenihan is set forth at least the spirit of Parnell. Faced with parliamentary Nationalists, Unionists, Sinn Feiners, all in hostility because he offered only ' your souls ' as a policy, Lenihan continues, " Do you expect Ireland to change and me to stand still ? But the world's crumbling to pieces under your feet and none of you seem to feel it. . . . History talks of the Parnell Movement, it succeeded because it was a movement, because it moved, changed its objectives, changed its tactics. You're not moving, not one of you. . . . But I passed away, it was left to others, I thought, to lead that battle. Each year that passed made that battle more necessary, for each year Ireland grew more prosperous—and more dead —until Home Rule became merely the exchange of government by English shopkeepers for government by Irish gombeen-men ". In a *fracas* that follows Lenihan is struck by a blind man and killed. *The Lost Leader* though daring and interesting was not a great success on the stage. The characters tended to be mere representatives, typical of aspects of current political thought, rather than the lively creatures of *The Whiteheaded Boy*. It is now almost forgotten, and it was the last of Lennox Robinson's political plays for the time being.

A short novel which had been destroyed in the offices of a Dublin publisher during the bombardment and burning of part of the city at Easter 1916 was re-written and published in 1917. In this Novel, *A Young Man from the South*, the evolution of Robinson's own political views are strongly exemplified in the personality of Willie Powell, who had been born into the strictest Unionism and had gradually come to have strong Nationalist views. Though published after the Easter Rising the novel had been completed before that event, and in the re-writing the author refrained from making any capital of the tragic time. Except for a small volume entitled *Eight Short Stories*, and a little brochure called *Dark Days*, being short sketches of the Easter events, Lennox Robinson eschewed political subjects for several years after the production of *The Lost Leader*. The five plays produced between 1918 and 1926, between *The Lost Leader* and *The Big House*, have nothing distinctively Irish about them ; they might have been written by any English dramatist of the time. *The Round Table*, first produced in January 1922, and since revised for production in London by Miss Sybil Thorndike in 1925, is a study in personality under pressure of monotonous conditions and family responsibilities. The title is symbolical, standing for the most hated thing in the life of

Daisy Drennan. The entire Drennan family depended upon
Daisy for its cohesion, and its comfort. Christopher Pegum
wanted to marry her, but having successfully married off her
brothers and sister she decided to vanish from the railway
station where the parties were starting for their honeymoon.
In the earlier version of the play Daisy is brought face to face
with her *alter ego* in person, but in the later version this is
replaced by a vision. In neither version is the method of
enlightenment quite convincing, and perhaps the idea which
Mr. Robinson attempted to develop has been more successfully dramatised by Elmer Rice in *The Adding Machine*, or
by Karel Capek in *R.U.R.* In any event it was certainly a
welcome innovation on the part of an Irish dramatist, writing
for an Irish audience, to attempt a play which had nothing
peculiarly local about it.

In *Crabbed Youth and Age*, produced in November 1922,
is a little masterpiece of satirical comedy. It is probably the
most delightful one-act play of the contemporary theatre in
any country. There is little or no plot, no story, just a portrayal of a vivacious, well-informed, mother who is a good
conversationalist, and who by her wit and her charm attracts
the attentions of young men to herself at the expense of her
very modern and ill-informed daughters. This little comedy
is Lennox Robinson's best play so far. Technically it is
perfect, every move depending upon every other, and every
word springing from its predecessor. It gives the impression
that a new Robinson is in the making, an impression that
seems to be shared by W. B. Yeats, and that he will develop
into a master of the comedy of manners, a genre in which the
Irish drama has been singularly deficient. As a satirist
Robinson has always been strong, and this new development
would give him the scope his peculiar genius demands. It is
probable that credit for this development must be given to the
Spanish dramatists Sierra and Benevente, in whose work
Robinson has taken a deep interest. *Never the Time and the
Place*, produced in April 1924, is just a slight sketch which
may be further extended in course of time.

Studies in character is the only label that can be affixed
to his next two plays, possibly dependent to some extent upon
a growing interest in the work of the Italian dramatist Luigi
Pirandello. *Portrait*, produced in March 1925, is accurately
described by its title. It is a portrait, a group of portraits of
individuals and a collective portrait of the face of our time.
Satire is once more the strong point in what is essentially
what Arnold Bennett would describe as 'a fantasia on modern
themes '. If the play were taken seriously it must be labelled
tragedy, but it is really a gesture of contempt before the
increasing ' jazzmania ' of the post-war years. To the group
of young people portrayed nothing is serious, life is to be
grabbed and snatched. It is the brief life of the butterfly, and
the same inglorious end. It can hardly be said that the play
is a success ; it is too heavy in its structure to convey its
mood, and it was taken for tragedy in the theatre. The same
may be said of *The White Blackbird*, produced on 12th October, 1925. Here one son in a family is so different from all
the rest that he resembles the hero of George Gissing's *Born
in Exile*. A frivolous family with one serious member. The
result is certain to be disastrous, maybe even tragic. As
Lennox Robinson treats the theme there is no tragedy, the
audience is more disposed to laugh at the serious one as a prig
and a pedantic bore. Perhaps *The White Blackbird*, too, is
intended to be political, but if that be so not even six people
are aware of it. The characters, however, are all carefully
studied and drawn, but somehow the play is unreal. It might
refer to Ireland, but just as easily it might refer to any other
place. In September 1926 was produced what is for the
present Lennox Robinson's last play, *The Big House*.[1] In this
play is the biggest theme that Robinson has yet treated—the
fate in the new Ireland of the Anglo-Irish landowning and
professional classes. In a nation of peasants these have long
been the centres of what culture the country had, and if they
pass away or are absorbed in their environment the future of

[1] Since this was written another play, *The Far-off Hills*, has been
staged at the Abbey Theatre, and *Give a Dog* .... has been published.

Irish culture will be difficult to forecast. Even now Irish booksellers know what the immediate result of the departure of so many of these old Anglo-Irish has been for them, and if the process be continued indefinitely the result may well be disastrous. The St. Leger Alcocks of Ballydonal House were Irish and English, and the family was quite clear of the dividing line between its members and the countryside. There was always ' we ' and ' them ', but that did not prevent the Alcocks from taking their part in the life of the country. Then the war and the ' troubles ' came, sides had to be taken. Ballydonal House was raided by ' Black-and-Tans ', and burned by the Republicans. The older Alcocks will never change, but the end of the play shows the daughter of the house in the process of becoming ' more Irish than the Irish themselves '. Plainly this play reveals the divided allegiance of its author. He would regret the loss of what the Alcocks represent in Ireland, but he nevertheless welcomes the new Ireland that is now coming into being. *The Big House* might have been a great play, its theme is great but its characters are so petty that one cannot grieve for them. The passing of a great tradition is a fitting theme for great tragedy, but Mr. Robinson's mixed sympathies enabled him to miss its greatness and to present what is at best only a fairly good play. Like all his work it is tinged with melodrama from which he seems unable to escape when he goes outside satirical comedy, but as the years pass he has worked himself clear of the obvious thesis which marred his earlier plays. Now that Synge is dead, and Lady Gregory and W. B. Yeats no longer at their best, Lennox Robinson is the sole representative of the Abbey Theatre's earlier years. That he will write great drama there is no reason to doubt, he is experimenting always, and perhaps that is his only hindrance. The success of *The Whiteheaded Boy* and *Crabbed Youth and Age* shows clearly enough that his great strength is in satirical comedy, and if he would use his great gifts of satire to their fullest extent in future years the Irish theatre may have reason to rejoice. Ireland needs the salted comedy, more perhaps than does any other European country to-day, and there are humbugs and hypocrisies in abundance to provide material for the skilled dramatic instinct of Lennox Robinson. But as he has said he can see the faults of his friends as well as those of his enemies, and that may stay his satirical genius.

Seventeen years have passed since *Birthright* was named by competent American critics as the " best new play presented in America during the season 1911-1912 ". Yet despite that praise, and the fact that nearly all books on the drama mention his name in commendation, the plays of T. C. Murray have achieved little beyond a local recognition in Ireland. It was not until *Autumn Fire* was recently presented both in London and New York that the playgoers of these cities had an opportunity of judging his quality. With critics he has fared little better, some have said that he is merely a writer of melodrama, and one, at least, has hailed him as one of the world's great dramatists. In truth both estimates are far from the fact, but T. C. Murray is certainly one of the most considerable of the Irish dramatists, and the outstanding Irish Catholic dramatist. Perhaps the greatest obstacle to the wider fame of Murray as a dramatist is his own incurable modesty. He is one of the shyest and most retiring of living writers, shunning publicity of every kind. He is now in middle-age, and all his life he has been teaching in primary schools. Born in County Cork he began his teaching and play-writing careers in that county, and only after his plays had attracted the favourable attention of critics was he appointed to a school in Dublin.

His first play, *The Wheel of Fortune*, was produced by an amateur company in Cork city in 1909, and in the years that have since intervened he has written only seven plays. Three plays had been produced before he left his native county, and since 1913 he has resided continuously in Dublin. There is nothing lurid or startling about either the man or his work ; he is like deep water, as clear and as strong. That he holds strong convictions will not take long to discover, but these convictions do not obtrude in his plays. The one exception is his deep religious feeling, which forms the undercurrent in all his plays. In the Irish drama his plays are the Catholic counterpart to the essentially Protestant viewpoint expressed by Lennox Robinson. No one who either reads or sees one of Murray's plays can escape the knowledge that its author is a devout Catholic. It must, however, be said that the people he knows best, and who are portrayed in his plays, are those of West Cork, who are generally regarded as being the most ostentatiously religious in Ireland. It is therefore in keeping with the strictly realistic method which he invariably uses that his characters should all be deeply religious, and that they should make parade of their religious beliefs and practices.

The Wheel of Fortune was afterwards re-written and pro-duced at the Abbey Theatre in 1913, after his more serious plays had made him well known. The title, *Sovereign Love*, refers to the gold coin which was once so familiar, and which figured so prominently, in marriage arrangements throughout rural Ireland. Many plays have been written around this subject of ' matchmaking ' as it is called in Ireland. The arranged marriage is not peculiar to Ireland, it may be studied at its best and worst in France. In *Sovereign Love* the sub-ject is treated as comedy, but the play degenerates into farce as the action proceeds. The scene is laid in the parlour of 'The Granuaile' public-house, where the Kearney family is assembled awaiting the appearance of Andy Hyde, a returned Irish-American and prospective husband of Ellen Kearney. Hyde is late and the family is impatient at the delay. The landlady brings the information that the O'Donnell family, come to 'make a match' for its son David, is in a similar plight in an adjoining room. The two families are brought together and begin the process of 'making a match' between Ellen Kearney and David O'Donnell. They haggle about the amount of the 'fortune'; the negotiations breaking down several times, only to be resumed through the intervention of interested relatives. Finally, agreement is reached at a figure of £250 and half the priest's fees, which are said to be five per cent of the 'fortune'. All are drinking to the future happiness of the young couple when the 'Yank' arrives. He and old Kearney have a discussion during which Hyde agrees to pay £300 and the entire fee. The discussion is interrupted by the father of young O'Donnell, who discovers what is afoot and denounces Kearney's trickery. He leaves the room in a rage, leaving the Kearneys with Hyde. As the curtain falls old Kearney says to Hyde, " Well now, who'd ever think there was such villainy in all the living world ". He is self-righteous, unctuous, triumphant.

Even in the revised and re-written form *Sovereign Love* is not a good play. It is mechanical in its action, and the characters are types rather than individuals. Only the excellence of the dialogue saves the play from the extremity of farce. What can be said in its favour is that it extracts healthy laughter at the expense of a custom which is generally condemned but which nevertheless continues to flourish. Usually plays which deal with 'match-making' are tragic, Murray has himself treated it tragically in *Aftermath*, but it is upon this theme that Murray has built his only comedy. Though the play is popular with Irish audiences the only virtue which it may be deemed to possess for the critic is that it is the first play of a dramatist whose later work is of great value.

The career of T. C. Murray as a dramatist really began when *Birthright* was first staged at the Abbey Theatre in October 1910. This play also has been revised and altered several times, but only in incidentals ; essentially the play is the same to-day as when it was first staged eighteen years ago. Throughout the years it has retained its place as one of the most popular plays in the Abbey Theatre's repertoire. The play is a variant of the oft-told tale of Cain and Abel in terms of Irish conditions and character. The Morrissey family consists of Bat Morrissey, a dull, hard-working, tyrannous farmer, his wife Maura, and his two sons Hugh and Shane. Hugh is the elder ; a sportsman, full of life and spirit, with little inclination for the humdrum life of the farm. He is the pride of his mother and something of a popular hero in the neighbourhood. Shane is the pride of his father, whom he resembles in his love for the farm and a complete lack of interest in everything which does not minister to its prosperity. As the small farm would be unable to support two adult sons Shane, as the younger, must go to America. He is on the eve of departure when the curtain rises. Bat Morrissey resents the necessity for the departure of his farmer son, and throughout the two acts of the play every incident tends to increase and strengthen his resentment, and drive him to fury. When Hugh's services are needed on the farm he is found to be absent at a hurling-match. The music of a band and the shouts of a cheering crowd, applauding Hugh's victory, so frighten a favourite mare that she injures herself and has to be destroyed. Then Hugh is asked by the priest to preside over the entertainment of the visiting team, and is unable to remain at home for the evening. On hearing this Bat goes to the trunk and cuts from it the label bearing Shane's name.

BAT. What are you stopping for ? Don't you understand plain talk.

SHANE. But, father . . .

BAT. Write it, I tell you, at wanst.

MAURA. But surely, surely, Bat . . .

BAT. Shut your mouth, woman ! 'Tis none o' your business ! (*To* SHANE) Write it—and write it at wanst, I say, or 'twill be worse for you ! (SHANE *writes slowly and carefully, and hands back the label to his father.*)

BAT. (*Looking at label in the stupid manner of the half-illiterate and handing it back to* SHANE.) Read it for me.

SHANE. (*Reading.*) " Hugh Morrissey, Passenger Queenstown to Boston via Canpania ". (*He returns it to his father, who goes towards the trunk, and with a grim smile re-attaches it to the handle.*)

BAT. Now, my fine captain, you may feast and drink to the devil.

The second act opens at midnight of the same night. Hugh is still absent, and the unfortunate coincidence of a sow farrowing keeps Bat and Shane out of bed. Hugh returns and explains that he had been detained by the rowdy conduct of some of the visitors. His father, tired and angry, shouts at him the news that he, and not his brother, must go to America. Unable to credit the words Hugh is shown the label, and noting the handwriting of his brother he jumps to the conclusion that Shane has played a mean trick. He calls Shane a 'dirty grabber', than which there is no worse accusation in Ireland, except it be informer. Shane accuses Hugh of being drunk, and goes on to accuse their mother of persistent favouritism—Hugh always got the best of everything since they were small children. Both get furiously angry, they grapple with each other, and Shane strangles Hugh before they can be separated.

The action of the play is so swift that it carries the conviction of inevitability in the theatre. More careful study, however, shows that a series of coincidences really carries the plot. Accidental noise causes the mare's death, a sick call keeps the priest from the entertainment and makes Hugh's presence necessary, the sow farrows prematurely, keeping Shane and his father up late. So a number of small accidental happenings makes Hugh's murder appear inevitable by bringing to a head the long suppressed jealousy of the younger brother, and the fundamental divergence of character and temperament within the family. With great dexterity the quarrel is transferred from the father and son, as it would have been in the Repertory Drama, to the brothers. But it is character which gives the play its undoubted merit, particularly the character of Maura, the mother, who is drawn with a loving-kindness that gets over the footlights and escapes from the covers of the book. The dedication to the published play makes it clear that Maura is drawn from life. She is the most human of the mothers in the Irish drama.

Two years elapsed before *Maurice Harte* was produced on 20th June, 1912. *Maurice Harte* again is a tragedy of environment and parental affection. Maurice is the pride of the Harte family, and every nerve is being strained to pay for his education for the priesthood. His parents have sacrificed themselves and their other son, Owen, to that great ambition ; but the end is in sight when the play opens. In a short time Maurice will be ordained, and then he will perform the marriage ceremony for his brother and Bride Burke, whose dowry will clear the farm from debt. Maurice is home on holiday from Maynooth, and by relating the story of another student he tries to convey to his mother that he has no vocation for the priesthood. She fails to comprehend the significance of his words, so he discusses the matter with Father Mangan, his parish priest. Father Mangan makes the position plain to Mrs. Harte. Her agonised disappointment is so overwhelming that Maurice agrees to return to Maynooth for ordination. Nine months pass between the first and second acts, and at the end of that time Maurice has taken first place in his final examination and is on the eve of ordination. His father has arranged to be present at the ordination ceremony and will bring Maurice back with him to marry Owen and Bride Burke. All hope is centred upon these two great family events. The preparations are almost complete when Father Mangan brings news to shatter expectations. Maurice's mind has broken down under the strain, and he is brought back to his home a nervous wreck on the verge of insanity.

Maurice Harte is a tragedy of parental ambition and parental interference. Everything in the play is probable and logical—Maurice is sacrificed to the will and pride of his mother. Ellen Harte is a very fine portrayal of the Irish peasant mother, generous and mean, ambitious and benevolent, cruel and kind, ruthless and cunning when these qualities are necessary. All her qualities are used by the dramatist, producing a convincing study of a very difficult character. But the tragedy of Maurice himself dwarfs all else, and in his tragedy is contained much of the apparently paradoxical in the life of Ireland.

Spring, a little one-act play, was produced in January 1918, after Murray had written nothing for the stage for five years.

It is a grim satire upon the grasping meanness which is common in rural Ireland. An old man, Andreesh, lives in the house of his poverty-hardened daughter-in-law, Jude, who considers him an unnecessary burden and decides that he must go to the workhouse. As he is about to go the Old Age Pensions Act is passed, and Jude relents because the weekly pension will be useful to the house. Then suddenly the old man has a stroke and dies. The play is just an etching of a grasping peasant, but it displays in a marked degree T. C. Murray's chief defect as a dramatist, his tendency to rely upon accidental coincidence for his dramatic effects. This will be found in nearly every play he has written, but it is most marked in *Spring*. Another one-act play was published in 1917 which has not yet been presented on the stage. It is the tragedy of a young girl betrayed and then spurned by her lover, and condemned by the priest because he will not have scandal in his parish, who goes to drown herself as the curtain falls. It is a grim little tragedy, very moving and convincing to read. It is perfect in its characterisation and dialogue, yet it will probably never be produced in the Abbey Theatre because of its theme. It is undoubtedly T. C. Murray's best play and as such it ought to have a chance of being seen on the stage, but Ireland has not yet reached the plane whereon moral questions can be discussed openly. In time perhaps that plane may be reached, and then *The Briery Gap* will make many weep and many more think.

In 1920 there was presented a three-act play which has not yet been either publicly acknowledged or published. It was the author's first attempt to treat the three-act form, and it was followed in 1922 by another three-act play, *Aftermath*. Again the theme is parental pride interfering with, and ruining, the life of a son. Myles O'Regan is a schoolmaster with literary ambitions and in love with Grace Sheridan, a teacher in the school of which he is Principal. His mother, however, has other ambitions and designs for the future of her son. She is dissatisfied with the labourer's cottage in which they are compelled to live since they lost their big farm and she arranges for the marriage of Myles with Mary Hogan who is now the owner of the farm. By direct attack she frightens Grace into marriage with Doctor Manning ; and Myles marries Mary Hogan. At the end of four years he is a peevish miserable wreck, taking interest neither in his school nor in his farm. So he leaves his wife and his home— to return some day, perhaps.

Here may be noted another characteristic of Murray's plays : they never really end. With the single exception of *Spring* his plays do not end on the stage, the characters go off to something unknown and audiences are left to speculate on their future. In *Aftermath* Myles goes away with no more valid reason for going at just that precise moment rather than at any other ; the only reason would seem to be that the play had to end. The construction of this play is loose and laboured, and neither in characterisation nor in dialogue is it equal to the author's best work. It has failed to arouse interest either in the theatre or in the study. Perhaps it may be explained by the letter written by Murray to the American critic Barrett Clark (*Study of the Modern Drama*, p. 53), " After *Birthright* came *Maurice Harte* . . . and in the meantime I had devoured all that was significant in modern dramatic literature, making a study of the Russian, Norwegian Swedish, and German schools of drama ". There are traces of this study in *Aftermath*, but the theme is still that which served for *Birthright* and *Maurice Harte*, the influence of parents upon their children.

Autumn Fire, produced in September 1924, is yet the author's masterpiece in the three-act form. In this play, treating the same theme as Eugene O'Neill in *Desire under the Elms*, is a tragedy of quiet despair. The very vital widower father marries the young girl who is loved by his son. An accident renders him an invalid ; the poisonous gossip of his relatives makes him believe his wife deceives him. The end of the play is typical of the solution of such a problem in Catholic Ireland. The real tragedy is never enacted on the stage ; it begins only when the final curtain falls, leaving the victims of circumstance to endure their fate until one of them dies. The dialogue of this play is delightful, as near reality as literature is ever likely to approach. It is an exceedingly good play, one of the best plays of its time in any country, missing greatness only by its refusal to face the logic of its situations. When the Abbey Theatre allowed the rights of this play to pass out of its control it did one of the silliest things in its entire career. Yet this, one of the masterpieces of the Irish drama, was for so long ignored by the Irish theatre that its control lies now in London.

The Pipe in the Fields, a one-act play produced in October 1927, is part fantasy and part reality. Its theme is the awakening of artistic perception in the soul of a boy, the awakening being brought about by fairy music. It is a difficult theme to treat in the theatre, and it cannot be said that this play is altogether successful. But it is delightful either to see or to read, and it reveals the author in a new mood which he may exploit more fully in the future.

For his latest play, *The Blind Wolf*, which was produced on the evening of 30th April, 1928, Murray went outside Ireland for his scene, but the psychology of the characters is that of the West Cork peasants whom he knows so well. The play is also interesting for the fact that he has accepted a theme which has been used many times by dramatists in Ireland, England and Germany. Given in bald outline, the story of *The Blind Wolf* is almost identical with that of George Lillo's *Fatal Curiosity*, which was staged at the Haymarket Theatre in 1736, but the location, the names of the characters, the psychological content, and the environment, of Murray's play are entirely different. It is certain that he was quite unaware of Lillo's play, and that he only came to know of it after his own play had been written and was on the point of production. He says that he first got the outlines of his story from a newspaper account of an actual happening somewhere in Central Europe. Peter Karavoe and his wife Marina, with their little granddaughter and her mother, are on the verge of starvation ; so destitute that even the innkeeper refuses to give them any more food on credit. They are hoping that their son Franz will send something from America. Instead Franz himself comes to the inn and decides to give his parents a surprise. He orders everything necessary for a feast from the inn-keeper, and then decides to go as a stranger who had lost his way to his parents' house. There they fail to recognise him, and murder him in the night so that they may rob him. The play is interesting rather than distinguished, and the magnificent acting which it brought forth made it seem better than it actually is. *The Blind Wolf* adds nothing to its author's reputation, but it indicates an inclination to go outside Ireland for his themes in the future, and this may lead to something entirely different from anything Murray has hitherto done.

In his technique Murray is a realist—he presents real people in real situations—but he is a realist who presents without thesis or comment. He is too fond of accidents for his technique to be entirely satisfactory ; coincidence and accident may pass on the stage in moments of excitement but they become monotonous when used too frequently. The use of such devices damages the reputation of the artist by suggesting a deficiency in the inventive faculty. It is in his dialogue that Murray is supreme ; in that he is surpassed by no dramatist of his time. His characters, too, are all alive, and all recognisably Irish, even if they have a close family resemblance to each other. Murray is the dramatist of quiet desperation, one of the best of the Irish dramatists who is nevertheless closely akin to the best writers of the English Repertory School. He has tenderness and pity, a deep love for frail humanity which is probably religious in its source, he does not sit in judgment, and it is probable that he owes much to that English dramatist who is master of pity and realism—John Galsworthy. Much fine work may still be expected from him in the future as he is still in the prime of his writing career.

The name of Seumas O'Kelly is practically unknown

outside Ireland, and even in Ireland his work has never had a large or widespread appreciation. His work has been most highly appreciated by discerning critics wherever he has been read, and his death at an early age in 1919 removed one of the most considerable, and most potentially valuable, of Irish dramatists. He contributed one great play and a couple of very good plays to the Irish Theatre, but it is as a novelist and a short-story writer that he is best known outside Ireland. Seumas O'Kelly was a Connachtman, born in Galway, and he had that pensively meditative charm which seems to be the birthright of the people west of the Shannon. In physique he was frail and delicate, with a fervent belief in the fairy-lore which permeates his stories but which never found itself in his plays. A journalist by profession he had edited provincial newspapers for several years before he settled in Dublin in 1912. Before that year, however, he had become known to playgoers as the author of a play of outstanding merit which had been staged by the Theatre of Ireland in 1909. O'Kelly had been one of the political group which opposed the Abbey Theatre after the production of *The Playboy*, and he aided in the production of plays by several amateur companies before he finally came to the Abbey Theatre in 1910.

The Shuiler's Child had made a great impression upon literary and artistic circles in Dublin when it was first produced in 1909, with the notable actress Maire NicShuibhlaigh playing the principal part, but it was not until the play was staged at the Abbey Theatre in November 1910 that it became known to the larger playgoing public. The 'shuiler' is a familiar figure in Ireland ; he is the wanderer, the tramp, the tinker, somewhat akin to the roving 'gypsy' of England. *The Shuiler's Child* is a drama of renunciation ; a social problem set forth in stark terms. Moll Woods, the '*shuiler*', or vagrant beggar, singing from door to door for a livelihood, comes to the cottage of the O'Heas, a childless couple who have adopted a little boy from the local workhouse. Moll recognises the boy as her son, Phil, whom she had been forced to abandon to the workhouse. She longs to have him return to her, but the foster-parents have come to regard the boy as their own and are reluctant to let him go. An inspector from the workhouse arrives and threatens to remove the boy as he is not satisfied that proper discipline is being exercised by Mrs. O'Hea. The shuiler determines to save her son from returning to the workhouse, so she goes to the authorities herself to claim the child she had abandoned. Her request had, by law, to be complied with, and when the boy is restored to her she takes to the roads again, bringing him back to the house of the O'Heas. The O'Heas fear that the boy is to accompany his mother upon her wanderings, but as they are considering plans to keep the two close at hand the police arrive to arrest Moll Woods on a charge of child-desertion. Then the shuiler's motive in claiming her child becomes clear : she has admitted her relationship with the boy so that she can obtain the sole right to dispose of him without the intervention of the workhouse authorities. She leaves him to the O'Heas and stumbles out of the cottage to the prison to which the law must condemn her, and to that life of vagabondage, misery, and remorse to which she condemns herself. In the person of Moll Woods O'Kelly created a character that gripped the public, and in the development of her tragedy he proved himself very proficient in the technique of the stage. *The Shuiler's Child* is a play of great power and intensity, full of life and sympathy, which at the same time attracts attention to an important social problem.

In *The Bribe*, produced in November 1913, attention is again directed to a social problem of great significance. Nepotism was, until very recently, the outstanding vice of Irish public life, and to this vice and its possible consequences O'Kelly directed attention in his play. There is a vacancy for a doctor under the control of the public health authority and the sons of local people are candidates. The chairman of the board which controls the appointment barters his casting-vote to the highest bidder, the father of the least competent of the candidates, spurning at the same time the

claims of a brilliant son of a poor neighbour. The incompetent doctor gets the appointment, and when he later attends
the chairman's wife in her confinement his lack of skill has
fatal results. The probabilities are a little strained to fit the
thesis, but the play is nevertheless a very powerful presentation of a lamentable state of things. In technique it is in no
way inferior to *The Shuiler's Child*, and it has been exceedingly
popular with Irish audiences. *The Parnellite*, produced in
September 1917, presents in terms of stark realism the meanness, the treachery, the moral cowardice, and the tragic
consequences attendant upon the downfall of Charles Stewart
Parnell. There is something of the psychological basis of
The Playboy in *The Parnellite*, but O'Kelly's play is more
pedestrian in its stark presentation of the ugly facts, and more
bitter because he was a partisan and very obviously upon the
side of ' the Parnellite ' against the horde of cowards and
knaves who opposed him. The play is effective rather than
thrilling, but it is certainly much above the average Irish play.

O'Kelly also wrote at least four one-act comedies of which
only one has been produced by the Abbey Theatre, the others
have been produced many times by amateur companies
throughout the country, where they are popular on account of
their satirical content and droll dialogue. *Meadowsweet* was
staged at the Abbey Theatre in October 1919, and has been
revived many times since that year. It is a pleasant little play
without any of that distinguishing quality which made his
three tragedies notable. Indeed it may be said that in his
comedies O'Kelly never reached either the technical or
creative levels of his tragedies, but they are not in any way
inferior to numbers of one-act comedies which have been
staged by the Abbey Theatre, and their exclusion is somewhat
difficult to explain. But essentially O'Kelly's mind was
tragic, and it was the sombre aspects of life that attracted him.
There is no doubt that he had studied Ibsen to some effect ;
his three major plays have all the impress of that master. In
his three tragedies he depicted with great dramatic power
phases of Irish life in his own time. His language has none

of the rhythmic grandeur of Synge, nor the smooth poetry of
T. C. Murray, but it is true to his people and often reaches
poetic heights. In technique and dramatic power he is the
equal of any English-writing dramatist of the contemporary
theatre, but always he is the dramatist with a thesis. In
method he is thoroughly realistic, his men and women are
those amongst whom he lived and whom he knew intimately,
without romantic glamour of any kind. He dramatised the
problems of his time in terms of the people whom he knew,
and none who would know Ireland can afford to ignore his
plays. His early death deprived the Irish theatre of one of its
most promising playwrights, who would, had his life been
prolonged, undoubtedly have contributed many plays of
outstanding merit.

It is only incidentally, and perhaps accidentally, that St.
John Ervine is to be regarded as an Irish dramatist. True,
he is an Irishman, and he has written plays that are Irish in
theme and have been produced at the Abbey Theatre, but
never has his main interest been in Ireland or in the Irish
drama. He was born in Belfast in 1883, but at an early age he
went to London, where he joined the Fabian Society and came
much under the influence of Bernard Shaw and the English
Repertory Theatre movement. These influences, rather than
his youth in Belfast, seem to have formed his mind so that he
is something of an anomaly in the Irish theatre. He always
regarded the Abbey merely as one of a chain of Repertory
Theatres throughout the British Isles rather than the expression of a separate national consciousness which it was
founded to be. During the short term of his management of
the Theatre in 1915-1916 he avowed his intention to produce
such works as *Samson Agonistes* and *The Knight of the Burning
Pestle*, at the same time announcing that no acceptable plays
were being written in Ireland. Nevertheless, even if it be
accepted that his plays are all in the English Repertory
manner, it must also be recognised that he has given the
Irish theatre one play of surpassing distinction in *John
Ferguson*, and two others of more than ordinary distinction.

As early as 1913 he had given his *Jane Clegg* to the Manchester Gaiety Theatre, and had enabled Sybil Thorndike to achieve a triumph in the title-role. Since the end of the war all his plays have been in an English setting, and have been expressly written to meet the demands of the English theatre. Sometimes, as in *The Ship*, he glances at his native Belfast for his plot, but otherwise everything Irish that was in him except his vitriolic abuse seems to have been obliterated.

St. John Ervine's first play to reach the stage was produced at the Abbey Theatre on 30th March, 1911. It was *Mixed Marriage*, a play which has since been staged almost everywhere throughout Great Britain and America. Its theme was at the time one of burning controversial interest in Ireland, and great interest was manifested in its production. A short time previously there had been riots in Belfast, in which as usual religion had played a conspicuous part, and a girl had been shot dead whilst standing at the door of her house. The circumstances of the time gave the play a topical picquancy, but its instantaneous success depended entirely upon its dramatic merit, and it is this inherent dramatic merit which has given the play its wide appeal. The house of Rainey is divided against itself. On the one side stands John Rainey, barricaded behind his religious and political principles. " Yer conscience and yer principles causes a great dale of trouble to other people ", his wife tells him. Opposing him are his sons Hugh and Tom, conscious of new principles and wider possibilities. Mrs. Rainey believes that " a wumman has no right to be choosin' sides ", but her comments leave no doubt that her sympathies are against John. Hugh says his father's ' good training ' was nothing but bullying. A new idea is also arrayed against John in the person of Michael O'Hara, a young and enthusiastic propagandist of Labour principles, who believes that "onderneath the Cathlik an' the Prodesan there's the plain workin' man". John Rainey is an old man who had passed his life in an atmosphere of religious bigotry ; he is no villain, but a very human personality whose prejudices and traditions were the essential man. He is simple and

childlike in his acceptance of the things that are. The mere
suggestion that his son should marry a 'Cathlik' is too much
for his warped soul, it is too strong for his Labour enthusiasm,
and he will break any strike rather than have the religions
come together. So the flare of religious bigotry is set to the
movement of the workers, and in the resultant riots Nora,
Hugh Rainey's Catholic sweetheart, is shot dead. This
accidental happening rather obscures the real tragedy which
must have been in Ervine's mind in those years of his early
Fabian enthusiasm : the fact that religious bigotry can be
made to break any cohesion of the Belfast workers. All the
tragedy is in the quiet ending of the play when John Rainey
says, " A wus right. A knew a wus right ". Youth inspired
by a new ideal had broken itself against the hardened prejudices of age, and Ireland's dream of unity was shattered at
the same time. *Mixed Marriage* is not a great play, but it is
a play of great significance, and a study of character which
commands attention by its fidelity and sympathetic insight.
The ' revolt of youth ' was at the time when the play was
written a favourite theme of the younger English dramatists.
Stanley Houghton had staged *The Younger Generation* in
1910, and other members of the Repertory School were much
attracted by the same theme. It is Ervine's theme in *Mixed
Marriage*, rendered in terms of Belfast where the religious
atmosphere is more complex than elsewhere in the British
Isles, and where religious differences make effective revolt
impossible. The play was the outstanding success of 1911
at the Abbey Theatre, and it was the notable first play of a
man who has since achieved a wide recognition as an
important dramatist and critic, with the critic dominant.

When *The Magnanimous Lover* was produced in October
1912 it was very badly handled by the critics of Dublin. One
critic went so far as to suggest that only ' a sanitary inspector '
could deal with the play. Such a viewpoint might have been
expected, as Ireland is not habituated to the discussion of its
ethical and social problems on the stage. When Ibsen's
Ghosts was staged at the Dublin Gaiety Theatre by an English

touring company the storm of protest compelled the owners
of the theatre to close the gallery. Such an attitude is not
conducive to moral or social health in any community, but
Ireland must be accepted as it is, not as it might be. The
Ireland that existed in 1912 is in this respect identical with
the Ireland of to-day, and it is no more possible now than it
was then to discuss moral problems on the stage. That is
why Murray's *The Briery Gap* and Synge's *The Tinker's
Wedding* have never been produced in Dublin. St. John
Ervine was more fortunate in the fact that *The Magnanimous
Lover* was actually staged, but it is not one of the plays that
are revived. It is neither a good nor an important play, but
it does depict an aspect of Irish life which is too seldom even
mentioned. Maggie Cather had been betrayed by Henry
Hinde, and Henry had gone to England to escape the consequences. He had prospered in England, becoming the
owner of two shops and a van, and his religious scruples had
demanded that he return to ' make an honest woman ' of
Maggie. When Maggie suggests that ' they both fell together ' Henry will have none of it ; his contention being
that she is ' a fallen woman '. Maggie must be accepted
upon a basis of equality or else not at all, so when Henry
refuses that equality she sends him back to England alone.
It is exactly the theme of Houghton's *Hindle Wakes* which
was staged earlier although *The Magnanimous Lover* was
Ervine's first play, written before *Mixed Marriage*. The
scene is an Ulster village, and the Ulster dialect is used with
considerable skill and effect. The hypocrisy of Henry Hinde,
mouthing religion and behaving as a cad and a blackguard, is
cleverly contrived, and in Maggie Cather Ervine gave to the
Irish drama its only rebellious woman. The play, however,
was entirely in the English manner, and it was therefore not
surprising that his next play should be entirely English and
have its first production at the Manchester Gaiety Theatre.
This production of *Jane Clegg* in 1913 demonstrated the
divided allegiance of its author, and proved that he could not
be counted entirely one of the Irish dramatists.

By way of a reprisal to the criticism with which *The Magnanimous Lover* had been received in the Dublin press Ervine wrote *The Critics*, and it was produced at the Abbey Theatre in November 1913. It is only a slight skit, but it is accurate enough in its characterisation and bitter enough in its satire to be amusing. The incompetent nature of the criticism to which the Irish plays were subjected is mercilessly exposed; the same people who reported political meetings and dog shows did the dramatic criticism. Such Philistine criticism could only inflict annoyance upon the dramatists and the Directors of the Theatre, and at the same time keep the standard of public taste at a debased level. Ervine's great quality is his bellicose courage, and this quality was, and is, sadly needed in Ireland generally, in Belfast as much as in Dublin. It is therefore a matter of great regret that he should have chosen to live and work in England rather than in Ireland. In *The Orangeman*, another slight sketch produced in March 1914, he pillories his own fellow-citizens of Belfast. It is not at all an important play, being but a thumb-nail sketch, perhaps, for *Mixed Marriage*, but it is certainly amusing to those who know the fanaticism of the Orangeman, particularly in July.

On the evening of 30th November, 1915, while its author was manager of the Theatre, was produced *John Ferguson*, unquestionably Ervine's finest play, and one of the great plays of the modern stage. In this play is to be found the best and the worst of the Ulster Protestant character. John Ferguson is a fanatic, but he is at the same time a stoic. His religious zeal may make him act foolishly, but it also makes him act heroically. Like his derided compatriots of ' the South and West ' he, too, would sacrifice his life for his ideals. John Ferguson can stand the strain, it is his wife Sarah who breaks under it. John is frail of physique, affectionate by nature, and indomitable in his religious faith. He is held in the grip of Henry Witherow, a brutal tyrant, the local miller to whom his farm is mortgaged. Witherow threatens to foreclose. John is sick, and his son Andrew is quite unfit to make a success of the farm ; but they are expecting help from John's brother in America. When no letter is received their last hope vanishes. But another hopeful prospect opens when Jimmy Caesar, an obnoxious, mean little creature but a wealthy local grocer, who hates Witherow with a burning hatred, offers to clear the mortgage if Ferguson's daughter Hannah will marry him. It is a tempting offer to John, yet he does nothing to persuade Hannah to marry Caesar. He knows that she is reluctant, but that she feels the whole future of her family rests upon her sacrifice, and she consents. But soon she realises the impossibility of marrying a man she despises. Her mother would force her to keep her plighted word, but her father realises his mistake, and silencing his wife he sends word to Witherow to foreclose. Then Witherow seduces Hannah, and Jimmy Caesar driven to desperation swears that he will murder Witherow. John brings all his religious ardour to bear upon Caesar in an endeavour to dissuade him, but in vain. Caesar goes in search of his enemy, and Andrew is implored to go after him and stop a crime. Andrew refuses ; he hopes Caesar will avenge Hannah. So the sick man goes out into the night himself in an effort to save, not Witherow from the death he deserves, but Caesar from perdition. John fails in his quest, and next morning Caesar returns in a woebegone state after a night spent cowering under a hedge. He had gone to murder Witherow but he had quailed, he was too much of a coward. " I'm full of hate ", he whines in his debasement, " and I want to hurt them that hurts me, but I haven't the courage to do it ". Then news comes that Witherow has been found shot dead, and Caesar is stricken with terror. He swears his innocence, but the circumstances are against him and he is arrested. Hannah now begins to have respect for him, he has apparently proven both his courage and his love. She visits him in jail, and is certain that Jimmy's doom is sealed. Just then a letter arrives from America with the money needed to save the farm : John's brother explains that he has mistaken the date and had missed the mail by a day. Hannah's

religious basis is broken, her life and that of her family is in
ruins about her. " Where's the right in it, da ? Where's the
right in it ? It's not just ! It's not fair ! " So she protests
in anguish. Her father's faith remains unshaken : " We
can't understand everything. It's no good trying to puzzle
it all out. We must have faith . . . that's all ! Just have
faith ! " Then comes the greatest blow. Andrew confesses
that it was he, and not Caesar, who shot Witherow. He had
known that Caesar was too cowardly to do it, so he had made
sure by doing it himself. He is not sorry that he did it, but
he cannot see an innocent man suffer in his place. He will
go to the police and confess, " I must go, ma, for my peace'
sake ". Then the faith of John Ferguson totters ; he urges
his son to escape.

JOHN. (*To* ANDREW.) Come on, son, and get ready. You must
quit the place this night.

ANDREW. I can't go, da, and leave Jimmy in the wrong.

JOHN. Yes, yes, son ! That'll be all right ! We'll think about
Jimmy afterwards. Come and get ready now, son.

ANDREW. I must do right by Jimmy for my peace' sake.

JOHN. No, son, you must save yourself first.

His children bring him back to his faith, and Andrew with
Hannah go off to the police. John Ferguson and his wife are
left alone. Then John picks up the Bible which is always by
him, saying : " Come here, Sarah ! Sit down, woman, here
by the side of me, and give me a hold of your hand. . . .
Listen to God's word, Sarah, and that'll strengthen you. (*He
reads of David receiving the news of the death of Absalom.*)
" And the King was much moved, and went up to the cham-
ber over the gate and wept: and as he went, thus he said, ' O
my son Absalom, my son, my son Absalom ! Would God I
had died for thee, O Absalom, my son . . . my son '." (*His
voice ends in a sob. The Bible falls from his hands. There is
a low moan from his wife.*)

John Ferguson is a play deeply felt and sincere, and in the
character of John Ferguson Ervine created a man which the

stage had not previously known.   His faith did not brace him
to meet the facts of life, nor did it comfort him when action
was useless, but it was all he had to use merely as a drug to
deaden his sorrow.   For his wife it lacked even that.   Fate
plays with these little lives as Hardy made it play with Tess
or Jude, and there is as much of Hardy in the play as there is
of Ulster.   Nevertheless *John Ferguson* is a great play despite
the minor blemishes in its construction.   Like T. C. Murray
Ervine is apt to strain accidental happenings, and in this play
there are two upon which the entire action is made to turn.
The seduction of Hannah by Witherow is not made at all
probable or convincing, there was nothing to indicate that
Hannah was attracted by Witherow.   Then there is the loss
of the mail by John's brother in America when a day would
have avoided all the sorrow and destruction.   However, it is
John himself who makes the play great, he stands like Lear
against the buffets of fate, and at the end his ' head is bloody,
but unbowed '.   His body may be broken, his life-work
ruined, but nothing can break his 'unconquerable soul'.
These Fergusons are little people, but they can show life
great, life tragic, as well as the kings and the aristocrats.   Their
stoicism is ennobling to the audience, even if they wear no
crowns and work with their hands.   They do not speak a
language that rises to poetry, their emotions are all subdued ;
but they do present the Northern Irish peasant as he had
never before been presented to the world.   His very defects
come from his qualities, his dourness, his staccato speech, his
religious fanaticism, his contempt for his more soft-spoken
compatriots in Ireland's other provinces.   John Ferguson
would have enjoyed his creator's gesture when farewell was
bidden to Ireland in *The Island of Saints, and the Way to get
out of It*.   This little play was staged in 1920, and is as
unworthy of its author as of the Theatre in which it was
produced.   *John Ferguson* is Ervine's gift to Ireland, and it
is his greatest play.

Brinsley MacNamara is known outside Ireland as a novelist
of power and distinction, but in recent years he is better

known inside Ireland as a dramatist. Like Padraic Colum he is a native of the midlands, having been born in the County of Westmeath, and it is the people of this and the neighbouring counties who figure in his novels and his plays. His best known novel, *The Valley of the Squinting Windows*, aroused considerable anger when it was published, and led to personal attacks being made upon the author and his family. For a time he was a member of the Abbey Theatre Company, acting with the Company during its second American tour. His first play, *The Rebellion in Ballycullen*, which was produced in March 1919, is a satire upon the pseudo-patriotism of the inhabitants of an Irish village, showing their reactions to the militant movement in Irish politics. As a first play it showed considerable dramatic power which promised well for the future of its author. In his second play, *The Land for the People*, which was first staged in 1920 and has since been re-written and revived many times, the motives of a land agitator are ruthlessly exposed. Connor Cooney had led an agitation to recover ' the land for the people '. He had betrayed that movement and had himself become the largest landowner in the district. He had disowned his wife, and had invested his wealth in the name of his ne'er-do-well brother, Johnton, so that his wife could not claim alimony from him. His wife's father had been his companion in the great movement to recover the land, but he had been sincere and had been sacrificed. Cooney's son is being reared as a snob and a wastrel, ' a gentleman ' as it is called by the peasants, and his daughter is in love with the young leader of the new agitation for the breaking up of the land. This time the people get the land, because they take it by force and there is no treachery in their own ranks. Connor Cooney is broken, and in the end the only consolation he has left is the wife he had spurned. As re-written and staged in 1927 *The Land for the People* is a very convincing play, vividly realistic in its treatment of the conditions, and bitterly satirical with the characters, under which Land Agitations are conducted in Ireland. The play is rather an earnest of great achievement in the future than a great achievement in itself. It is nevertheless one of the plays of considerable merit which the land hunger of the Irish peasant has made possible.

It is by his two comedies, *The Glorious Uncertainty* and *Look at the Heffernans !* that Brinsley MacNamara is popularly known as a playwright, and his success as a writer of light-textured plays came as a pleasant surprise to all who were familiar with his earlier plays and his novels. In *The Glorious Uncertainty*, which was first produced in November 1923, and revived very frequently since that date, the author deals in witty fashion with what are known as 'flapper', or unofficial, race meetings, and with the efforts of one Gabriel Cunneen, the owner of a public-house magnificently styled ' Hotel ', to retrieve his fallen fortunes as an amateur book-maker. The play is replete with all the slang of the turf, and many of the characters have the tattered reputations of the racecourse. As a laughter-maker this play is one of the outstanding successes of the Abbey Theatre in recent years, and it has borne revival frequently every year since its production without any apparent diminution in its popularity. *Look at the Heffernans !* first staged in April 1926, is as popular as its predecessor. It is a comedy of intrigue, in which the wiles of the Widow Molloy and the immaculate character of the brothers Heffernan give many opportunities for unrestrained laughter. The two Heffernans are the models for the neighbourhood, and their efforts to retain their reputations, while simultaneously carrying on a flirtatious intrigue, are extremely diverting. In these two humorous plays the characterisation is almost perfect. All the well-known types of the racecourse, the shop, and the village are utilised to induce laughter that is a social, no less than an individual, tonic. Audiences laugh at these people on the stage as they laugh at them in the ordinary intercourse of every day. Fidelity to the actualities of Irish rural life is not the least of Brinsley MacNamara's virtues as a novelist and a playwright.

The Master, Brinsley MacNamara's latest play and his best to date, was produced for the first time at the Abbey Theatre on 6th March, 1928. To some extent it is indebted to his first play, *The Rebellion in Ballycullen*, inasmuch as its theme is concerned with the effects of revolution in Irish politics after the General Election of 1918. The central character is the schoolmaster, James Clinton, but the theme of the play is really the power of the priest and the public-house owner to control political effort in Irish villages. In the midst of the Anti-Conscription agitation of 1917-1918 the schoolmaster is dismissed his school on a trivial pretext, and he blames the parish priest for his dismissal. Never had James Clinton been popular with his neighbours in the village of Clunnen ; he had been domineering and, they said, cruel. His own opinion was that ' the mob is always wrong ', and upon that opinion he based his conduct. So no one mourned when he was dismissed. His chance to achieve popularity presented itself, and he undertook to lead the armed revolt in the village. From this vantage-point he would dictate his terms to priest and traders alike. He established a ' Sinn Fein ' school in the village, and to this school the children were driven while the National School, to which the parish priest had appointed a woman teacher over the head of Clinton's son Michael, was boycotted. The ' respectable traders ' did not like the dictation of James Clinton, so they plotted against him and in a short time they undermined his power over the Volunteers. When the menace of Conscription had passed it was seen that Clinton had no power at all ; and then the ' mob ' turned against him, under the leadership of a public-house owner named Jasper Branagan, who had his eyes fixed on a local manor-house deserted in fear by its owners. Branagan and his followers attempted to drive ' the Master ' from the official residence which he occupied, but in this he is foiled, and it is Michael Clinton, ex-commandant of Volunteers, who is ' exiled '. The frightened schoolmistress having resigned almost in terror the parish priest solved the problem of the school and the residence by re-appointing James Clinton to his old position.

As played in the Abbey Theatre on its first production the

theme of the play was rather obscured, and the bumptious behaviour of the schoolmaster tended to alienate the sympathy of the audience.   But a little consideration will make clear that *The Master* is another portrayal of the disillusionment which has overtaken young Ireland since the establishment of the Irish Free State in 1921.   Brinsley MacNamara shows in his characters, particularly his young men, something of the idealism which fortified Ireland during the troubled years from 1918 to 1921, and he shows no less clearly the selfishness and the desire for power actuating the older people.   In the end it is the ideas of the older people which predominate, and the grand dreams of those who fought, and died, for an idealised Ireland are shattered by the realities of rural life. ' The more things change the more they are the same ' might be the motto for *The Master*, as it shows the New Ireland settling down to become as like the Old Ireland as possible.   In his presentation of this New Ireland Brinsley MacNamara approaches the view-point of Sean O'Casey, but in no other point is there any similarity between the two playwrights.   MacNamara's play is more closely woven than anything O'Casey has yet done, and his dialogue is modelled upon the speech of the Irish Midlands.   There is no rollicking humour in MacNamara's play, as there is in O'Casey's, as there is no attempt made to introduce that ' comic relief ' which seems to be so much desired, and admired, by the controllers of the commercial theatre.   This play definitely ranks Brinsley MacNamara as one of the most promising playwrights upon which the Irish Theatre must rely in the immediate future, as it ranks him also as one of the most uncompromising realists.   He has, so far, made no attempt to break with the realist tradition and method ; he carries the banner of Ibsen as well as any in the range of Irish dramatists.

Sean O'Casey is the great discovery of the post-war Irish theatre.   A few years ago his name was known only to the workmen who were his mates in the service of the building contractors of Dublin.   Now he is known wherever the

English language is spoken or read as a dramatist of considerable importance. His plays have brought a new popularity to
the Abbey Theatre, as they have brought to that Theatre an
audience which had never known it before. It was an unusual
experience for the Abbey Theatre to be compelled to turn
away hundreds of people from its doors every night, yet the
plays of Sean O'Casey have given it that prominence for
almost the first time. He has been described as 'the greatest
Irish dramatist since Synge' by competent critics, and there
is no doubt that he is now the most popular dramatist of the
Abbey Theatre. There is really no basis for comparison
between O'Casey and Synge : Synge was a poet, with all the
attributes of a poet ; O'Casey is a photographic artist who
retouches his films with an acid pencil to produce an effect of
grotesque satire. All his characters are taken directly from
the Dublin slums, placed in positions and surroundings which
give the appearance of caricature. In the streets they would
pass unnoticed—they are normal—but on the stage they are
as figures from Dickens pictured by ' Phiz '. His plays
resemble those of Eugene O'Neill rather than those of Synge ;
and when compared with the plays of O'Neill they fail to
realise the expectations raised by the extravagant praise of the
press of Dublin and London.

In the circumstances of his life, too, O'Casey somewhat
resembles O'Neill. O'Casey is some few years older than
O'Neill, and he has not roved the world. He has passed his
years as a manual worker, and as a permanent resident of
the slums of Dublin. He was born and was reared in a
Dublin 'tenement', that is, a house which once sheltered the
Irish aristocracy but now houses sometimes several families
in a single room. He never went to school, but earned a
livelihood from a very early age by selling newspapers in the
streets. Like the majority of his class he drifted into that
vague section of workers known as ' general labourers ',
engaged from time to time on any work that offered, from the
docks to a bricklayer's mate. In the effort to organise, and
improve the conditions of, these workers he took his place

with Jim Larkin, and he was for some time connected with the Irish Transport Workers' Union. He aided in the organisation of the Irish Citizen Army which fought under the command of James Connolly in the Dublin Rising of 1916. The *History of the Irish Citizen Army* was his first published work ; it appeared in 1918 under his Gaelic name. Since that date he has devoted himself entirely to drama, and to his daily work. He was a regular attendant at the performances at the Abbey Theatre, and any technique that he has was learned by watching the plays there. He has written many plays, but so far only five have been staged. It is said that as many as eight of his plays had been rejected before his first was accepted for the Theatre in 1923.

The first production of *The Shadow of a Gunman* in April 1923 made his reputation in a single night. The play packed the Theatre for weeks with enthusiastic audiences, and made the name of Sean O'Casey the best known in Dublin. Since then four other plays have been staged, and the three longer plays have been published. His plays have been received with enthusiasm in London, and somewhat coldly in America, but he has shared at least one distinction with Synge ; his *The Plough and the Stars* provoked riotous scenes in the Theatre when it was produced in February 1926, because it was alleged he defamed the memory of the men who were executed in 1916.

O'Casey is not by any means, as is generally supposed outside Ireland, the first Irish dramatist to stage the slums of Dublin, and to portray the hardy vivacious race that inhabits them in a play. There is no doubt, however, that he is the best. Some years ago two plays staged the types from the slums, and both passed almost without notice. They were *The Slough*, by A. P. Wilson, and a blistering social satire by one who named himself ' Alpha and Omega ' called *Blight*. There was also *The Labour Leader* by the Cork novelist and dramatist Daniel Corkery which, incidentally perhaps, used the same material. Where O'Casey scores over those dramatists is in the use he makes of the period of war and bloodshed through which Dublin has so recently passed, and with which his audiences are all familiar. The plays mentioned were all serious social dramas ; they contained no comedy elements, and they were not calculated to make audiences laugh. They were all in the manner of the English Repertory School, and they have all been dropped from the repertoire of the Theatre. Such is the usual fate of plays which deal seriously with serious subjects. " Life is a comedy to those who think, a tragedy to those who feel ". The dramatists all felt tragedies, but the audiences demanded comedies. Sean O'Casey gives the audiences what they want, and they can laugh uproariously at satire of themselves.

" I forget ", said Sarcey, " what tyrant of ancient Greece it was to whom massacres were everyday affairs, but who wept copiously over the misfortunes of a heroine in a tragedy ". Dublin audiences resemble that Greek ; they endured the bloodletting of several years with stoical calm, then laughed at the tragedy of Juno. They were indifferent to the fact that Juno is of infinitely greater significance to Dublin and to the world than the spectacular melodrama which was enacted upon the political stage. That significance did not reach the audiences ; they had handled their guns like men, and it was time to laugh. Life is a rollicking farce to the audiences, and a harrowing tragedy to the dramatist ; but it was not entirely the fault of the audiences that they failed to be harrowed by O'Casey's tragedies. As they were played at the Abbey Theatre it was the comic rather than the tragic aspects of the plays that were emphasised. In the two more important plays audiences were entertained with the antics of two typical Dublin loafers, exemplified, and acted, as such characters had never previously been on any stage. Dublin audiences simply loved these loafers in the theatre, but they would spurn their originals at the Theatre door.

The two more important plays are both tragedies of disillusionment ; they were played and accepted as comedies of errors. The two one-act plays are unworthy of serious attention ; they are at best but slightly expanded anecdotes.

Juno and the 'Paycock' is modern tragedy at its best, almost at its greatest. *The Shadow of a Gunman* is that parody of tragedy called melodrama. *The Plough and the Stars* is a social and political satire which is very effective in its delineation of Irish disillusionment. Tragedy must present a solemn view of life with depth, with feeling, so that the action depicts the concern of all humanity. There may be sorrow, sin, death, blood, tears, and suffering, but if the imagination be not led upwards and onwards from the individual to the universal, the play containing them is but superficial melodrama. Because of its superficiality, and because of its close resemblance to an Irish weekly newspaper in the year 1921, *The Shadow of a Gunman* is merely melodrama which must inevitably lose its significance with the passage of time. *Juno and the 'Paycock'* has its superficial qualities, but it is uplifted and ennobled by the character of Juno. Juno is the great, the universal, mother, as great as the greatest mother in drama, even though her influence be limited to two rooms in a Dublin slum. The tragic significance of Mrs. Alving, in *Ghosts*, is small when compared with the tragic significance of Juno. Her son dead ' for his country ' ; her daughter betrayed by a worthless liar and deserted by a braggart coward ; her husband a boasting, lying, drunken wastrel ; she rises superior to her slum surroundings and prepares to begin her life-struggle anew.

O'Casey's plots are difficult to summarise ; in a sense it may be said that his plays are without plots, and all who think that a play and a plot are synonymous will rule him out of the list of dramatists in company with Schnitzler, Tchechov, and Eugene O'Neill. His plays depend for their significa..ce upon personalities rather than upon plots ; upon Davoren, Shields, Maguire, and Minnie Powell, in *The Shadow of a Gunman* ; upon ' Joxer ' Daly, ' Captain ' Boyle, and Juno, in *Juno and the 'Paycock'* ; and upon 'Fluther' Good, 'the Covey', Jack Clitheroe and Nora, Uncle Peter, in *The Plough and the Stars*. Many others play minor, unimportant parts ; but story there is none, they are all ' slices of life ' in the strictest and most literal sense of the term. But a story must be made if the plays are to be summarised in a form that will be intelligible to anyone who has not seen or read them. In *Juno* 'Captain' Jack Boyle, the 'Paycock', his wife Juno, with Johnny and Mary their two children, live in a two-roomed flat in a Dublin tenement house. Jack Boyle is a public-house lounger who got his title of 'captain' from being " wanst on the wather, in an oul' collier from here to Liverpool". His other title, 'the paycock', was bestowed upon him by his wife because she thought he was as useful and as vain as the peacock. Juno herself is nicknamed because every thing of importance in her life has happened in June. Juno and her daughter work while the 'Paycock' struts the floor or lounges in public-houses. Mary is on strike against the victimisation of a fellow-worker. Johnny is an invalid who was " only a chiselur of a Boy Scout in Easter Week, when he got hit in the hip ; and his arm was blew off in O'Connell Street ". ' Joxer ' Daly is the ' butty ', or drinking companion, of Jack Doyle. He is a typical Dublin wastrel of the worst kind ; lazy, deceitful, hypocritical, and engaging withal, but detested by Juno. Mary Boyle is being courted by Jerry Devine, who has dreams of being a great leader of Labour and a champion of democratic freedom, but she throws him over in favour of Charlie Bentham, a school-teacher studying law. Into the Boyle household comes Bentham with the story of a legacy which is coming to Jack Boyle, and upon the prospect the Boyles proceed to buy new furniture and give a party to their neighbours to celebrate their good fortune. The festivities are interrupted by the funeral of the son of another resident in the house, whose body has been found on the roadside " beyant Finglas, riddled with bullets ". The entire party goes to view the procession. Only Johnny, the crippled boy, remains ; and to him is brought a message " to attend a Battalion Staff meetin' the night afther to-morrow ". Johnny, nervously passionate, refuses to take any note of the message. " I done enough for Ireland ", he says. To which the messenger retorts : " Boyle, no man can do enough for Ireland ". Soon rumour begins to cast doubt upon the Boyle legacy. Bentham has gone to England ; the tailor takes away the ' captain's ' new clothes ; the furniture dealers take away the furniture ; and Mrs. Madigan, a neighbour, takes the gramophone in lieu of her unpaid loan. Juno takes Mary to a doctor ; the verdict makes Jerry Devine spurn where once he had loved. Johnny and his father disown Mary for having ' disgraced ' them, and the ' captain ' goes out to get drunk, vowing vengeance upon his return. Johnny is taken away for execution as a spy, he being responsible, it is alleged, for the death of his neighbour's son and his own chum. The room is desolate, cheerless, bare.

MRS. BOYLE. We'll go, Mary, we'll go ; you to see your poor dead brother, an' me to see me poor dead son.

MARY. I dhread it, mother, I dhread it !

MRS. BOYLE. I forgot, Mary, I forgot ; your poor oul' selfish mother was only thinkin' of herself. No, no, you mustn't come —it wouldn't be good for you. You go on to me sisther's an' I'll face the ordeal meself. Maybe I didn't feel sorry enough for Mrs. Tancred when her poor son was found as Johnny's been found now—because he was a Die-hard ! Ah, why didn't I remember that then he wasn't a Die-hard or a Stater, but only a poor dead son ! It's well I remember all that she said—an' it's my turn to say it now : What was the pain I suffered, Johnny, bringin' you into the world to carry you to your cradle, to the pains I'll suffer carryin' you out of the world to bring you to your grave ! Mother o' God, Mother o' God, have pity on us all ! Blessed Virgin, where were you when me darlin' son was riddled with bullets ? Sacred Heart of Jesus, take away our hearts of stone and give us hearts o' flesh ! Take away this murdherin' hate an' give us Thine own eternal love. (*They all go slowly out.*)

(BOYLE *and ' JOXER ' return very drunk, talking patriotic nonsense.*)

BOYLE. I'm tellin' you . . . Joxer . . . the whole worl's . . . in a terr . . . ible state of . . . chassis. (*Curtain.*)

'Patriotism is not enough', this play shouts with Nurse Cavell, and the audience laughs at the drunken antics of Boyle and Daly ! Sacrifices are made for, and in the name of, the Motherland, but the mother of flesh and blood is spurned, derided, sacrificed, or ignored ! Ireland, the Motherland, is loved as an abstraction ; Juno is compelled to live in a slum, to see her children sacrificed, but she is ignored because she is merely a reality. Even her own son will fight for the abstraction instead of working for his mother ! Not in Ireland only does this happen. For four years all the world knew it when the war-drums sounded and the battle-flags were unfurled. And in time the same thing will happen again.

In comparison with *Juno and the 'Paycock'* the poverty of *The Shadow of a Gunman* manifests itself very quickly. Here again a woman is sacrificed to the cowardice of men ; but the play is little more than a chronicle of events, with a satirical commentary. The scene is a Dublin tenement house in which live Shields, a pedlar, and Davoren, a poetic dreamer. Shields is a loquacious patriot, a hero in speech and a coward in action. Davoren is above and outside the battle. He is, however, believed by his neighbours to be a ' gunman on the run ', and he is respected accordingly. Maguire, ostensibly a pedlar, leaves a bag in the room. Minnie Powell, another resident, falls in love with Davoren, 'the shadow of a gun-man '. A raid is made upon the house by the Black-and-Tans. The pseudo-pedlar, Maguire, had been killed in an ambush. Hasty examination of the bag reveals bombs. Minnie takes the bag to her room, where it is found by the raiding-party. She is arrested, and is killed ' trying to escape '. The lesson is the same : the innocent are goaded to destruction by the men of words, the speech-makers and the poets, who live themselves to be known as 'the men who won the war '

The shattering of dreams and the survival of communities seems to be the theme of *The Plough and the Stars*, produced in February 1926. Over the dreams and hopes of John and Nora Clitheroe, newly married, is the shadow of political strife. They live in a tenement, but they are different from the normal tenement inhabitant. With them lives Peter Flynn, Nora's uncle, and the young Covey, Clitheroe's cousin. Peter is a showy patriot who dresses like Robert Emmet and mouths platitudes. The Covey is a class-conscious proletarian, anti-religious and anti-patriotic. Jack Clitheroe is a Commandant in the Citizen Army unknown to himself, as his wife had destroyed, without his knowledge, the letter appointing him to the position. Into the quiet home comes Captain Brennan to acquaint Clitheroe that he is to command a battalion at a big demonstration. His wife's appeal is vain ; he throws her off and goes. The demonstration is a success ; but a public-house near which it is held is packed, patriots and viragos mix indiscriminately, and even the ' Plough and Stars ' banner of the Army is borne into the bar while its bearer has a drink. Back at the tenement again a consumptive child is brought to the door to take the air ; three men play pitch and toss and discuss the fighting ; the women and the men go off to loot. Nora Clitheroe is brought home by Fluther Good after a fruitless search for her husband, and a stray lady wanders aimlessly. Then comes the great moment of the play. Jack Clitheroe comes to the door covering the retreat of a wounded volunteer. Nora hears him and comes to the door, she clings to him, beseeching him to give up the fight and come back to her. "They are all afraid", she says, " don't you be afraid to be afraid ! " Again he throws her from him, and she lies inert upon the steps until she is taken into the house. A doctor is fetched. The consumptive child has died, and men are playing cards on the coffin. Nora Clitheroe's baby has been born dead and she has become demented. Captain Brennan brings to her a last message from Jack, who has been killed and left in a flaming hotel. Soldiers come to escort the funeral of the dead child, and when the coffin has been taken away Nora appears in a state of delirium. She prepares the table for a meal oblivious of the sleeping neighbour who tends her. The rattle of musketry wakes the sleeper, and attracts Nora to the window. The nurse is killed by a volley, and Nora is taken away by another neighbour. Soldiers had herded the men away, and they now return to sit down to the meal Nora had prepared.

They sing ' Keep the Home Fires Burning ' as the play
ends.

Death, destruction, suffering, waste ; all in the sacred name
of patriotism ! Again it is the women who suffer, the women
who are great. " Is there anybody goin' with a titther o'
sense ? " asks the consumptive child. The men talk and
dream, loot and die for their dreams ; the women live and
die for the realities. The play has many memorable scenes,
but it is not so good as *Juno*. It is little better than a series of
disconnected scenes with the fighting as a background, and
the theme gets lost in the multiplicity of incidents. There is,
too, a tendency to make the characters talk in 'literary'
language which makes them stilted and unreal. Its form owes
something to the cinema, but it undoubtedly is one of the
most popular Irish plays of recent years. It quickly ran
through the storm of protest with which its first week was
made notable, and achieved a popularity in Dublin which was
repeated in London.

Whatever may be the future of Sean O'Casey there is now
no doubt that he is a considerable dramatic artist, and a man
who is so intimate with the people of his plays that he could
not fail to portray them justly. That his work since *Juno* has
shown no advance, and that he is disposed to change his
locale to London, is disquieting.[1] His success is attributable
entirely to his intimate knowledge of his native city, and it is
there that his future must be decided. He is a realist of the
most uncompromising kind, an ironist, and a traditionalist,
much to the diappointment of some critics who expected him
to write ' proletarian ' plays in the new German manner. He
has accepted the realist tradition of the Abbey Theatre, and
no Irish dramatist since the death of Synge is more likely to
influence the Irish playwrights of the immediate future.
Already it is plain that the methods of O'Casey are being
imitated, even by dramatists whose reputations were high

[1] The rejection of *The Silver Tassie* in May 1928 led to an acri-
monious correspondence between Sean O'Casey and the Directors of
the Abbey Theatre. See *The Irish Statesman*, 9th June 1928.

before the name of O'Casey had been known. The disillusionment of Ireland has aided O'Casey to popularity, and
the success of his plays makes it certain that Irish drama will
remain realistic for a considerable time to come. The Abbey
Theatre will continue to be the home of realism in Ireland,
and George Moore's statement will remain as true as when
he made it.

CHAPTER X

THE NECESSITY FOR COMEDY

Comedy Necessity to gather an Audience, and to provide Relaxation—
Stimulation Necessary to induce Comedy—The Earliest 'Comedies':
Yeats, Ryan, Lady Gregory—Irish Humour essentially Intellectual—
Irish 'Comic Characters' for Foreign Amusement—Comparative
Scarcity of Pure Comedy—Irish 'Comedy' is mainly Farce—The
Best Irish Comedies already Noted—The Plays of William Boyle—
W. F. Casey—Edward McNulty—George Shiels.

THE 'Comic Poet', George Meredith has stated, requires a
cultivated society with quick perceptions, a community
without giddiness, a period free from feverish emotion and a
reasonable equality between the sexes. Some of these might
have been found in the Ireland of the end of the nineteenth
century, but that was certainly not a period free from feverish
emotion, nor was the community entirely without giddiness.
The quickness of perception, and the reasonable equality of
the sexes, were then, as now, marked features of the Irish
community. If the opinion of Karel Capek be accepted that
period was ideal for the development of Irish comedy. " The
actual state of change and flux in everything is rather the
opportune time for writing comedies" (*Observer*, 12th February, 1928). Both of these opinions would suggest that
comedy ought to have developed with spontaneity in Ireland,
and to have flourished without any resort to artificial stimulation. There was at the time in the country the quick perception, the equality of the sexes, and the beginnings of the
change which has eventuated in the creation of the Irish Free
State. In politics, economics, the arts, and social affairs, the
change was notable to all with the necessary experience of the
country to enable them to judge. But the 'Comic Poet' did

not find his environment sufficiently inspiring to make his presence manifest to all. So the Irish Theatre began its career with tragedies in verse and in prose, and the appeal was quite definitely to the limited audiences which such plays would be likely to attract in almost any city of a size comparable with that of Dublin. No one anticipated that the Irish Literary Theatre could be popularised with the plays it intended to stage ; but then it was never intended to popularise the Literary Theatre. It was only when the idea of a National Theatre had definitely superseded that of the original venture that the necessity for popularisation presented itself to the minds of the founders and directors. It was then that the urgent necessity for comedy began to be noted, and comedy began to be written.

The function of the 'comedy' in the Irish Theatre was to be that which Socrates accorded to the jest : it was to be 'a *pleasant* interruption' in the more serious dramatic work. But according to Lady Gregory (*Our Irish Theatre*, p. 78), " The well-to-do people in our stalls . . . say, ' We have had enough of verse plays, give us comedy '." The verse plays of Yeats and Moore, and the psychological problem plays of Martyn, were no more calculated to become popular successes in Dublin than they were in London ; they were all plays with a strictly limited appeal, likely to gather an audience of very small dimensions, an audience smaller than the requirements of the enterprise were certain to demand. The gathering of an audience is a problem which all Repertory Theatres must solve in the early stages of their careers ; if that problem be not solved the Theatres are unlikely to have any careers at all. To solve the problem Directors have had to resort to all kinds of stratagems, and just as ballad-opera is said to pay for grand opera the Directors of Repertory Theatres have usually been compelled to gather audiences upon the plays which were known to have the widest possible appeal. Of course this policy has been criticised in Britain and America where it has been practised, but critics have not pointed to any better way of gathering an audience, and hold-

ing it when it has been gathered. If all the supporters of
Repertory Theatres were of the 'earnest' kind the Directors
could go on supplying them with what was considered to be
the best in contemporary drama ; but the supporters are
usually a very mixed company, every section of which must be
satisfied if the venture is to be a success, and become a permanent institution. So in the lists of the plays produced by
Repertory Theatres in England and America it will be seen
that so-called popular plays receive at least as much attention
as the masterpieces of drama, and so it will continue to be as
long as the people go to the theatre primarily to be amused
rather than to be enlightened. That Ireland was not an
exception to this universal experience is not extraordinary,
even though some of the confident anticipations of the
founders had to be discarded very quickly.

Thus it became necessary for the founders of the Theatre
themselves to supply the ' comedies ' which were demanded,
and in October 1902 the first plays of the new Irish Theatre
charged with the definite purpose of providing audiences with
material for laughter were staged. Actually the first of these
laughter-making plays was *The Laying of the Foundations*, by
Fred. Ryan, who was for some time the secretary to the
Theatre. Ryan was for a considerable period one of the
notable figures in the literary and revolutionary life of
Dublin. A socialist and a rationalist in religious thought he
attracted a good deal of attention by his propagandist work
on behalf of his beliefs. For a time he acted as editor of an
Egyptian Nationalist newspaper in Cairo, was an intimate
friend of Wilfrid Scawen Blunt, for whom he did a lot of
political work and at whose house he died in 1913. Ryan
wrote only one play, which was popular for a time but is now
entirely forgotten. It was never printed, and the manuscript
is generally believed to be irretrievably lost. Like everything
else that Ryan wrote the play was political, being a skit on the
dominant politics of Dublin at the period, which anticipated
some of the popular plays of later times such as *The Eloquent
Dempsey* and *The Lord Mayor*. *The Pot of Broth*, by W. B.

Yeats, was, however, the real forerunner of the long line of little one-act 'comedies' which came to be a marked feature of the programmes of the Irish Theatre. This slight sketch, farcical rather than pure comedy, has held its popularity throughout the years, and has always been well received upon its numerous revivals. To Lady Gregory it obviously owes much, and in a sense it may be said to be her first contribution to the repertoire of the Theatre. Actually the first play of Lady Gregory to be staged was *Twenty-Five*, a one-act 'comedy' produced on 14th March, 1903, and since that time Lady Gregory had been the chief writer of these 'comedies'. They are all slight in matter and manner, being anecdotes in dialogue, short tales in action, rather than comedies in the strict sense. But that they performed their main function there is no doubt, they made audiences laugh in the Theatre, and they brought people there.

It may appear to be something of a paradox to people who are accustomed to regard all Ireland as a comedy, and all Irishmen as comedians, that stimulation should be required to secure comedies in Ireland for the Irish Theatre, and that it should have been the very serious-minded founders of that Theatre who supplied the first laughter-making plays. There is, however, nothing paradoxical to those who are familiar with Ireland, and are intimate with the really serious mentality of its people. It was quite in accord with that mentality that the first plays of an Irish Theatre should be verse-plays, and plays which treated psychological problems in dramatic terms. Despite all opinion to the contrary, it must be said that Ireland is not a country of natural humorists. " Lands where the Comic spirit is obscure overhead are rank with raw crops of matter ", George Meredith says (*Essay on Comedy*, p. 98), and Ireland is one of the lands where the Comic spirit is obscure. Irishmen are actors, talkers, but it is difficult to know how they ever came to be called comedians. Perhaps because the line of dramatists which Ireland gave to England wrote mainly plays at which English people could laugh without restraint it came to be expected that Irishmen were always those who could be depended upon to provide the material for a laugh. But it must be remembered that when English people laugh at comedies by Sheridan, Wilde, or Bernard Shaw they laugh at their own follies displayed by one who is in every essential a foreigner. English people will laugh at their follies, and enjoy the fun, but Irish people will not ; there is personal laughter, that is laughter at things that are personal, in Ireland, but there is none of that communal laughter which can treat the affairs of the entire nation as its object. Synge very quickly discovered that when his *Playboy* was mobbed and *The Tinker's Wedding* was banned from the Irish stage ; and within the past few years Sean O'Casey discovered it when *The Plough and the Stars* became the object of noisy demonstrations in the Theatre. This limitation is so very serious that it cramps all Irish dramatists who might be disposed to write true comedy. " Comedy . . . is an interpretation of the general mind and is for that reason of necessity kept in restraint. . . . The Comic poet is in the narrow field, or enclosed square, of the society he depicts ; and he addresses the still narrower enclosures of men's intellects, with reference to the operation of the social world upon their characters. He is not concerned with beginnings or endings or surroundings, but with what you are now weaving. To understand his work and value it, you must have a sober liking of your kind and a sober estimate of our civilised qualities. The aim and the business of the Comic poet are misunderstood, his meaning is not seized nor his point of view taken, when he is accused of dishonouring our nature and being hostile to sentiment, tending to spitefulness and making an unfair use of laughter. Those who detect irony in comedy do so becaues they choose to see it in life. . . . Humorist and Satirist frequently hunt together as Ironists in pursuit of the grotesque, to the exclusion of the Comic. That was an affecting moment in the history of the Prince Regent, when the First Gentleman of Europe burst into tears at a sarcastic remark of Beau Brummell's on the cut of his coat. Humour, Satire, Irony, pounce on it altogether as their common prey. The Comic spirit eyes but does not touch it. Put into action it would be farcical. It is too gross for Comedy " (Meredith, *Essay on Comedy*, pp. 85-87). If this opinion of George Meredith be applied to the Irish Comedy as strictly and as logically as he would himself apply it the effect would be almost a denial that in the Irish drama there is any Comedy at all. And in fact that is very nearly the case. The vast majority of the plays which have been labelled comedies when staged in the Abbey Theatre are in reality only farces. The little plays of Lady Gregory are usually only farces, but in *The Image* the comic spirit had its way, and a delightful comedy is the result. Synge would have satisfied Meredith with *The Playboy*, *The Well of the Saints*, and *The Tinker's Wedding*. Colum's *The Fiddler's House* would pass the test, as would George Fitzmaurice's *The Country Dressmaker* and Lennox Robinson's *The Whiteheaded Boy* and *Crabbed Youth and Age*, but from the level of these there is a very steep descent to the average of what is called Irish Comedy. True, the Irish Theatre has never been disfigured by the caricatures which still hold the stages of Britain and America, and which still can pose as Irish Comedy. The Irish Drama has never had to depend upon the antics of drunken clowns, with caubeens and shillelaghs, to produce laughter, even though it must be said that at times it verged upon that preserve more closely than either art or patriotism would warrant.

Outside Ireland, evidently, if publishers' lists of ' Irish Plays ' may be accepted as a criterion, only the very crudest farce or slapstick foolery is supposed to be genuinely Irish. From the days of Shakespeare until the beginning of the present century it was the custom of the stage in English-speaking countries to accept the Irishman only as a buffoon, and that figure is still accepted in those places which are either invincibly ignorant or politically malevolent. The work that Shakespeare began seemed to be the Irish view of themselves when Lever and Lover emphasised it in the novels in which they pretended to deal with Irish life. The clothing, the speech, the pugnaciousness, the wit, and even the poverty, were all used in the effort to turn an honest penny by making the English people laugh. But it must be emphasised here that when Irish people were used in this way the authors showed that they had a keener appreciation of English psychology than of the realistic presentation of Irish life. The aim of these works was to make English people laugh, and as English people will laugh at the crude rather than the subtle it was the crude caricature that was presented to them. The esteem in which the authors came to be held proved that they were correct in their estimates of the market, if not exactly complimentary to their own people. Landor has said that " genuine humour and true wit require a sound and capacious mind, which is always a grave one ". The humour of the music-hall suggests that there was only a small audience for the genuine kind in either England or Ireland. Ireland accepted the stage-Irishman and laughed as heartily at his antics, whether he was presented by Samuel Lover or Lady Gregory, as the people of any other country. It must have been from the buffoons of Irishmen in the works of dramatists and novelists that the outside world came to believe that Irishmen were all buffoons, and were all 'comic'. It were much nearer the truth to say that the Irish mind is always grave, and to this extent would satisfy Landor, even if it be not always sound or capacious.

The Irish mind is always intellectual, and the humour of Ireland is of an intellectual kind. Rarely does it fall into the sentimentality which is so marked a feature of the humour which appeals to English audiences. The plays of Sir J. M. Barrie, for example, fail to satisfy Irish audiences because at every point when he is confidently expected to face his problems he evades them or becomes sentimental. In the plays of those Irish dramatists who have written entirely for the English stage it will be found that all the laughter is induced by wit, satire, or irony. Even the famous 'screen scene' in Sheridan's *School for Scandal* depicts an Irishman's view of the higher grades of English society. English people

could laugh at it, but no one can say that Sheridan laughed at
it himself. Oscar Wilde spent his life endeavouring to 'live
up to his blue china', and by this it may be suggested that
he meant the opinion which other poeple had formed of
himself and his work. Wilde laughed at England and English
ways to such good purpose that he induced the English
themselves to laugh with him. To-day it is recognised that
George Bernard Shaw is one of the most serious-minded
dramatists who ever wrote a play ; but only a short few years
ago he was regarded by all people in England as a licensed
buffoon. He has himself attributed his clear vision of English
ways to his 'normal vision', but it is permissible to suggest
that by 'normal vision' he means 'Irish vision', or the fact
that he could view English life without preconceived notions
and without those prejudices which always encircle a human
being in his native environment. The vision of Synge,
Gregory, Robinson, Colum, or Fitzmaurice, when viewing
the life of Ireland is no less clear than the vision of Sheridan,
Wilde, or Shaw when viewing the life of England. In none
of these is the vision so clear that it can 'have a sober liking'
for its kind, and 'a sober estimate' of our civilisation.
Always there is the desire to change and to improve ; nowhere
is there the serene onlooking at the follies and perversities of
humanity that is to be found in Molière or Cervantes. Of
the English George Meredith said (*Essay on Comedy*, p. 78),
" The national disposition is for hard hitting, with a moral
purpose to sanction it ; or for a rosy, sometimes a larmoyant,
geniality, not unmanly in its verging upon tenderness, and
with a singular attraction for thick-headedness, to decorate
it with asses' ears and the most beautiful sylvan haloes ".
When making that generalisation he was taking the Irish
contribution to English Comedy into account, more particularly, perhaps, in the first part of the sentence. Irish comedy
certainly is disposed to hit hard, and there is always some
moral purpose.

" If instead of falling foul of the ridiculous person with a
satiric rod, to make him writhe and shriek aloud, you prefer

to sting him under a semi-caress, by which he shall in his anguish be rendered dubious whether indeed anything has hurt him, you are an engine of Irony " (*Essay on Comedy*, p. 79). In all the greatest Irish comedies there is always that dubiety whether anything has hurt : the laugh at Christy Mahon in Synge's *Playboy* or at Denis Geoghegan in Lennox Robinson's *The Whiteheaded Boy* must always be restrained by a lingering doubt whether some wound has not been inflicted. It will be remembered that Lennox Robinson has himself said that *The Whiteheaded Boy* is political from beginning to end, and *The Playboy* is certainly a play with a moral purpose no matter how much that moral purpose may be covered by the trappings of farce in acting. Irishmen are too much in earnest to laugh merely for the sake of laughing, always they are trying either to improve the community of which they are a part, or they are trying to wound their neighbours by laughing at them. Irish humour rarely resists the temptation of "driving into the quivering sensibilities", as Meredith said, nor is it good at "comforting them and tucking them up ". There is always the appeal to the intellect, driven home by wit and a regard for the fine phrase. In language that is more highly-coloured than any other stage language of our time the so-called comedies of the Irish Theatre conveyed moral lessons and wounding lashes to the audiences of Ireland. It may be doubted if the audiences of other countries ever see Irish comedies as Irishmen see them.

Because of this national earnestness, and high moral purpose, there has not been in the Irish Theatre any comedy approaching in purity the comedy of France, or even the comedy of England. The Comedy of Manners, for instance, is quite unknown in the Irish drama, it has but one little specimen in Lennox Robinson's *Crabbed Youth and Age*. The absence of such comedy may be ascribed to that statement of Mr. Yeats about drawing-room plays, which were for people who live in drawing-rooms, and the absence from Irish social life of a strong middle-class. The Comedy of

Manners is essentially an urban thing, and as the life of Ireland is mainly rural in its psychology the development of such a comedy is not to be expected for some considerable time. It is true that the social life of Dublin is undergoing rapid change since the foundation of the Irish Free State ; there is growing in the city a new governing class, and perhaps from, and about, that class there will in time be produced something approximating to the Comedy of Manners. There is now in process of development a class which finds the drawing-room as much of a necessity as the silk hat, and with the adoption of both the satirical gifts of Irish comedy-writers will sooner or later come to play. In fact the growth of this new governing class will provide the comedy-writers with a variety of material which in the past was lacking from Irish life. When that material comes to be used it is probable that Irish comedy will learn more from Jacinto Benevente or William Congreve than it will from Molière. The most striking thing about the Irish comedy of the past twenty-five years is its adherence to individuals rather than to types. In every case the characters are highly individualised, closely observed and faithfully reproduced. The Irish comedy is at the same time imaginative and realistic ; there is little of the photographic about it, even if there be much of the record of peasant speech. It is the result of close observation and the sensibilities of the dramatist, producing an imaginative study which is true to life. The verbal felicity of Irish comedy, while owing much to the imaginative sensibilities of the dramatist, owes a great deal to the wit and love of metaphor inherent in the Irish people. In a sense it is true that Irish comedy is almost entirely a comedy of words, depending upon fine speech and witty repartee for its best effects. This is true as much of the comedy of the Irish drama in Ireland as of that drama which has been the contribution of Irish dramatists to the English stage. Wilde would be small indeed if he were without his epigrams, and it was the wit of Bernard Shaw which first secured him a hearing in England and America. Witty dialogue is a characteristic of all Irish comedy, as it is no less the staple of Irish conversation, and it cannot be said that Irishmen are entirely unaware of the fact.

But despite what may be termed a national predilection for comedy it is a peculiar fact that the Irish drama is somewhat deficient in comedy, and it is rich in farce where situation takes the place of character. Some of the most popular plays of the Irish Theatre are little farces that are no better than music-hall sketches, or the curtain raisers that once were popular in the English theatre. Other countries, however, are little better in this respect, and perhaps when its age and the material at its disposal are borne in mind it will be thought that the Irish drama is more rich in comedy of the best kind than any of its contemporaries. With the names of Synge, Colum, Gregory, Fitzmaurice, and Robinson it can bear comparison with the comedy of any contemporary theatre, but as these have all been considered as Folk Dramatists or Realists the lesser writers of laughter-making plays are here to be examined.

The first recruit for the provision of the necessary laughter, to the great business of what Mr. Arnold Bennett has called ' cheering us all up ', was William Boyle, whose first play, *The Building Fund*, was staged at the Abbey Theatre in April 1905. William Boyle is a Leinster man who has lived a great part of his life in London and other parts of England, and before he began his career as a purveyor of light entertainment to the Irish Theatre he was known as the author of a book of short stories, *A Kish of Brogues*, published in 1899. He had, unlike so many of the newer dramatists, some experience of writing, and some experience in the delineation of the Irish peasant character as it presents itself in the Leinster counties, the old counties of the English Pale. In these counties there is not to be encountered the richness of phrase or extravagance of metaphor that the counties of hill and bog and sea produce in such abundance, and consequently there is not in William Boyle's plays or stories any of the glamour of language which is one of the marked features of Synge and Lady Gregory,

nor is there any of the poetic rhythm of Colum or Murray.
The language of William Boyle's plays is as flat as is the land
of the counties of Louth and Meath from which his characters
are drawn. There is, too, a conventionality of structure in
his plays which suggests that he was familiar with the ' well-
made play ' of the London theatre of the eighteen-nineties,
the theatre of Sardou and Pinero. He might indeed, be
called the Irish Robertson because of the lack of distinction
of dialogue or structure in his plays. Nevertheless, William
Boyle's plays are among the most popular in the Irish theatre ;
they have made thousands of people laugh during more than
twenty years, and they were the first plays to cause a ' House
Full ' notice to be placed at the doors of the Abbey Theatre.
Large numbers of people in Ireland consider the plays of
Boyle to be the best in the whole range of the Irish Drama,
but that, of course, is just one of the perplexing problems
which beset every appraiser of the drama in any country.
When *The Building Fund* was produced in 1905 there were
many good judges who thought that a new dramatist of
considerable power, and even more considerable promise,
had been discovered, but that play has remained Boyle's best
work. *The Building Fund* is concerned with a miserly old
woman and the manoeuvres of her grasping son and grand-
daughter for the reversion of her farm and fortune. The play
opens with the attempt of Michael O'Callaghan and Dan
MacSweeney, local farmers, to extract from old Mrs.
Grogan a subscription to the building fund of a new church
for the parish. She will give nothing, and in her determination, her plea of poverty, she is seconded by her son, John.
The visit of her neighbours, however, suggests a way in which
she can defeat the hopes of her son and grand-daughter,
whom she imagines desire her early death so that they can
enjoy her savings. John is openly concerned about her
money and its proper disposal ; the girl is more guarded,
hiding her hopes under a tender solicitude for the old woman's
welfare, and doing everything possible to make her comfort-
able. But Mrs. Grogan is certain they are both interested

only in her money, and is equally resentful against both. In time the collectors, knowing that only pertinacity will secure the fund from their neighbours, make another effort to extract a subscription from Mrs. Grogan. During this visit she uses the collectors to witness her signature to her will, and on her death, a short time after, it is found that she has left all her property to the building fund. The two younger people will be kept on to manage the farm for Father Andrew, its new owner, but their greed had been defeated by the malevolence of the old woman. This is comedy where the laugh is bitter ; the dead Mrs. Grogan laughs best.

William Boyle has never reached the standard of this play in his later work. The characterisation of the play is admirable, its dialogue is on the level that would be expected from his people, and the construction of the play is masterly. The dialogue is not picturesque, and there is little distinction in the handling of it. There is, in fact, no style, no romance, none of that beauty that illuminates even the most grimly grey of Ibsen's comedies. But there is skilled craftsmanship ; and there is bitter satire in the idea of the building fund itself, and in the way that it is used by the miserly old woman. As it is customary to laugh at the discomfiture of others Irish audiences have laughed long and loudly at the discomfiture of the crafty son and grand-daughter of Mrs. Grogan.

The Eloquent Dempsey, produced for the first time in June 1906, and still popular at the Abbey Theatre, is farce-satire of the most obvious kind. Jeremiah Dempsey is the kind of local politician, of whom there were many in Ireland when the play was written, and perhaps there still are some remaining, who desires to make the best of all sides. He is not content to sit upon the fence, he must be active in opposing camps. So he is a Nationalist who is willing to receive Chief Secretaries for Ireland and present addresses of welcome to them ; an Emigration Agent who deplores emigration ; a temperance advocate who owns a public-house. But he over-reaches himself, or at least he is out-manoeuvred by the strategic plans of his wife who desires to get him away from both politics and public-house to a farm in the country. Typical of the cheap humour of the play is the statement of Dempsey, after he had shown himself to his supporters with the orange side of his dressing-gown outermost, " Last time I appeared before you I was inside out ". The double-dealing and the loquacity of the petty politician are so effectively satirised that laughter is inevitable, but the figure of Jerry Dempsey is nevertheless a caricature of the crudest kind, and the play is unredeemed by any nobility of language or structure. Its appeal is to the cheapest laugh, and as the cheapest laugh is the easiest to secure *The Eloquent Dempsey* has had, if anything, more than its share in the twenty years during which it has held its place on the stage of the Abbey Theatre.

In *The Mineral Workers*, produced for the first time in October 1906, an attempt was made to deal dramatically with a serious social and economic problem, and to widen the circle of persons with which patrons of the Abbey Theatre had become familiar. The theme of the play is the attitude toward the development of mining activities in the country of the different sections of the community. Stephen J. O'Reilly is a returned Irish-American mining engineer who is anxious to develop the minerals in his uncle's land. The consent of the farmer, Ned Mulroy, is obtained after considerable debate, but he never really forgives the miners for tearing up his precious land. Not even the increased prices which he can obtain for his produce reconciles him, so he is not displeased that the mine should fail. Dan Fogarty had held out against the development until the company was compelled to force him into compliance by diverting the water supply and obtaining the mortgage which Sir Thomas Musgrove, the aristocratic bank director, held upon his land. Dan Fogarty's ofttimes repeated 'Oh, Lord! Aye' anticipated by nearly twenty years the use of the same trick in the plays of Sean O'Casey. Ultimately it is Dan Fogarty who wins : he comes into the venture as a Director. In many ways the characterisation of *The Mineral Workers* is the best of any of Boyle's plays, but there is always the suggestion of Pinero in both characters and situations. Sir Thomas Musgrove and his sister, Mrs. Walton, might easily have come direct from any of Pinero's plays, while the Irish-American was at the time a new type on the Abbey stage and, therefore, welcomed by the audiences. But on the whole the characters are stereotyped and convey the impression that their creator had little or no knowledge at first hand of the life he desired to portray. *The Mineral Workers*, however, has made Irish audiences, in all parts of the country, laugh for more than twenty years, and no plays in the entire Irish drama are more popular with the hundreds of parish amateur dramatic societies than those of William Boyle. In a sense he may be said to have taken the place that Boucicault held in the esteem of an earlier generation, and his plays, too, are made to the pattern which Boucicault had popularised.

Family Failing, produced in March 1912, is notable only for the remarkable acting of Miss Cathleen Nesbitt as the only energetic person in the play. Without Miss Nesbitt the play is a paltry thing purporting to be a study of the ' family failing ' of laziness. Neither *Family Failing* nor *Nic*, which was staged for the first time in October 1916, is of the level of Boyle's other three plays.

The failure of William Boyle as a dramatist is remarkable when all the advantages at his disposal are taken into consideration. He had shown that he could write short stories of Irish life with grace and some artistic accomplishment ; his plays prove him to be a dramatic technician without superior in the range of Irish dramatists ; and he had the great advantage of living for long periods in different parts of the country in his capacity of Government official. He seemed, however, to be unable to blend all these when he came to write a play. The stage tricks are all used, but the characters are never quite life-like enough to be convincing, and nowhere does the dialogue reach above the mediocre. Perhaps it is that Boyle had known too many places to become thoroughly impregnated with the spirit and the speech of any

one of them, and perhaps, also, his work as a Revenue Officer
tended to make him suspect to the people so that they never
expanded in his presence. He was not a young man when he
came to write plays, being considerably older than any other
of the earlier Irish dramatists, with the possible exception of
the four founders of the Literary Theatre. He was, therefore,
of an earlier tradition, which had accepted Boucicault, and
his familiarity with the English theatre of the eighteen-
nineties is obvious in all his plays. It was probably his
patriotic leanings, in addition to his knowledge of the stage,
which prompted him to write plays for the Irish rather than
the English Theatre. Whatever be his shortcomings he
certainly fulfilled the early requirements of the Abbey
Theatre by providing it with those vehicles of amusement
which taxed nothing more than the power of laughter.

When two plays by a new dramatist named W. F. Casey
were produced in 1908 it seemed that the Theatre would have
another laughter-maker who would have continued to send
forth amusing plays for many years. This half-formed hope
and desire was destined never to be realised, as W. F. Casey
went to London as a journalist and has not since contributed
to the Irish Theatre. He has written other plays, but they
have been staged in England as they are concerned entirely
with English life. One of his plays which was staged last year
in London, *Old as the Hills*, has a superficial resemblance to
the earlier play, *The Suburban Groove*, which was staged at
the Abbey Theatre in October 1908. In this play the author
extracts much laughter at the expense of the inhabitants of
the Dublin suburb of Rathmines, which was supposed by the
Dublin populace to ape everything English, particularly the
English accent and ways of speech. The play is a good study
of a suburban family, and it is only the silly Claude Callan
who is something of a caricature. On the whole the play is
fair comedy and fully deserves the popularity it has long
enjoyed. The same cannot be said of Mr. Casey's first play,
The Man who Missed the Tide, first staged in February 1908,
and for many years revived regularly. For this play the

author did not seem to be quite certain of his intentions, and in consequence the action slips from comedy to melodrama and finally to farce. The theme, a man held by circumstance from taking advantage of his opportunities, had great possibilities which were never exploited, so that the author himself 'missed the tide' as much as his principal character. There was no doubt that these two plays promised a comedy-writer of considerable power, but that promise was never fulfilled, and Mr. Casey remains the only dramatist in the Irish Theatre who has successfully placed the suburban Dubliner on the stage with all the surroundings and para-phernalia of his actual life. In the suburbs of Dublin, as in the suburbs of any large city, there is material in abundance for comedy, and tragedy too, but that material remains unused in the Irish Theatre. Perhaps some day the Dublin suburbs will produce a dramatist for themselves as the Dublin slums have produced their dramatist in Sean O'Casey.

Another playwright who responded to the need for amusement is Edward McNulty, also a novelist who deserted the book for the stage. It is very doubtful if Edward McNulty has seen Ireland or Dublin at all; certainly his writings give no indication that he has understood, even if he has seen. He seems to see Irish life through a haze of Lever and Lover, and he bestows upon it a patronising smile such as the novelists of Irish life usually popular in English lending libraries like to bestow. Edward McNulty captured the popular applause when his play *The Lord Mayor* was produced in March 1914. It is said that the author intended this play to be a withering satire upon the municipality of Dublin, to do for Dublin public life what *An Enemy of the People* had done for some Norwegian town. But if that were the intention it was frustrated by the comic genius of Arthur Sinclair, who created the part of Jimmy O'Brien, 'the strong, silent man of the Corporation'. The municipal politics of Dublin were, at that time, generally believed to be corrupt, but Edward McNulty shot his bolt too far, and the result was a roar of laughter instead of an awakening of the civic conscience. The play shows how a man who is bankrupt in his business is enabled to pay off his creditors, fellow merchants and colleagues in the Municipal Council, from his salary as Lord Mayor of the City. But when they try to use him for the extraction of an exhorbitant price for some land they own, and which the corporation intends to buy as a site for baths, he turns upon them and declares himself ' the people's Lord Mayor '. There is a sub-plot in which intriguers from Dublin Castle offer a title to O'Brien if he will present an address to the King, and an attempt at symbolism on the part of a clerk named Kelly, who says that when he writes " England, the tyrant, grinds the face of Ireland " he really means to say, " Gaffney, the tyrant, grinds the face of Kelly ". Neither of these is effectively combined with the main plot, and in consequence the play was treated as a burlesque farce, and as such it retains considerable popularity with Abbey Theatre audiences and amateur dramatic societies. The second play, *The Courting of Mary Doyle*, produced for the first time in November 1921, is farce pure and simple, without any saving grace which would justify its inclusion in the repertoire of a National Theatre. A third play by Mr. McNulty, dramatised from a novel of the same title, *Mrs. Mulligan's Millions*, was relegated to the music-halls, which was certainly its rightful place.

In 1921 there was produced the first play by a playwright who has since achieved considerable popularity as a purveyor of amusement in Dublin and in London. The little play was called *Bedmates*, staged on the 6th of January, 1921, and the name of the author George Shiels. It was a one-act play, and beyond the fact that it provoked laughter there was nothing very notable in it. This was followed by another little farce-comedy called *Insurance Money* in December of the same year, and again there was little of distinction about the play beyond its power to amuse. But the power to amuse both plays certainly have. Then in October 1922 there was produced a three-act comedy called *Paul Twyning* which showed that the playwright possessed the power to create really living characters on the stage. Paul Twyning is an itinerant plasterer who becomes involved in the affairs, chiefly matrimonial, of the family in whose house he happens to be working. The play is obviously of the 'contrived' or 'built' kind, inasmuch as it is mainly plot, but it is the realisation of the character of Paul Twyning which makes the play something more than a mere laughter-maker. In Paul there was the material for a fine comedy, but the author, probably through lack of experience, was unable to make the most of the material in his hands. When it is understood that the author is an invalid unable to leave his house, and that he has never seen one of his plays actually staged, it will be known that he is severely handicapped in his effort to write plays which will be more than plot-controlled puppet shows designed to induce laughter. His sense of the theatre is very pronounced, and he writes dialogue which is amusing and interesting without being in any way distinguished. In Paul Twyning, however, there is a character which was at one time a familiar figure in all parts of Ireland, but the itinerant craftsman has now almost ceased to exist. Despite the reality of the central character *Paul Twyning* is no more than a fairly good specimen of the humorous 'well-made play'. It is possible that the author during his residence in America came to consider that machine-made plays of that country as the ideal to which his own work should aspire ; whatever be the explanation his plays have a rigidity of structure unusual in the Irish drama. It was during his residence in America that George Shiels was disabled in a railway accident, and he has never had intimate contact with the Abbey Theatre for which his plays were written.

In December 1923 *First Aid* was staged without exciting any interest, and in May 1924 another three-act play, *The Retrievers*, was produced. The plot of this play is so involved that the characters have difficulty in extricating themselves from its toils. There did, however, emerge a character study of a comic American who disentangles things to his own satisfaction, and is so delighted with himself that he waves the Stars and Stripes in exalted glee as the final curtain falls. The play did not have a very cordial reception, and it has now probably faded completely from the public mind. In *Professor Tim*, which was first staged at the Abbey Theatre in September 1925, George Shiels has found his most successful play to date. It has been revived several times in Dublin, and in addition it had an enthusiastic reception in London when it was staged there by the Irish Players in 1927. The English critics, no less than the public, received the play with a warmth that was somewhat disconcerting to the critics of Dublin. And in truth the play is not by any means a masterpiece. Again it is a plot-play, in which interest is sustained by the reliable methods of slapstick farce and the drunken antics of 'The Professor'. The Professor was the pride of his family, which maintained its dignity upon the fame he was alleged to have achieved in Australia, and upon the wealth he was believed to have amassed. He was, in fact, a water-diviner, and when it was learned that he was about to visit his family great things were expected. There was consternation when he arrived drunken and dishevelled, with every appearance of being no better than a beggar. And as a beggar he posed until the time arrived to make the course of true love run smoothly, by making possible the marriage of a relative with a bankrupt, but true-hearted, sporting farmer. When that time arrived the Professor revealed himself as a man of wealth and position, which his family had always believed him to be. The plot is novelettish and antiquated, but in its development the author has certainly provided material for laughter. There is, however, no attempt to effect a contact with the life of the Ireland in which the scene is supposed to be laid. The same is true of *Cartney and Kevney*, produced in November 1927, which uses the well-worn stock characters in the time-honoured humorous situations. In all his plays the author tends to repeat himself, there is little variation in plot or characterisation, and in none of the plays except *Paul Twyning* is there displayed more than a merely casual acquaintance with the realities of Irish peasant life. Perhaps in the future George Shiels may write a true comedy, but the disability which he suffers prevents that immersion in contemporary life from which true comedy must come.

On the whole, therefore, it will be seen that Irish comedy is a poor and a paltry thing. In the plays of none of the authors who have specialised in ' comedy ' will there be found anything which would have satisfied the fastidious standard of George Meredith. The few genuine comedies which have been given to the world by the Irish Theatre are all the work of authors who are primarily known for the excellence of their more serious, and more realistic, work.

CHAPTER XI

FANTASY AND SYMBOLISM

Irish belief in the Fairy World ought to have provided a great abundance of Fairy Plays from Irish Dramatists—Belief outside Ireland that Irish Dramatists have actually done so—The Catholic Church and Clergy in Ireland endeavouring to eradicate all surviving belief in Fairies—Success of the Effort—Only very few Fairy Plays by Irish Dramatists—And only a few authors who treat themes as Fantasy or in Symbols—Lord Dunsany the most prolific and best known—Edward Martyn one of the early Symbolists.

IT is the belief of some commentators upon the modern drama that Ireland is the home, and the source, of the Fairy Play. This belief seems to be more strongly held in America than elsewhere, and it cannot be held by anyone who has at the same time a knowledge both of Ireland and the Drama. It is possible that the work of W. B. Yeats is responsible for misleading many people ; but Mr. Yeats is the only Irish dramatist who has written a Fairy Play, and even he has written only one, *The Land of Heart's Desire*. That much of the older Irish literature is concerned with the fairies, and fairy-lore, is undoubtedly true, and that much of the poetry of the last twenty years is also to a considerable extent ' fairy-poetry ' is equally true ; but the Irish novel and the Irish play are invariably realistic in conception and execution, so that the horny hands of the farmer or the labourer are of greater significance than ' milk-white arms ' tossed in rings. It is possible that a faith in the existence of the fairies, 'good people' or 'little people', may still survive in remote parts of rural Ireland, but no Irish resident fails to be impressed by the fact that the choicest antics of the fairies are reserved for credulous tourists. It is the stories which are told to tourists that gives the impression abroad that Ireland is inhabited

241

mainly by fairies, whereas a more blunt generation would make use of a different noun. The career of the fairy on the stage of the Irish National Theatre is not in accord with the place which the fairy occupies in the non-Irish conception of Ireland ; only W. B. Yeats has used him in the English language, and Dr. Douglas Hyde in Irish. It may be that fairies are not good dramatic material, approximating too closely to the classical gods, too fragile for the modern stage ; or, which is the more likely, the logical faculty in the post-Ibsen audience would be bored by fairies, or would be so much uninterested in their doings as to stay away from the theatre.

But, it may be said, the desire to escape from the ordinary world of reality to a world of infinite attainment is inherent in all humanity, and for that reason alone the fairy play ought to be popular. Dreams, we are nowadays told, are but the unrealised strivings and yearnings of actual life, and if that be so the dream play, which is akin to the fairy play, ought to be popular also. ' To get out of oneself ' is supposed to be an actual need of human nature at some time or other, and for that reason the tawdry simulation of other worlds and more colourful lands is given the high title of Romance. To satisfy the need for extra-corporeal experience is one of the greatest functions of art, but it has been so often, and for such long periods, debased and lowered to conform to the popular taste that art has come to be somewhat shy of Romance and tends to remain on the plane of actuality in the theatre as in its other manifestations. It is to the childish instincts in mankind, to the eternal ' Peter Pan ', that the fairy, and the so-called romantic, plays make their appeal, but when the years of childhood are passed the spirit craves for something deeper, something which will interpret and explain the actual in terms of the dream. The Symbolists attempted to do this, and in the plays of Maeterlinck the appeal to popular sympathy was made in the theatre. With the exception of *The Blue Bird*, which is accepted as a play for children, it can hardly be said that an overwhelming response was made to the appeal. Sir James Barrie fared better ; but here again the play which concentrates his philosophy of life is generally regarded as a children's play in which pretty young actresses display themselves as ' the boy who wouldn't grow up '. In *Peter Pan* Sir James Barrie appeals to the child that is in Everyman, but the very vigour of the response to the request for a declaration of belief in fairies, which is usual in the theatre, suggests that the belief is neither profound nor sincere. In an age of scientific scepticism, when the bonds of religion are loosed or broken, it could not well be otherwise.

Nevertheless, a well-known writer on the drama could say in 1925 : " Dramatists in England and Ireland are steadily moving along the paths already traversed by Evreinov and his companions. It is not that all or any of them have achieved such fantasy of expression, but that each informs his works with a peculiar atmosphere which is distinct from the symbolism visible in Ibsen's better-known works. Whereas Ibsen normally lays stress upon the problem or upon the men and women, utilising suggestion and symbolism to raise his plays above the particular to the general, these poetic writers lay their stress on the forces that exist beyond man, on fate, on the spirit of nature, on the fairy world. Their atmosphere is the atmosphere of mystery, not the atmosphere of so-called reality, wherein are seen only the visible phenomena of life " (*British Drama*, Allardyce Nicoll, pp. 403-4). In the British drama such signs may be visible, but in the Irish dramatists of the younger generation after W. B. Yeats, J. M. Synge, and Lady Gregory, there are no such signs, and an examination of the plays of the earlier dramatists of the Irish Theatre, whose plays constitute but a small fraction of the works produced by the Theatre, is likely to give a somewhat distorted impression of the Irish Dramatic Movement as a whole. The great majority of the Irish dramatists have stressed the actuality of Ibsen rather than his symbolism, and have placed all the emphasis upon the problem or upon the characters, so that there is only a small fragment of Irish drama which has been raised above the particular to the

general. Of the influences upon Irish drama Ibsen has undoubtedly been the greatest from without ; and while it
might have been expected that the great Russians would have
been at least equally influential little or no effort has been
made to utilise the models provided by Tchechov or Evreinov.
The Irish mentality, and the Irish environment, offer
remarkable approximations to those of Russia ; so remarkable
in fact, that with changes in the names of characters and
places the plays of such Russians as Tchechov, Gogol, or
Turgeniev might easily pass for the work of Irishmen. There
is much of Ireland in the atmosphere and the people of *The
Cherry Orchard ;* the fatalism, the kindliness, and the little
irritations ; Gogol's *The Government Inspector* could have
been located as easily in the province of Connacht as in rural
Russia, because the Government Inspector was as much
a feature of the recent life of Ireland as he was of that of
Russia, and any inspector could have acted the part, but only
George A. Birmingham has made use of the possibility ; and
the pastoral simplicity of Turgeniev's *A Month in the Country*
might easily have been equalled by many Irish dramatists.
For such Russian dramatists as Gorky, Tolstoy, Andreyev,
and Evreinov, however, there can be no Irish comparisons.
In all these dramatists there is a philosophic earnestness and
a questioning of current morality which are entirely alien to
Ireland. In Ireland morality is a fixed thing not to be
questioned, and the religious feeling, organised and regi-
mented, of the people makes it reasonable to suggest that such
dramatists as Evreinov or Andreyev are very unlikely to have
their plays imitated by Irish writers.

Fundamentally, the causes which preclude the appearance
of a rival to Evreinov in Ireland are also the causes which
have prevented any development of the fairy play. It will
be remembered that Yeats' first attempts to bring fairy, or
occult, lore upon the stage led to uproar in the theatre,
and to a consistent propaganda being organised against the
Irish Literary Theatre. The reason for the uproar and the
propaganda was that Yeats was alleged to offend the religious

susceptibilities of the people. Of course he did nothing of the kind ; but the religion of the Irish people is very sensitive and very well ordered, so that a protest is certain to be made if anything even remotely touching the supernatural is put upon the stage, or if anything suggesting that all the clergy are not saints is included in a play. It is for this reason that Synge's great comedy, *The Tinker's Wedding*, can be played in Birmingham or Boston but never in Dublin. There is little reason to doubt that at one time belief in the power of the fairies, for good and evil, to influence human life and human destiny was widespread in Ireland. Everywhere throughout the land the visitor will be shown the mounds and the raths which were the dwelling-places of ' the good people ' and ' the little people ', and widespread still is the belief that the fairies exist and use their spells. A cow goes dry, it is the fairies ; a child dies, it is the fairies ; the butter is slow in the churn, it is the fairies ; so the people say, and so the people believe in many parts of rural Ireland even to-day. But the saying and the believing is contrary to the teaching and the stern exhortations of the Catholic clergy. The clergy has set itself to the work of rooting out these beliefs in the fairies and such pagan superstitions, and the work is so nearly successful that probably in another genera- tion or two Peter Pan will plead vainly in Ireland for the life of Tinker Bell. It is this clerical ban which has prevented the exploitation of the rich fairy-lore of the country on the stage of the Irish Theatre, and in the plays of Irish dramatists. Sir James Barrie can exploit the childish belief in fairies, or Maurice Maeterlinck, and Irish audiences will applaud, but it is significant that no Irish fairy play has appeared in Ireland since Yeats' *Land of Heart's Desire* in 1911, with the exception of Lady Gregory's *The Golden Apple*, which is a play ' for Kiltartan children ', or the children of other places, only. For nearly twenty years there has been no fairy play which would appeal to adults no less than children written by an Irish dramatist, and that is surely something to be marvelled at in the land which is the last resting-place of the fairies of

Europe. In future, evidently, fairies will not be permitted to reside outside of Persia, nor to exercise their powers nearer Europe than Ispahan.

Lord Dunsany is Ireland's only practitioner in magic in the contemporary theatre, but Lord Dunsany has had to invent not only a geography but a theogony of his own so that he could exploit his magic on the stage, or in his tales. Beyond the fact that his family and title are Irish, and that he has a castle and estates in the Irish county of Meath, there is little that can be called distinctively Irish about Lord Dunsany. Edward John Moreton Drax Plunkett, 18th Baron Dunsany, comes of a very old Anglo-Irish family which has given much distinguished service to Ireland and to England. He was born in 1878, was educated at Eton and Sandhurst, served for a time in the Coldstream Guards, and during the Great War served in the Royal Inniskilling Fusiliers as a Captain in France and Gallipoli. He had served with distinction also in the Boer War, and after that had given up soldiering for the comparatively milder excitements of big game hunting, cricketing, and the creation of a new theogony. On the whole he is more Anglo than Irish, and his reputation as a dramatist is mainly American, although he has had considerable success in the British theatre. The greater part of Lord Dunsany's life has been lived out of Ireland. He has a home and estates in Kent, and it is there, or in London, Africa, or America, rather than in Ireland that he prefers to live. He has done in England something that he might have done in Ireland were he so inclined ; he has organised and to some extent trained a band of village players which has given performances to the satisfaction of some most exacting critics. It seems probable that Lord Dunsany's sympathies are mainly English, as his viewpoint is certainly English, and that Ireland occupies little or no place in his consciousness. That he has no sympathy with the political and social aspirations of the Irish people may be deduced from a paragraph in the Introduction which he contributed to the late Francis Ledwidge's *Songs of Peace* in 1916. In that paragraph

Lord Dunsany said, " There follow poems at which some
may wonder : 'To Thomas McDonagh', 'The Blackbirds',
'The Wedding Morning' ; but rather than attribute curious
sympathies to this brave young Irish soldier I would ask his
readers to consider the irresistible attraction that a lost cause
has for almost any Irishman ". The 'curious sympathies'
which Lord Dunsany refused to attribute to Francis Ledwidge are sympathies with the leaders of the Dublin Rising
of Easter 1916, who were executed after that amazing episode
had concluded. It is at least permissible to suggest that the
poet who wrote

> But, harpers, leave your harps aside,
> And, poets, leave awhile your dreams.
> The storm has come upon the tide
> And Cathleen weeps among her streams,

and who had enlisted to fight for the liberation of small
nations included his own amongst the number. There is
nothing ' curious ' in Francis Ledwidge having sympathy
with the aspirations of those amongst whom he lived, and
which he shared. What certainly is curious is that Lord
Dunsany should have found it necessary to emphasise the
content of these poems ; it is that emphasis that divides Lord
Dunsany from the Irish literary movement. As for the ' lost
cause ' which is supposed to have attracted Ledwidge's
sympathy, all that need now be said is that it is known to the
world as Saorstat Eireann, or the Irish Free State, and with
that Lord Dunsany has no sympathy whatever. No play of
his has been staged at the Abbey Theatre since the Irish Free
State came into being.

Lord Dunsany is the author of more than twenty plays, in
addition to some novels and volumes of tales. He is one of
the most popular dramatists in the American theatre, and
the majority of his plays have been staged in England, but so
far only four have been produced in the Abbey Theatre. It
was, however, in that Theatre that his first play was staged on
29th April, 1909. That first play, *The Glittering Gate*, was
revived many times with popular approval, but for many years

now it has ceased to be part of the regular repertory of the Theatre. That first play also demonstrated what have since become so well known as characteristics of its author ; a bitter irony and a scepticism that despairs of mankind. No greater contrast to the plays which the Abbey Theatre had staged up to this time can be imagined than *The Glittering Gate*. The curtain rises to reveal Jim and Bill, ' both dead and lately burglars', before what they believe is the Gate of Heaven : " A lonely place strewn with large black rocks and uncorked beer bottles, the latter in great profusion. At back is a wall of granite built of great slabs, and in it the gate of heaven. The door is of gold. Below the lonely place is an abyss hung with stars ". With great skill the dialogue reveals the past lives of the pair, and their chief desires while they were on the earth. Beer bottles descend from the upper air, are wearily uncorked, and are always found to be empty, but the hope that one may be full persists.

BILL. You'll cheer up when I tell you what I've got. I say, Jim, have you got some beer ? Why, so you have. Why, *you* ought to cheer up, Jim.

JIM. All the beer you're ever likely to see again. They're empty.

BILL. (*Half rising from rock, on which he had seated himself, and pointing his finger at* JIM *as he rises, very cheerfully*) Why, you're the chap that said there was no hope here, and you're hoping to find beer in every bottle you open.

JIM. Yes ; I *hope* to see a drop of beer in one some day, but I *know* I won't. Their trick *might* not work just once.

Bill talks of his mother, and hopes she is inside : " They won't have brought me up against her, will they ? That's not fair evidence, Jim ".

JIM. It would be just like them to. Very like them.

BILL. If there's a glass of beer to be got in heaven, or a dish of tripe and onions, or a pipe of 'bacca she'll have them for me when I come to her. She used to know my ways wonderful, and what I liked. And she used to know when to expect me almost anywhere. I used to climb in through the window at any hour and

she always knew it was me. (*Creak, creak.*) It will be all a blaze
of light, and I'll hardly know it's her till I get used to it. But I'll
know her among a million angels. There weren't none like her
on earth and there won't be none like her in heaven. Jim ! I'm
through, Jim ! One more turn and Old Nutcracker's done it.
It's giving ! It's giving ! I know the feel of it. *Jim !* (*The gates
swing out an inch and are stopped by the rock.*)

When the gates swing open fully nothing is revealed but
' empty night and stars '. " Stars. Blooming great stars.
There *ain't* no heaven, Jim ". As the mocking laughter
increases in volume, ever louder and louder, Jim says "That's
very like them. Yes, they'd do that ".

The Glittering Gate, though it was no more than a dialogue
in one act, proved that a dramatist of great power and infinite
fancy had come to the Abbey Theatre. Already known as
the author of three of the most remarkable works of fancy
written in the early years of this century, it seemed likely that
he would use in drama the unique mythology which had come
from the richness of his own imagination. Lord Dunsany
did not turn to the rich mine of Irish mythology and rural
folk-lore to find the basis or the colour for his work ; instead
he created a very hierarchy of gods whom he enshrouded in
glowing colours of the fabulous East and permitted in complete freedom to control the destinies of their fantastic
cosmos. If the gods of Pegana have never themselves
appeared upon any stage they have certainly given their
benediction to many of Lord Dunsany's later plays. There
was nothing of Pegana in *The Glittering Gate*, it was not one
of the pleasant jokes of the beneficial deities, rather was it a
grim satire on the eternal Hope that is the very basis of human
life. *The Glittering Gate* dismissed Hope as a fraud, or, as
Dean Inge has said, "Hope was regarded as a gift of dubious
value, an illusion which helps us to endure life, and a potent
spur to action; but in the last resort an *ignis fatuus*" (*The Idea
of Progress*). It is evident in this early play, and more marked
in the plays that have succeeded it in time, that Lord Dunsany
regards humanity as altogether fatuous, and that human

effort is doomed to eternal frustration. That viewpoint was not at all common or popular before the outbreak of the Great War, but since that catastrophic event belief in human perfectability and the inevitability of human progress has suffered serious injury. Democracy is in eclipse throughout the greater part of Europe, and the newer doctrine that man is but the creature of the state shines in its stead. Lord Dunsany will not be grieved by this change, indeed there is every reason to believe that he will rejoice in so far as his pessimistic temperament will permit him to indulge that emotion. He is himself enthroned among his gods in Pegana.

King Argimenes and the Unknown Warrior, which was staged for the first time in January 1911, is another illustration of Lord Dunsany's characteristic attitude of aristocratic detachment. In this two-act play he again demonstrates his technical equipment, and from the rise of the curtain the attention of an audience is gripped. In this play will be found the beginning of the line of plays of Eastern glamour and Eastern cruelty which have made the name of their author so well known to audiences in two continents. The theme of *King Argimenes* is not without its touch of arrogant snobbery ; a king will be a king, and will act as a king, be recognised as a king, even when he is actually a captive and a slave. The assertion of aristocratic superiority in blood could hardly be more explicit, and it is, perhaps, to be counted to Lord Dunsany for excellence that the assertion has given no offence, even in the ' sweet land of liberty ' itself where it is very popular. In Ireland the play was never really popular, it failed to impress its first audience although it was produced with all the technical excellence of the Abbey Theatre company, which included Sara Allgood, Maire O'Neill, Maire NicShiubhlaig, J. M. Kerrigan, Arthur Sinclair, and Fred O'Donovan. It is doubtful if a better group of actors could be assembled in any other theatre in the English-speaking world at the time, but all their art failed to make the play impress the audience. In technique and in dialogue, in characterisation and in setting, the play is excellent ; its theme is too sharp for any Irish audience which is itself essentially snobbily aristocratic, and with its quota of the impoverished and enslaved descendants of kings.

King Argimenes is in the fields with other slaves of King Darniak engaged in the exciting search for bones to gnaw, all attention concentrated upon the discovery of a bone substantial enough to dull the pangs of hunger.

KING ARGIMENES. This is a good bone ; there is juice in this bone.

ZARB. I wish I were you, Argimenes.

KING ARGIMENES. I am not to be envied any longer. I have eaten up my bone.

ZARB. I wish I were you because you have been a king. Because men have prostrated themselves before your feet. Because you have ridden a horse and worn a crown and have been called Majesty.

KING ARGIMENES. When I remember that I have been a king it is very terrible.

The terrible remembrance gives Argimenes an inner life which is unshared by his comrades in misfortune. He is a master, a commander, and his mastery is discovered and recognised by the envy of Zarb, in whose speech may be discerned, perhaps, Lord Dunsany's interpretation of social-ism as it appeared to him in 1910. In the process of digging Argimenes unearths a sword which he apostrophises as " holy and blessed thing " ; it is the symbol of his, and his op-pressor's, power. He remembers the sufferings and indig-nities to which he has been subjected while in the power of Darniak : " And these things they have done to a king, and a king of the House of Ithara ". With the sword he slays the palace guard, and imposing his authority upon his fellow-slaves the mob captures the armoury and throws down Darniak's idol. King Darniak himself is killed ; Argimenes ascends the throne and is acclaimed ' Majesty ' by the populace. Darniak's overseer is dragged before the throne holding a parchment in his hand, the plan of the great garden which was to have been a wonder of the world. Argimenes will have none of it.

KING ARGIMENES. (*Grimly*.) Show me the place that I digged for three years. (*The king's overseer shows it with trembling hands ; the parchment shakes visibly*.) Let there be built there a temple to an Unknown Warrior. And let this sword be laid on its altar evermore, that the ghost of that Warrior wandering by night, if men do walk by night from across the grave, may see his sword again. And let slaves be allowed to pray there and those that are oppressed ; nevertheless the noble and the mighty shall not fail to repair there too, that the Unknown Warrior shall not lack due reverence.

As they worked in the fields the slaves with Argimenes had speculated upon the death of the king's dog, hoping that a lingering death would not waste all the flesh from his bones. The entire polity of the kingdom had been revolutionised in the interim but the slave mentality survives. So the end of the play is as grim as the beginning. A man announces the death of the king's dog, and the memory of past suffering is too strong.

KING ARGIMENES AND HIS MEN. (*Savagely and hungrily*.) Bones !

KING ARGIMENES. (*Remembering suddenly what has happened and where he is*.) Let him be buried with the late king.

ZARB. (*In voice of protest*.) Majesty.

Despite the technical excellence and brilliant phrasing the play is one of the most bitter commentaries upon current events that the modern theatre has presented. " Not in our stars, dear Brutus, but in ourselves that we are underlings ", Lord Dunsany repeats with scathing emphasis. The master is the master, and come what may nothing will alter his mastery. A bitter philosophy surely to present to a British populace that was at the time engaged in a life and death struggle with the hereditary legislative powers of the House of Lords. Lord Dunsany could crack the whip, but the slaves in this instance failed to make the usual obeisance, they forgot to say ' Majesty '.

Lord Dunsany's best and longest plays have never been

produced at the Abbey Theatre, and have never been accepted as part of the Irish drama. In *The Gods of the Mountain*, which was produced at the Haymarket Theatre in London on the 1st of June, 1911, will be found the quintessence of Lord Dunsany's irony. *If*, which was produced with great success in London in 1921, is a slighter thing suggesting that accident plays as great a part as fate in human destinies. But *If* has in it all the glowing colour of the fabled Orient, and it was this, perhaps, rather than its theme that accounts for the great popularity the play achieved in Britain and America. The elaborate staging which both of these plays require may account for their non-production at the Abbey Theatre, but as they share that distinction with some sixteen other plays, most of them simple one-act pieces, it is probable that other reasons must be sought. The malicious gossip of Dublin explains the non-production of Dunsany's plays at the Abbey by saying that such a small theatre has room for only one titled person.

Whatever may be the reason for the non-production of his plays at the Abbey Theatre it is certain that eight years elapsed between the production of *King Argimenes* and *A Night at an Inn*. The United States had seen *A Night at an Inn* staged in 1916, London had seen it in 1917, but it was not until 2nd September, 1919, that the play was staged at the Abbey Theatre. It is a grimly terrible one-act play, calculated when well acted to inspire an audience with the same terror that its characters must simulate. The Toff and his three sailor companions are the survivors of a party which had stolen a great ruby from the forehead of an Indian idol. They have been followed by priests from the temple which they desecrated, had ' given them the slip ' in Hull, and had come to hide in a lonely inn on the Yorkshire moors until the priests should give up the search. The Toff has rented the inn with the hope that the priests will follow and be murdered in the lonely spot. After a discussion about the disposal of the stolen gems the three sailors get a small ruby and depart for refreshment and amusement. They return quickly in alarm : the priests have tracked them. Dispositions are made for attack. A faked struggle, in which each of the sailors in turn is supposed to be killed, is enacted so that the shadows will be visible upon the window. Then the sailors hide behind the properties in the room. The Toff sits to read a newspaper with a revolver on the table before him, hoping to lure the priests to the attack so that the conccaled sailors may fall upon them. Stealthily and slowly the three priests enter singly, and each in turn is stabbed to death. All are delighted at the success of The Toff's ruse, whose cleverness they extoll and whose health they proceed to toast. Suddenly stony heavy footfalls are heard without, and the victims cower before the idol itself, which enters the room, walks slowly to the table and places the ruby back in its forehead. Out again it goes, and from without calls in turn the names of the sailors. Some irresistible force draws them singly from the room and only a muffled shriek tells the fate that meets them outside. Finally the voice of the idol calls : " Meestaire Arnold Everett Scott-Fortescue, late Esquire, Able Seaman ", and The Toff, too, is forced to respond, muttering "I did not foresee it " as he goes to his doom. This little play is wonderfully effective in the theatre, making real for audiences all they have ever heard or read about the sinister power of the gems which are the eyes of idols in eastern temples. Such fabulous gems have always fascinated Europeans, and in this play Lord Dunsany infuses terror into his story. It is one of the most thrillingly powerful one-act plays of the contemporary stage, and its popularity throughout the English-speaking world is only what is deserved and might be anticipated. As an exercise in the technique of the one-act form the play is flawless, slowly concentrating its effects for the cumulative terror of the last few moments. Nevertheless its appearances at the Abbey Theatre have been rare, and the real appreciation of the play has been found in the United States.

The latest play of Lord Dunsany's to be seen on the stage of the Abbey Theatre was *The Tents of the Arabs*, which was produced for the first time on the evening of 24th May, 1920. *The Tents of the Arabs* had been staged in Paris six years earlier, and it was well known in Britain and America before its production in Dublin. It relates simply, in two short acts, how the King who desired a simple life was fascinated by the desert and followed a caravan on its journey to Mecca, and permitted a camel-driver to usurp his throne rather than reveal his identity. "I have done the work of a King now for five years and listened to my councillors, and all the while the desert called to me ". In this play will be found a love motive which is usually absent from Lord Dunsany's plays. The King comes to love the gypsy girl, Eznarza, and his love determines his decision to choose the tents of the Arabs rather than return to his throne. The opening of the second act, with the love scene between the King and Eznarza, is probably the most beautiful in Lord Dunsany's dramatic work. And in the final scene, when the King has chosen the tents rather than the throne, the dialogue assumes a metrical form with a faint echo of Synge in its measured cadences.

KING. We will dwell a little apart in a dear brown tent of our own.

EZNARZA. We shall hear the sand again, whispering low to the dawn wind.

KING. We shall hear the nomads stirring in their camps far off because it is dawn.

EZNARZA. The jackals will patter past us slipping back to the hills.

KING. When at evening the sun is set we shall weep for no day that is gone.

EZNARZA. I will rise up my head of a night time against the sky, and the old, old unbought stars shall twinkle through my hair, and we shall not envy any of the diademed queens of the world.

Since 1920 no new play by Lord Dunsany has been staged at the Abbey Theatre, but during the years since the end of the war his fame has grown in all other countries. It is in the United States, however, where he is most highly appreciated, and perhaps the Little Theatre Movement in that country is mainly responsible for that appreciation. The majority of Lord Dunsany's plays are in one-act, and these American Little Theatres specialise to a large extent in the production of plays in that form. Beyond his exotic colouring there is little in Lord Dunsany's plays to attract the European. His attitude to life is so aristocratic as to be almost contemptuous, and his snobbery is repellent to any but snobbish people. Occasionally he seems to verge on bad taste, as in *The Amusements of Khan Kharada*, and in none of his plays is there displayed the slightest sympathy with humanity as it exists in the contemporary world. There is a superficial resemblance in some of his plays with those of Sir J. M. Barrie, but the resemblance is only in the mechanics of drama, it is never in the content or the underlying philosophy. Where Barrie sympathises and smiles Dunsany derides and sneers ; where Barrie is the ministering angel Dunsany is the Olympian god judging and condemning. So *If* may be read as a corrective to *Dear Brutus*.

Much has already been said about Edward Martyn as one of the founders of the Irish Literary Theatre and only his contribution to the Irish drama remains to be considered. Martyn did in Ireland the same propagandist work for Ibsen and ' Ibsenism ' that Bernard Shaw did in England, but in his plays it was the Ibsen of *The Wild Duck* and *The Lady from the Sea* rather than the Ibsen of *The Doll's House* that he followed in his major, and best known, work. The adventurous career of his first play, *The Tale of a Town*, has been so very adequately, and wittily, described by George Moore in *Ave* that little remains to be said about it beyond the fact that it was not staged until 1905 when Martyn had a little theatre of his own. *The Tale of a Town* is in the naturalistic Ibsen manner, merely transferring to Ireland something of the matter of *Pillars of Society* and *An Enemy of the People*. The petty snobbery of an Irish town, and the corrupt influences in municipal life, are the main themes of the play ; but the characters are just puppets and the dialogue is so stilted

that the play could never come alive on the stage. It became
the basis for George Moore's *Bending of the Bough*, which was
produced by the Irish Literary Theatre in 1900. Edward
Martyn's great play was *The Heather Field*, which was first
staged by the Irish Literary Theatre in 1899 and several
times revived by other Irish companies. It is a psychological
analysis in three acts of an Irish landowner whose reality is
his dream-world but who is forced by circumstance to
undertake the administration of his estate. He idealises his
estate and undertakes the reclamation of a large tract of land
from the heather, believing that it can be made to yield rich
crops of hay and corn. The opposition of his wife and his
more practical relatives and friends only made him more
determined to proceed with his scheme, until finally it
developed into a mania. Large sums of money are required
for the reclamation work and he mortgages his property so
that the money may be available. He is utterly oblivious to
everything but his scheme, and his wife becomes so alarmed
that she endeavours to secure control of his affairs and prevent
the bankruptcy towards which she sees they are drifting.
Tyrrell is exalted by alternating hope and fear, and his wife
is so haunted by the fear of ruin that she develops an intense
hatred and intrigues to have him restrained. In a scene that
recalls Strindberg's *The Father* she seeks to have her husband
declared insane, and the doctors are on the point of giving her
the verdict when they are dissuaded by Tyrrell's close friend,
Barry Ussher. Ussher fears catastrophe, but he refuses to
believe that his friend is insane, so the restraint is prevented
and the catastrophe postponed. Driven by his creditors
Tyrrell has become a hard landlord and, like so many Irish
landlords, turns to eviction of his tenants to cover his own
mismanagement. The tenants resort to violent opposition
and the usual police escort is provided for Tyrrell, but this is
repulsive to him and he prefers to remain indoors brooding
and planning, without any actual contact with his land. In
this solitary state his dream deepens, he remembers the
heather field of his boyhood, where the winds sang to him and

the colour was a riot of beauty. Into this dream one day came his little son with a handful of heather, the only flowers he could find. He had gathered them in the heather field, and Carden Tyrrell's dream was shattered. Nature had triumphed, and the land he had wasted so much to reclaim had become waste once more. Fortune and ideal are both gone, and Carden Tyrrell's mind goes back to his boyhood, there to remain for the remainder of his life. He believes his son to be his younger brother and speaking to him says : " See, even now the sky is darkening as in that storm scene of the old legend I told you on the Rhine. See, the rain across a saffron sun trembles like gold harp-strings, through the purple Irish spring ". As he sees the rainbow he says (with fearful exaltation), " Oh, mystic highway of man's speechless longings ! my heart goes forth upon the rainbow to that horizon of joy ! "

There is something of *The Wild Duck*, and a suggestion of *Ghosts* in *The Heather Field*, and the symbolism also is twofold. Ireland itself is symbolised in the actual field, and the hopes and fears of ardent patriotism given voice. But there is also the struggle between man the idealist and woman the materialist, the universal human story of absorption by an ideal. When the ideal is shattered all is lost and life becomes but an empty mockery, a state of being undead. George Moore has said that *The Heather Field* was " the first play written in English inspired by the examples of Ibsen ", but if that be so it was Ibsen the poet that inspired it. In it there is no didactic purpose, no moral to be drawn, no lesson to be learned. It is just one of the great plays contributed by the Irish theatre to the drama of the world. It is true that the dialogue is sometimes stilted and unreal, and that there is a tinge of sentimentality, but despite these defects the play is powerful on the stage and no audience can witness its performance without being very profoundly moved.

Maeve, Edward Martyn's second important play, was produced by the Irish Literary Theatre in February 1900. It is described as " a psychological drama in two acts ", and in it Martyn gave free rein to his poetic fancy. Again the idealism of the visionary is contrasted with the practical values of the worldling, and again there is symbolism of double significance. Maeve O'Heynes, daughter of the hereditary Prince of Burren, is an idealist who has submitted to betrothal with a wealthy Englishman, Hugh FitzWalter, so that the wealth of the Englishman may aid in re-establishing the impoverished fortunes of the family. FitzWalter is tolerant and easy-going, giving complete freedom to the moody temperament of Maeve. Peg Inerney, Maeve's old nurse, believes that a peasant legend which identifies her with the Great Queen Maeve of Irish story is true, believing that Maeve had undergone metamorphosis at the hands of the fairies one night on the mountainside. Maeve O'Heynes is only too willing to believe this also, and when the old woman invites her to go to the mountain to meet the legendary figures and the noble lover of her dreams the girl forgets that it is the eve of her wedding and goes. She is entranced for hours on the mountain, and when she returns to her home her whole being has been disturbed by the ecstasy of her vision. As she sits by her window the spirit world again opens before her vision, and there passes a procession of Queen Maeve and her retinue as it comes from its cairn on the mountain to her castle. " I see them now, and I see others who lived long before them, and are buried in that green cairn. Oh, I am dying because I am exiled from such beauty ". As the spirit procession returns to the cairn it carries with it the soul of Maeve, and when her sister, Finola, comes to prepare her for the wedding Maeve is found sitting cold and lifeless at the window. Maeve had gone in search of " that silvery beauty which survives in the human heart, which we see shimmering to the horizon, leading our longings beyond the world, and we hear it in our hearts like silver harps and strings, sounding seemingly of themselves, for no hand is by ". And George Moore continues in his preface to the printed version of the play : " Therefore Maeve is made of moonlight and hoar frost and light of morning. We do not discover her among our acquaintances, but everyone discovers her when he wills to do so in his own heart ".

The play opens coldly and slowly enough, but it gathers warmth and force as it develops, and in the scene where the vision of Queen Maeve comes to the young girl is a climax which cannot be forgotten when once it has been witnessed. *Maeve* is a delight in the theatre, portraying " the spirit and sense of an ill-fated race " in an atmosphere that is magnificently conceived and splendidly sustained.

None of Martyn's later plays reached the high level of *The Heather Field* or *Maeve*, and none of them has evoked anything of the interest that these two earlier plays had for audiences in Ireland and elsewhere. In his later work Martyn seems to have been somewhat soured, and indeed the treatment he received in the Irish Theatre would have soured a nature more optimistic and gregarious than he was gifted with. He became realistic and satirical and his plays lost the poetic quality which had distinguished them in the earlier years. *An Enchanted Sea*, however, retained some of the qualities of the two more important plays. This play was produced in 1902, but it has never been part of the repertory of any Irish theatre, nor has it ever attained to popularity elsewhere. Here the supernatural and the actual are so very imperfectly blended that something of the ludicrous results. Guy Font, a young squire, is not entirely human ; there is supposed to be a mixture of fairy blood in his veins. Like Ibsen's Lady from the Sea, he is held in thrall by the Sea-Spirit. Through the machinations of his aunt he is drowned, but in the result he seems not so much to have ceased to live as to have entered into the life of his natural element. In this play the inspiration of Ibsen is perhaps more obvious than in any other play of Martyn's, and in it also is that spirit of Irish folk-lore which seems to pervade, rather than to fashion, his plays. In *An Enchanted Sea* it is the young and imaginative Lord Mask, and not the elfin Guy, who is likely to attract and hold the attention of an audience. There is more than the usual incidental violence, which is so often mistaken for drama, in this play ; there is the murder of Guy by his aunt, the discovery of the crime, and the suicide of the aunt.   But despite all this crude violence, so alien to Martyn, the play is not really dramatic, as the characters are never wholly convincing, never quite fully alive, and the dialogue is, as always, literary rather than living.

From this point the dramatic work of Edward Martyn deteriorated to an extent that is almost incredible.   It is difficult to believe that the man who wrote *The Heather Field* and *Maeve* is he who wrote *The Placehunters*, *Grangecolman*, and *The Dream Physician*, yet the two last named plays were produced as recently as 1912 and 1914 respectively.   The theme of *The Placehunters* is plain from the title ; it is a dull satire upon the drab conditions of the Ireland of 1902, a kind of throw-back to *The Tale of a Town*.   It never aroused the interest of anybody in the theatre and is quite forgotten.

In *Grangecolman* the characterisation is stronger and the dialogue more close to life than is usual in Martyn's plays, but there is much talk that is unrelated either to characters or incidents.   The atmosphere of the play is suggestive of Tchechov, and the characters have close affinities with the shiftless, negative existence of the people in *The Cherry Orchard*.   The scene of the play is laid in an Irish country house where all humanity is stifled by disappointments and misunderstandings.   Only once is there anything approaching a thrill ; the catastrophic end when Catherine is inadvertently shot by Clare Farquhar, who fires at what she believes to be a ghost.   But the thrill leaves the emotions unmoved, because interest in the people as human beings had never been excited.

In *The Dream Physician*, staged in 1914, Martyn essayed psychological comedy, with a satirical eye on George Moore, who had been baiting him in *Hail and Farewell*.   The humour is, as might be expected, somewhat heavy, and the attempt to blend the dream and the actuality is not successful.   It is an essay in the manner of *An Enchanted Sea* in which sly humour takes the place of tragedy.   It also failed to make any deep impression in the little theatre where it was staged, and the small audience which witnessed its performance will perhaps remember its author's nervousness more than the play.

Martyn cannot be said to have influenced the Irish drama to any extent through his plays, as everything he attempted has been done better and more often by others. Nevertheless his work is of some importance, and the two plays, *The Heather Field* and *Maeve*, by which he is most favourably and widely known will give him an abiding place in the Irish theatre. It was as an inspirer, a courageous and sympathetic critic, and a pioneer, and not as a dramatist that Martyn influenced those about him. Had he been less fastidious, less literary, less European, he would probably have made a greater contribution to the Irish drama. But it is as a man, and not as a dramatist, that he will be remembered. That, perhaps, is his tragedy.

CHAPTER XII

MELODRAMA AND FARCE

The Melodrama of Politics : Conal O'Riordan, Thomas MacDonagh, Maurice Dalton, Dorothy Macardle, Terence MacSwiney, F. J. H. O'Donnell—Plays about Irish Social Problems : R. J. Ray, Walter Riddall, A. P. Wilson, A. & O., Daniel Corkery, J. Bernard Mac-Carthy—Writers of Farce : Seumas O'Brien, S. R. Day and G. D. Cummins, Martin J. McHugh, Bernard Duffy, M. M. Brennan.

DURING the second decade of its existence the Abbey Theatre failed to live up to the great standard which it had set in its earlier years. The acting tended to be stereotyped, and the quality of the plays produced was in very marked inferiority to that of the great days. Of course it was not to be expected that such dramatists as Synge, Yeats, Lady Gregory, Colum, and Fitzmaurice would continue to come forward indefinitely, nor could it be expected that a company of players acting in a new play every week would retain its pristine freshness of manner and expression. The ascendancy of Arthur Sinclair first drew attention of regular playgoers to the obvious tiredness of the company. Sinclair could, and still can, be a great actor when he chooses, but he permitted himself to get into a rut, and by his staccato speech to play for a laugh every time. In this way almost every play at the Theatre was reduced to the level of farce. The audience could be induced to laugh uproariously at Sinclair even in such plays as *The Shadow of the Glen* or *The Playboy of the Western World ;* the greatest tragedy in the repertory of the Theatre could be made the occasion for laughter. As a consequence, perhaps, of this domination of the comic element in the acting only comedies and farces seemed to be received with favour by the company, and audiences awaited the opportunity to laugh.

The makers of the Theatre seemed to have ceased writing, new dramatists were slow in making their appearance, and for a time it almost seemed that the Irish Dramatic Movement had worked itself out. There was an abundance of little one-act farces, blood-and-thunder melodrama, and a considerable quota of crude political propaganda. Here and there gleams of hope showed themselves, in the little farces perhaps the promise of comedy to come or in the melodrama the hint of a purpose that with experience would develop into high tragedy, but it must be said with regret that these gleams rarely got beyond their first faint flush. Many of the authors never got beyond a first play, while others continued to write without making any marked progress.

So long as the primary function of the theatre is amusement rather than entertainment in its full meaning, it may be supposed that audiences will go to the theatre for laughter and ' thrills ', to laugh or to cry. In every country the theatre that is anything more than an amusement booth has to struggle against this demand and to make its appeal to the small section of the population which is sufficiently cultivated to require intellectual entertainment and the stimulus of art. The population of Ireland is so small, and the population of Dublin so representative of the population of Ireland, that this section of the population would be quite inadequate to maintain a theatre of any considerable size. It has been said that London, with its population of twice that of all Ireland, has only some 20,000 people who would be attracted by the intellectural drama, and if that be so in a world-capital what could be expected in an island which is the outpost of Western Europe ? Even Caesar ignored Ireland ! Dublin had been accustomed to the travelling companies sent out from London for its more expensive theatre fare, and the populace had revelled in melodrama of the crudest kind for many generations. It would have been too much to expect that the habits and outlook of the two sections of the population could be altered radically within the short space of ten years. What might have been expected was what actually came to pass :

the Theatre came to meet the people when the people failed
to rise to the standard of the Theatre. The plays at the
Abbey Theatre began to be derivative and imitative; the
worst traits of the more important dramatists being copied
and imitated, and the so-called ' peasant ' speech reproduced
with the accuracy of a gramophone record. This was
supposed to be ' faithful realism ', but it drew from George
W. Russell (' A.E.') a vigorous and a well-timed protest.
" We have developed ", said ' A.E.', " a new and clever school
of Irish dramatists who say they are holding up the mirror to
Irish peasant nature, but they reflect nothing but decadence.
They delight in the broken light of insanity, the ruffian who
beats his wife, the weakling who is unfortunate in love, and
who goes and drinks himself to death ". To this criticism
one of the minor dramatists was led to reply. " To many
honest persons ", says J. Bernard MacCarthy in the Preface
to *The Long Road to Garranbraher*, " undoubtedly the so-
called ' Abbey ' peasant in a serious play is anathema; and
their chorus of disapproval rivals the roar of Niagara. They
are sunny, well-fed folk, who stoutly refuse to think that the
Irish peasant (or any other humble dweller in the countryside)
is anything else save a good-natured giant singing at his work
all day long out of sheer joy in existence, and dancing merrily
at the cross-roads of evenings. It is a pleasant picture : pity
it is not a true one. . . . If you come as a sentimental writer,
you will be ready to enthuse about the ' simple tillers of the
soil ', their ' unworldliness and courtesy ', and ' contentment
with their lot ', the very things you came prepared to witness ;
but you will have merely stirred the surface of the pool.
There are deep waters you will never sound, fierce under-
currents you will never suspect. You have not discovered
the real peasant, and you never will. You have passed over
the grim passions, the primitive hungers and desires beneath
the crust ". It was the grim passions and primitive hungers
that the lesser dramatists of the Abbey Theatre saw and
attempted to reproduce in drama, and when they came to
clothe their visions in speech the echoes of Synge and Lady

Gregory resounded in every line. To such an extent was this
carried that a witty Belfast writer, himself a dramatist of some
accomplishment, was tempted to caricature the entire movement in a play entitled *The Mist that does be on the Bog*, but
neither that nor 'A.E.'s ' protest could prevent that imitative-
ness which is common to all literature. Anyhow melodrama
and farce were inevitable in the Theatre, in Irish drama no
less than in the drama of all other lands, and it was certainly
to be preferred that these should be home-made rather than
imported. If the Irish Theatre had to have melodrama and
farce, and it had, it was better that such plays should be
written by Irish apprentice dramatists, some of whom might
move on to better things. But, of course, there is nothing
very distinctively national in such plays ; they are the same
in all countries, made of the same materials with only slight
variations in the texture and in the speech. There is little to
be gained by any detailed analysis of such plays, but no
account of the Irish drama would be complete if the suggestion were left that its contribution to the world-theatre
consisted of masterpieces only. The fact is that the Abbey
Theatre has produced as large a proportion of bad and
indifferent plays as any other theatre in the world, and that
not by any means all of these poor plays were written by
obscure or minor dramatists. Therefore in order that this
survey may be as complete as possible a glance will be given
to some of the minor dramatists and to a few of the indifferent
plays.

With a very close approximation to absolute truth it may
be said that all the plays of the Irish theatre are political, even
The Whiteheaded Boy is claimed by its author to be entitled
to that label, but generally the political content was sufficiently hidden to pass unnoticed. The symbolism of Yeats
and Martyn, the lyricism of Synge, the kindliness of Lady
Gregory, or the humanity of Padraic Colum, all obscured the
political current which passed through their plays. But there
was also a school of dramatists which obtruded its politics and
attempted to make the drama a vehicle for political propa-

ganda. Generally these plays were produced outside the Abbey Theatre by amateur groups attached to the political clubs, but occasionally one of them would get to the stage of that Theatre, and always the play had some dramatic merit which surpassed its political content. One of these plays, *The Piper*, when it was staged for the first time in 1908, led to a noisy protest in the Theatre by people whose patriotism was stronger than either their knowledge or their sense. Norreys Connell is now better known by his real name of Conal O'Riordan, the author of some of the most successful novels and plays published in England since the war, but this little play marked him as one who was destined for such success. In its single act it contrasts the character of the Englishman and the Irishman as that character is shown in time of war. An English officer is a prisoner of the Irish Rebels in 1798. The Rebels are all in favour of celebrating their victory at Vinegar Hill, but the Englishman suggests that sentries should be posted to prevent a surprise attack. This leads to an outburst of discursive talking, and to an attack upon Englishmen as cowards who desire watchful protection. Black Mike, a leader of the Rebels, turns the attack upon his followers, accusing them of a moral cowardice beneath contempt. His words have little effect, and the play ends as the captive officer had foreseen by a victorious onslaught of the English mercenaries. This, and the two other one-act plays which Conal O'Riordan contributed to the Abbey Theatre, give cause for regret that one of such promise, and later of such achievement, should have found it necessary to desert the Irish drama. That he would have contributed greatly to that drama had he remained in Ireland there is now no possibility to doubt ; but London has gained what was lost to Dublin and no one will grudge Conal O'Riordan the great success he has achieved in England and America.

In 1916 the drama suffered another loss when Thomas MacDonagh was executed for participation in the Easter Rising. A poet of distinction and probably the ablest critic in the Irish Literary Movement, he was also the author of a few plays of which one had been produced at the Abbey Theatre. MacDonagh's politics provided the motive for all that he did during his short life ; everything that he did was ' for the greater glory of Ireland ', as all his activities were directed towards the political liberation of the country. His play, *When the Dawn is Come*, was produced in October 1908, and presents a somewhat fanciful picture of the effects of political liberty in the future. There was no attempt made to disguise the propagandist motive of the play, and it cannot be said that it was effective as drama. The only abiding impression that the play has left is that of the sickly pink uniforms of the soldiers, and that is more a tribute to the producer than to the dramatist. The play has never been revived, but later work of the dramatist proves that the Irish theatre lost a man of potential worth when Thomas Mac-Donagh fell before the firing squad in 1916.

A new dramatist made his appearance when *Sable and Gold* was staged for the first time on the 16th of September, 1918. This play deals with the events of 1916, showing the effects upon the life of one family of that outbreak. As it was the first play to deal with such a recent event considerable attention was attracted to it and to its author, but no other play has since come from him. *Sable and Gold* is melodramatic enough to satisfy the most fastidious seeker after such plays, but in its construction and its dialogue it gave more than a hint that something much better might be expected from its author. But that expectation has not yet been realised, although it may be at any time. The play has been extremely popular with amateur dramatic companies in all parts of Ireland, and has probably been played by such companies more often than any other Irish play of recent years. The political content of the play, together with the poignant situation in which its characters are placed, no doubt accounts for this popularity with audiences in all parts of Ireland ; but these have not been sufficient to keep the play in the regular repertory of the Abbey Theatre.

Another new dramatist who made her appearance in 1918 is also one from whom fine work may be confidently anticipated in the future, indeed she has since proven that she can improve with every play that she writes. In *Atonement*, which was staged in December 1918, Miss Dorothy Macardle gave promise of fine work, but it was when *The Old Man* was produced on 24th February, 1925, that it was seen that she was capable of tragedy no less than political propaganda or melodramatic effects. In this play Miss Macardle deals with events attendant upon the deportation of John Mitchel in May 1848. Mitchel has been sentenced to transportation to Van Diemen's Land, and is imprisoned in Dublin awaiting the arrival of the ship that is to take him. A vast assemblage marches past the jail ' to cheer him ', and to assure him that the work he has striven to do will be continued in his absence. An attempt at rescue is discouraged by the Council of the Confederation and by Mitchel himself, yet Robert Emmet Sheridan decides that an attempt must be made at the docks when Mitchel is about to embark. His old grandfather tries to dissuade him, but aware that his entreaties have been vain the old man goes out while his grandson sleeps and informs Thomas Francis Meagher and William Scully of the project. These two appear at the house as young Sheridan is preparing to depart on his effort at rescue ; a struggle ensues and the young man is shot. Thus the Old Man loses as much by his attempt to frustrate the effort at rescue as he would have done had it been made and unsuccessful. The play is an allegory upon current events in Ireland, where the old men were at the time endeavouring to hold the young in check. The political intention of the play is obvious enough, and the atmosphere is melodramatic, but the play succeeds in rousing the emotions. If Miss Macardle could free herself from the more morbid aspects of politics she would be capable of much finer work than she has yet given to the theatre. Technically she is very well equipped, and the dialogue of her three plays leaves little to be desired, so that when she can break free of the political obsessions which cramp and fetter her something memorable will come from her pen. She is yet young, and she has a contact with the theatre in Britain and in Ireland which few Irish dramatists are so fortunate as to have. For all these reasons her future will be watched with some anxiety by all who are on the look-out for really good Irish plays.

Something more than a purely dramatic interest attached to the production on the 24th of February, 1921, of a play by Terence MacSwiney. The author was the famous Lord Mayor of Cork who had conducted the record hunger-strike in Brixton Prison, and who had died there as a result in October 1920. His play, *The Revolutionist*, had been published in 1914, but it had not been staged until the public concentration upon the manner of his premature death attracted attention to it. The play cannot be said to be possessed of any marked merits beyond its definitely ' literary' dialogue, and on the stage it failed to hold the attention of an audience. Its construction is purely experimental, suggesting the manner of the post-war German dramatists, and the way in which the action is broken into a large number of short scenes proves that the author was not quite sure of himself. But that he had ideas for drama, and that he had the will to produce drama, there is no reason to doubt ; what is open to doubt is that he would ever have produced drama which would have satisfied his own requirements. " Since the common cry of the critics ", he wrote, " is for imagination, we need not urge it ; but that we may truly appreciate this high faculty of the soul, let there be a plea for intellect. How far there is evidence of intellect in our contemporary drama is a matter for reflection. The return of philosophy, what Meredith pleaded for the Novel, will be likewise the saving of the Drama ". It is possible that, had he lived, he might have done something to bring philosophy into Irish drama, but the single example that has been seen on the Irish stage did not give much room for such a hope. Politics absorbed Terence MacSwiney, and the high ideals, the austere literary style, the love of the theatre, were all sacrificed in that agony in Brixton Jail. His death was one of the most dramatic events of this generation, and in that long-drawn drama he gave to the world an example of heroic fortitude which is likely to remain unique. It was in his life, and in the manner of his death, that he brought his philosophy into his drama. It was his great faith that sustained him in his struggle, and perhaps had he lived he might have given that faith expression in heroic drama.

In September 1920 the first play of Frank J. Hugh O'Donnell, *The Drifters*, was staged at the Abbey Theatre. It was a one-act play which did not attract much attention, nor did it arouse much interest, and there was a lapse of nearly five years before another play by the same author was produced. In the interval at least one other play had been published, but it had not been staged at the Abbey Theatre although amateur dramatic societies presented it in different parts of the country. With *Anti-Christ*, which was produced for the first time at the Abbey Theatre on St. Patrick's Day, 1925, O'Donnell challenged criticism with his first long play on a big theme. The very title of the play suggested that it was not solely concerned with an Irish subject, and when the play was staged it was seen that the theme was no less than War, and its effects. In structure the play resembles those of C. K. Munro in that there is a series of scenes instead of the conventional act-form : and another departure from convention is the description of the play as ' A Commentary '. The author dislikes the world as it is after the storm of European War and the calm of the Versailles Peace. His ' commentary ' opens with a glimpse at a couple of journalists, without belief in the work they do, concerting plans. John Boles who lost his sight in the war comes to visit them. He castigates their insincerity, points to the purity of the motives which led millions to death and disablement in the War, and ends with an attack upon the anti-Christian spirit which animates post-war governments. He will, himself, endeavour to bring London and England back to a sense of Christianity. In this the two journalists see nothing but the opportunity

for sensation, and they reserve columns in their papers for a
scare heading: " Anti-Christ is Here ! " In pursuit of his
plan Boles makes a long speech to a meeting of disabled
soldiers. Sandwichmen parade the streets with lurid posters,
and a boy selling newspapers in the street has some cross-talk
with a policeman. Boles is arrested, and the Prime Minister
decides to have him detained as a lunatic. There is the
material of a great play in *Anti-Christ*, but that material was
never exploited. The points are too obvious, and the contrasts too crude, to give the play that quality of sincerely felt
emotion without which there can be no tragedy. John Boles
is ' tragic ' only in the newspaper sense of the word, but the
conditions to which he returned from the idealism of the war
period are sufficiently ironic to provide tragedy of the
classical kind. The tragedy of John Boles is the tragedy of
all idealists : disillusionment. If the author of *Anti-Christ*
had been less of an idealist himself he might have produced
a better play. Since the play was staged in Dublin it has
been seen in London, where also another play of O'Donnell's
has been produced. This last play, *O'Flaherty's Star*, shows
the author in a different mood, a mood of peasant symbolism,
and it is perhaps in this, or in social problem plays, that his
future work will be done. He is a young man still experimenting, full of energy and enthusiasm for the drama, and it
is possible that he will yet give the Irish drama some plays of
distinction. He comes from the county of Galway, and he
has, in consequence, the stock of Connacht folk-lore which
no native of that province seems to be without. With the
experience which he has gathered he may decide to make use
of this, and he may thus discover the material he has sought.

Another group of more or less melodramatic playwrights
has given its attention mainly to the presentation of social
problems in dramatic form. As the drama throughout
Europe during the latter part of the nineteenth century had
been concerned with such problems it was but natural that
Irish dramatists should attempt to stage some aspects of the
problems as they were presented in twentieth-century

Ireland. It is to this group to which special attention must be directed if the primitive passions and hungers of contemporary Irish life in town and country are to be seen and understood. Mainly the problems dealt with were the land and the town wage-earner, but others of a less compelling kind also received some little attention. Without doubt the best writer of melodrama for the stage of the Abbey Theatre is R. J. Ray, who has produced five plays between 1909 and 1922, most of them conspicuous for their portrayal of almost incredibly brutal types of humanity. Probably the best of R. J. Ray's plays is *The Casting-out of Martin Whelan*, produced in September 1910, as the second play of its author. Here is depicted a community so depraved that it will stop at nothing to achieve its end, which is control of the land it tills. Crime is resorted to, and a malicious burning, perpetrated to achieve this end, and because Martin Whelan still retains the vestiges of decent behaviour he is boycotted and finally driven away. On the stage the play is effective enough, the characterisation is good if never completely convincing as having been carefully studied, and the dialogue is brusque enough to fit the violent people who use it. In *The Gombeen Man*, produced in June 1913, Ray attempted to dramatise a problem and a type which had both scourged Ireland for more than half-a-century. The Gombeen-man is a type of trader peculiar to Ireland : he supplies his customers with all the requirements of their farms and their homes and in return he takes from them the produce of their farms and dairies. On the face of it that does not seem too awful, but when it is borne in mind that the poor peasants were usually illiterate and that they never knew what prices were being charged for what they received nor the amounts credited for what they gave, the enormity of the problem may be glimpsed. From year to year those in the clutches of the gombeen-man never knew how they stood, and in the end their lands were usually distrained to meet their alleged debts. So the gombeen-man flourished, becoming in numbers of instances the successor to the expropriated landlord, and the boorish

tyrant of a district. A good theme for a play, but unfortunately R. J. Ray was not the man to write it. He was too
easily attracted by the violent side of the theme's possibilities,
and to these he succumbed, leaving entirely ignored the
psychological, social and economic aspects which were easily
the more significant. No new work by Ray has been staged
since *The Moral Law* in August 1922, and it is probable that
no other plays of his will be seen at the Abbey Theatre where
the audience has become accustomed to melodrama of a less
crude kind. It is, perhaps, the knowledge that his plays were
for the stage only which has prevented R. J. Ray from having
them published : whatever be the reason he is the only
prominent author in the Irish dramatic movement who has
not yet had any of his plays printed. He belongs to the
outmoded past when Boucicault ruled the Irish stage, but
that does not invalidate the statement that his plays were
strong theatrical fare in every sense of the term.

A writer who might have done some fine work was the
author of *The Prodigal*, which was staged in September 1914.
But unfortunately Walter Riddall died before his play was
produced, and another promising dramatist was lost to the
Irish theatre. In this play Riddall shows how the passion for
' goodness ' in a strait-laced family may drive some of its
members to the lowest depths of infamy. The play is
melodramatic in form, lurid in spots, but its psychology is
much superior to that of any of the minor writers of Irish
melodrama. Upon the ' prodigal ', and the reasons for his
' prodigality ', Riddall lavished all his sympathy, and the
result was a very convincing piece of character-drawing, no
less than a fully-developed moral tale. That the scene of the
play was laid in Belfast made it all the more piquant to the less
puritanical audiences of Dublin.

It might have been anticipated that the great strike in
Dublin in 1913, when the figure of James Larkin loomed
menacingly upon the Irish mentality for the first time, would
have been the occasion for some contributions to drama.
And if there were any such anticipations they were more than

realised during the following half-dozen years. First came A. P. Wilson with *The Slough* in November 1914, ere the echoes of the struggle had ceased to be heard. The author was for a time Manager of the Abbey Theatre, and he is now one of the prominent members of the Scottish Theatre. His sympathies were entirely on the side of the strikers, and he had rendered some assistance during the progress of the struggle. The theme of the play is sufficiently indicated by its title, it is, in effect, little more than a picture of the terrible conditions of the slum districts of Dublin, and it has since been used as a propagandist play by labour dramatic groups in Dublin and elsewhere. *Blight*, produced in December 1917, although similar in theme is entirely different in every other respect. It, too, depicts the filthy conditions in which the Dublin worker was compelled to live, but it does not place all the blame for these conditions upon the employing class. *Blight*, in fact, castigates the workers as much as the employers, and is therefore without any propagandist intent. It is an objective study, by two people who preferred to be known as A. & O., presenting a problem for the audience, rather than prescribing a remedy. This play is marked by a critically ironic insight into social conditions in Dublin, and by a characterisation which marks its authors as keen psychologists. It is a play which would bear revival, as it is also a play which anticipated Sean O'Casey in its portrayal of the typical Dublin wastrel. *Blight* is undoubtedly the best play yet produced by an Irish dramatist dealing with a specifically Irish social problem. But it is to Daniel Corkery's fine play, *The Labour Leader*, that attention must be directed if it would be seen how that social problem may be exploited with greatest dramatic effect. *The Labour Leader* was staged at the Abbey Theatre for the first time on 30th September, 1919, but it would seem to have been written some years earlier. Immediately it suggests that it is a study of ' Jim ' Larkin in his heyday, as in the person of David Lombard, the secretary of the Quaymen's Union, there is portrayed all the egoism and all the arrogance of that stormy petrel of Irish Labour. But it is a study marked by all the sympathetic insight that made *The Threshold of Quiet* the most attractive Irish novel of recent years, in which the characterisation is meticulous, the dialogue is pleasing as it is effective, and the sincerity obvious. It is the work of a man who is at the same time a connoisseur of words and a stage craftsman of considerable ability. Unfortunately *The Labour Leader* is the only full-length play he has yet had produced, but he has produced a few short plays, one of which was staged at the Abbey Theatre. Nowadays he would seem to have deserted the theatre and devotes his time to novels, short stories, poems, and the painting of pictures. Altogether a versatile man is Daniel Corkery, and withal he is one of the most distinguished figures in the Irish literary movement. Nowhere, however, does his work seem to have anything like the appreciation that its excellence deserves. Much may be expected from him in the future, but it may be doubted whether he will ever again be lured into the theatre.

Occasionally much is made in the press about ' navvy poets ' and such unusual literary phenomena, but no fuss will ever be made of such people in Ireland for the very simple reason that nearly all the Irish writers have been also workers at some other business. Irish writers are school teachers or chemists, clerks or shop-assistants, builders' labourers or farmers, rarely are they in their beginnings professional writers. It remained to J. Bernard MacCarthy to add a rural postman to the list, and this he has done with some little distinction. He is the author of many plays, and several of his novels have been published in London, but he still continues his work as a postman in the district of Crosshaven near the city of Cork. He is not by any means a great dramatist, but he has written at least two plays which are of more than average distinction. His first play, *Kinship*, was staged at the Abbey Theatre in 1914, and since that date he has produced a long list of plays which would have justified the whole-time work of a professional dramatist. Originally he was attracted by plays of a more serious type, but latterly he has shown a disposition towards comedy and one-act farces. The play by which he is best known, and which is also his best work in the full-length form, is *Crusaders*, which was staged for the first time at the Abbey Theatre on the 19th of January 1917. It is an inverted version of *The Prodigal*, illustrating the revolt of a son against what he considers an immoral way of making a living by his family. Father Tom Moran is a young priest who has become a crusader in the cause of total abstinence from alcoholic liquor. With his burning eloquence he has swept the country as once did Father Theobald Mathew, so that he had achieved a national reputation as a preacher against alcoholic intemperance. In time he was invited to come and conduct a temperance crusade in his own native district, where his own family kept a public house, and pressure is brought to make him abandon his mission. His parents come to him with plaintive appeals.

STEVE. (*His father.*) God knows it's little pleasure we find in coming.

MRS. MORAN. Tom, my son, don't be harsh with us. 'Tisn't for ourselves we want you to give over the temperance business but for the sake of the childer.

FATHER TOM. I know, I know. You said all that yesterday ; and no one can tell how hard a struggle it was to refuse your request (*is moved*). Ask me anything but that.

MRS. MORAN. Oh, Tom, Tom, how can you ? And it's the only favour we ever asked of you. This morn your father got word that the worst would happen if you went ahead with this crusade.

STEVE. Do, lad.

FATHER TOM. I cannot (*passionately*). You know I cannot. I would not mind the ruin of my own career—of the scorn that men would heap upon me, but I cannot desert the men whom I have led into the movement. I cannot desert them.

STEVE. No, maybe you'll prefer to desert your own. Pat, come here.

Then Father Tom is told that his brother Pat had been charged with embezzlement and forgery, but that he can escape imprisonment if the money is repaid within two years.

" *If* he can refund the money ", says Steve, " D'you hear me ". " By saving and contriving I can manage to pay it back ; I'll work my fingers to the bone to do it, but I won't be able to do it if my business is ruined, and the anger of the brewery brought down on me. There, that's how we're situated ". At length Father Tom is broken : " I give in ", he says. " The name of Moran must not be disgraced save by me alone. But let the world think what it will (turning to his brother tenderly). Pat, they shall not send you to prison". The cheers of the crowd outside indicate that the people are already assembling for the beginning of the mission, and the committee of the Temperance Society comes back into the room. Addresses of welcome are about to be read when Father Tom stops them, and announces that he will preach no temperance crusade in that town or elsewhere ever again. The members of the committee are angrily disappointed and taunt him with desertion, hinting that they are aware of its causes. The crowd outside still cheers, and the music of a band is heard. Father Tom is induced to speak to the people from the window, but he collapses in the effort. The committee leaves the room, and Canon Kelly is heard announcing that the mission will not be given, amidst the indignant protests of the crowd.

FATHER TOM. It's all over, mother. I am going to retire to a monastery, and spend the rest of my life there.

MRS. MORAN. Oh, Tom.

FATHER TOM. Mother, what brings you here ? Why did you not go home ?

MRS. MORAN. I could not leave you, lad. I knew you would be upset and troubled, God help us. Tom, you'll be coming home with me now—won't you ?

FATHER TOM. Yes, mother. (*He pulls back hangings and glances out window. In a voice trembling with emotion.*) Look at them. There they go . . . crowding into the public-houses. . . . (*With a heart-breaking cry of agony he throws himself on his knees and bows his head on the table.*) There they go. . . . My God ! My God ! The men I would have saved.

The probability that this situation had actually been presented to some young priest in Ireland, where very many of the clergy come from families owning public houses, gave an added poignancy to the play, and there is no denying that it was tremendously effective on the stage. But nevertheless the play is a not very distinguished specimen of melodrama, crude enough in its construction, and never rising beyond the commonplace in its dialogue. The characters are sharply defined, but never is the young idealist quite convincing, and consequently his surrender is not the tragic thing it might have been. The claims of a family when weighed against ideals have been so much more convincingly staged by other Irish dramatists, notably by Padraic Colum in *Thomas Muskerry*, that MacCarthy's play is by comparison without any distinctive quality. But it did stage a problem which is very real in Ireland, and for that alone the play merits some slight attention. The latest play by J. Bernard MacCarthy to be staged at the Abbey Theatre was *The Long Road to Garranbraher* in January 1923. This is a slight one-act tragedy in which Captain Peter Hanley, retired from the sea and on the point of eviction from his cottage, chooses his own degradation rather than rehabilitation by the dishonour of his son. The little play is reminiscent of Heijerman's *The Good Hope* inasmuch as the pivotal point of the play is the sinking of a ship so that its insurance money may be received by the owners. What is undoubtedly MacCarthy's best play has not yet been staged, although it was published in 1917 at the instigation of a Cork organisation known as The Twenty Club. The theme of *The Sea Call* suggests a comparison with *Riders to the Sea*, but the comparison could only be to the disadvantage of MacCarthy's play. The little play can come out advantageously from comparison with other Irish plays of but slightly varying theme, with Martyn's *The Enchanted Sea*, for example, or H. B. O'Hanlon's *The All-Alone*, which aroused the warm enthusiasm of Edward Martyn. It is in *The Sea Call* that Bernard MacCarthy's dialogue is at its finest, " beauty of imagination it has in a high degree, and atmosphere and rich music of speech as well ", T. C. Murray wrote in his foreword to the published play, and it is extraordinary that the play has never been staged at the Abbey Theatre. Recently the author has tended more and more to write short farcical sketches for amateur companies playing in village halls, and he is himself associated with a dramatic society in his native Crosshaven. His farcical sketches do not differ materially from the hundreds of such that are written weekly in all parts of the world.

The same, indeed, may be said of the vast majority of farces and so-called comedies which have been staged at the Abbey Theatre. They are produced to give ten minutes or a quarter-hour of laughter and having performed that function they are allowed to fade into oblivion. Lady Gregory is the only writer of poor farces who has been able to have her worst work accepted as literature equally with her best, but many of the others have had their work published in Ireland or in America. Of these Seumas O'Brien is probably the most important. When his *Duty* was first produced in November 1913, it was recognised as a masterpiece of its kind. Police who come to drink in public houses during prohibited hours may not be very funny, but when the beginning is made with a few civilians who have to be hidden to make way for the constable, and he in turn has to hide from the sergeant who flees from the coming inspector, and when all are hidden in the same coal-house, the fun and the laughter rise gradually almost to screaming point. The fun is at the expense of an Ireland that is now no more, and of a police force that has ceased to be, but it will be appreciated in any country with a primitive humour. Shortly after the production of this play Seumas O'Brien, who is a sculptor of considerable talent with a delightful specimen of his work displayed in the vestibule of the Abbey Theatre, went to live in the United States, and it is in that country where his recent dramatic work has been staged by the Little Theatres. That he has achieved a high reputation in America may be gleaned from the fact that his short one-act plays make their appearance with regularity in the anthologies of such plays which are now a feature of American publishing. He has not given all his talent to the writing of farce, some of his little plays are as grim as anything by Lord Dunsany, but he has never departed from the one-act form. His departure from Ireland was a loss to the Irish drama, but as his plays are still Irish in theme and atmosphere they must be considered as belonging to the Irish movement and still available for production at the Abbey Theatre.

The collaboration of Miss S. R. Day and Miss G. D. Cummins gave the Theatre two plays, one of which, *Fox and Geese*, is farcical comedy of the kind that compels laughter. When the play was produced in 1917 its three acts of fun seemed to promise a new stream of comic plays to the Theatre, but as no other play has since been staged it may be assumed that the collaboration is unlikely to write again. In *Fox and Geese* the fun is extracted from the schemings of match-making folk, and as much of the laughter is evoked by the dialogue as by the intricate complexities of the plot. Of its class, farce-comedy, it is a very good specimen, and it is as likely to evoke laughter in any other country as in Ireland. When the plays that pass as Irish outside Ireland are remembered it is somewhat surprising that such a laughter-maker as *Fox and Geese* should have escaped the attention of theatre managers in Britain and the United States.

In August 1914 the production of *A Minute's Wait* suggested that a new comic genius had been discovered in Martin J. McHugh, but again it was shown that he was only a single-play author. Two other short plays of his were afterwards staged, but neither of them was up to the standard of the first. That is not to suggest that the standard of *A Minute's Wait* is very high ; in fact it is not, there being nothing beyond the level of a music-hall sketch in its crude humour. But there is in it sarcastic comment on the methods of some Irish railway stations in the past which was thoroughly appreciated by the audience. It was this sarcasm, and not the match-making of the waiting peasants, that gave the little play its real humour for the Dublin audience, and probably the antics of the bewildered station-master would provide an audience anywhere with something more than ten minutes of wholesome laughter. No new play has come from Mr. McHugh since 1917, so it may be presumed that he has now done anything he is likely to do.

With the exception of those of Lady Gregory none of the one-act humorous plays of the Abbey Theatre has proven so popular in Ireland and abroad as those of Bernard Duffy. All three of his humorous plays were staged for the first time in 1916, and since that year *The Coiner* must be known as one of the most consistently revived plays in the whole range of Irish drama. In Ireland it is a stock play with amateurs, and its revival at the Abbey Theatre is always popular, while in England it has been played by the Arts League of Service travelling theatre for years, and it has several times been broadcast by the British Broadcasting Corporation. All Duffy's plays are simple stories simply told, and they depend for their humour upon the apparently guileless guile of the country folk, which is all carried in the dialogue and depends little upon plot or characterisation. In 1921 Duffy revealed himself as a dramatist of a wholly different kind when *The Piper of Tavran* was staged for the first and only time at the Abbey Theatre. In this play it is the music that makes the drama ; the dream being more real than the actual. Since 1921 no new play has come from Bernard Duffy, but he has published a charming novel and some short stories, so his writing career is not by any means ended and he may return to the theatre at any time.

The most recent accession to the ranks of writers of one-act farces is M. M. Brennan, two of whose plays were staged in 1922 and revived occasionally since that date. It is probable that Miss Brennan will continue to write these little farces, and it is even possible that she may do something much better than the crudely childish humour of *The Young Man from Rathmines*, which only a theatre at its wit's end for humour would ever have staged.

On the whole it must be said that when Irish plays are bad

they are very bad indeed, and the majority of Irish farces are bad. The only thing that can be said for them is that since Irish people, as others, must have farce it is better that their farces should be written by Irish people who may in time turn their attention and experience to other forms of drama.

CHAPTER XIII

MANAGERS, ACTORS AND PRODUCERS

The Amateur Company—The First Salaried Manager—A Manager from
England—The Ascendancy of the Brothers Fay—A Succession of
New Managers—Mr. Nugent Monck Introduces the Morality Play
—St. John Ervine as Manager—The Long Dominion of Mr. Lennox
Robinson—A Great Company of Actors—And Some Great
Actresses—The Group Breaks—The Supremacy of Arthur Sinclair
—The Failure in Staging—And an Improvement.

THE early venturings of the individuals who have founded
the most significant theatrical organisations of the past half-
century were mainly inspired by ideals, tempered by ignor-
ance, and maintained by enthusiasm. None of the founders
of the theatres which gave new life to dramatic art in Europe
or America had any professional or financial interest in
theatres : what they had was a great faith in the drama, a
belief in freedom, or an ideal of nationality. The renas-
cence of the drama in Europe was effected without any aid
from the theatre magnates or the leading actors ; indeed,
generally both of these treated the new movements with
active opposition or good-humoured contempt. Not theatre
managers, not dramatists, not actors, but idealists from
amongst the ranks of ordinary playgoers brought about the
great changes. In Paris an actor initiated the movement, but
an obscure actor whose fame is now securely based upon
something other than his acting ; in London a small clerk
founded the Independent Theatre ; in Berlin a group of
rebels ; in Moscow a few dreamers ; in Bergen a chemist's
assistant named Ibsen ; and throughout the United States
the great drama that is now emerging is largely due to the care
and enthusiasm of amateurs. It was so in Ireland also in the

beginning : first the ideal was art, and only art, but slowly there emerged the nationalist ideal which was no less than the creation of a new national drama in Ireland. Such ideals, artistic or national, could not have been found amongst those who controlled the theatre in Ireland towards the end of the last century : they were quite content to draw their companies and their plays from London, and to mark success or failure in financial terms. But as the ripple that had started in Bergen spread gradually outwards it touched London, and from London it spread to Dublin. Primarily it was Irish authors that seemed to have been affected, but later it was discovered that a few frequenters of the cheaper parts of the Dublin theatres were to be more influential in making the movement a living force in the national life.

The early ventures of the Irish Literary Theatre were only possible with the assistance of actors from London, as so far as was then known there were no actors available for such productions in Dublin. It is true that amateur acting has always flourished in Dublin, but the founders of the Irish Literary Theatre were not so familiar with some aspects of Dublin life as, perhaps, they might have been. London Literary Society was more familiar to them than the life of middle-class or working-class Dublin; and it was within these classes in Dublin that amateur dramatic production had flourished. So Mr. Yeats was aware that Miss Florence Farr spoke verse very beautifully in London, but he was not aware that Mr. Frank Fay spoke it no less beautifully in Dublin. It was from the little amateur National Dramatic Company of the Brothers Frank and William Fay, and not from the Irish Literary Theatre, that the real strength of the Irish theatre was derived. In the temperance hall attached to the Carmelite Church in Clarendon Street, Dublin, they had done some dramatic work, and it may be of interest to note that this hall is still used regularly throughout each winter for the production of plays by amateur companies. From Clarendon Street the group migrated to a small hall in Camden Street, not far away, and it was there that the company assumed a

definite existence as the Irish National Dramatic Society with
W. B. Yeats as President and George Russell (' A.E.') as
vice-president. Lady Gregory had sent a cheque to the
Society and in acknowledging it ' A.E.' wrote, " I will hand
the cheque to Fay. I know it will be a great assistance to them
as the little hall will require alterations and fittings and as
none of the company is in possession of more then artisan's
wages " (*Our Irish Theatre*, p. 31). All the work necessary to
make the little hall suitable for theatrical purposes was done
by the members of the company, without payment and
without hope of reward of any kind. An interesting picture
of the conditions under which the Irish theatre came into
being is presented in a letter from Mr. Frank Fay to Lady
Gregory in 1902 : "I received your kind note, also enclosures,
for which we are very much obliged. We are indeed getting
into very flourishing conditions, and if things only continue
in the present state, I have no doubt we shall be able to show
a fairly good balance at the end of the year. . . . About the
performance and how it worked out. I spent twenty-five
shillings on printing, etc., and we took altogether about four
pounds fifteen shillings, so I see no reason to complain
financially. But I find the stage very small, and the want of
dressing-rooms makes it very difficult to manage about the
scenery, as all our actors have to stand against the walls while
it is being changed. I think, however, we can struggle
through if we don't attempt very large pieces. The hall was
very cold, but I think I can manage a stove and get over that "
(*Our Irish Theatre*, p. 32). Under such conditions it would
not have been surprising if the members of the company lost
heart and gave up the work in despair. That they persevered
against such odds proves that love for acting and the drama
which was to be afterwards recognised throughout the world.
" They did ", said Mr. Yeats later, " what amateurs seldom
do, worked desperately ". It was from such conditions that
the company went to play in London for the first time in May
1903. The company left Dublin on Friday night, reached
London on Saturday morning, played at a matinee and again

in the evening at the Queen's Gate Hall a series of five one-act plays, and its members were back again at their work in Dublin on Monday morning.

With the opening of the Abbey Theatre in 1904 the conditions under which the company had to work were revolutionised. The generous interest of Miss Horniman provided the company with a fully equipped theatre, so that no more need the cold hall without adequate dressing-rooms be used. With the opening of the Abbey Theatre, too, the amateur status of the company was abandoned, and several of its members received salaries while still retaining their business occupations during the day. Thus Mr. William Fay was appointed, on a salary that would release him from other work, as manager, producer, and leading actor, in 1903, and he continued to fulfil all these functions for several years. Then for a time the management was entrusted to Mr. Alfred Waring, an English actor of conspicuous ability who has for many years now conducted a Repertory Theatre in Leeds with great artistic and financial success. Some of the Directors of the Abbey Theatre were not in favour of the appointment of an Englishman to the position: " I felt ", says Lady Gregory, " as if I should be spoken of some day as one who had betrayed her country's trust" (*Our Irish Theatre*, p. 92). But her letter of protest did not reach Mr. Yeats in London in time to prevent the appointment. " I think ", Mr. Yeats wrote, " we should take Vedrenne's recommendation unless we have some strong reason to the contrary. If the man is not Irish we cannot help it. If the choice is between filling our country's stomach or enlarging its brains by importing precise knowledge, I am for scorning its stomach for the present ". Synge was enraged by some of the first productions of the new regime, and wrote vehemently against " many of the worst tricks of the English stage ". " That is the end of all the *Samhain* principles and this new tradition that we were to lay down ". The principles enunciated by Mr. Yeats in *Samhain* were being departed from in any case without the intervention of any English influence, and they were soon to be eliminated altogether by the departure of the brothers Fay from the theatre. The reign of this particular English manager was not long, but the influence of the school of acting with which Mr. Granville Barker's name must be for ever associated was to become very marked in the Irish theatre as the years passed.

For a few years Mr. Conal O'Riordan, under the pseudonym of Norreys Connell, undertook the management of the Theatre, and during his tenure of that office he produced three of his own plays which were his only contributions to the Abbey Theatre's repertory. Then came Mr. Nugent Monck to take control of the School of Acting and the second company which was to occupy the Theatre during the absence of the leading company in the United States. It was Mr. Nugent Monck who produced at the Theatre the series of Mystery Plays, *The Interlude of Youth*, *The Second Shepherd's Play*, *The Annunciation*, *The Flight into Egypt*, and *The Worlde and the Chylde*, which is so conspicuous a feature of the season 1911-12. This series was received with popular favour at the time and it is remarkable that Mr. Monck's experimental season has never been repeated. It was under the management of Mr. Monck also that the plays of two remarkable Ulster dramatists were staged at the Abbey Theatre : *Red Turf* by Rutherford Mayne and *Judgment* by Joseph Campbell. The plays of Rutherford Mayne have been the outstanding feature of the Ulster Literary Theatre, which attempted to do in Belfast what the Abbey Theatre had done in Dublin, but *Red Turf* is his only contribution to the repertory of the Abbey Theatre. Joseph Campbell is best known as a lyric poet, and *Judgment* is his only contribution to the Irish drama. For some years Joseph Campbell has resided in America, but even during his residence in Ireland he wrote no more plays : it is possible that the peculiar quality of Mr. Nugent Monck's acting led Joseph Campbell to submit even this single play to the test of stage production, as it was somewhat akin to the morality plays which were then being staged. *Judgment* has never been revived, and consequently there was only that single production by the School of Acting in 1912. The acting of Mr. Nugent Monck's pupils presented no marked departure from that of the brothers Fay, but it has left no permanent mark upon the Theatre. By his work at the Maddermarket Theatre at Norwich Mr. Monck is likely to influence the English Theatre more than he influenced the Irish Theatre during his short stay in Dublin.

More deep and apparently permanent, because more prolonged and more definite, has been the influence of Mr. Lennox Robinson as manager and producer. In 1909 he was appointed to the joint position after a two months' course of training at the Duke of York's Theatre in London. " I watched Mr. Bernard Shaw produce *Misalliance*, and Mr. Granville Barker produce *Justice*, *The Madras House* and *The Sentimentalists*, and Mr. Dion Boucicault produce *The Twelve Pound Look*", he wrote later in a brief autobiographical sketch (*T.P.'s and Cassell's Weekly*, 6th February, 1926). Such a course of training, under such instructors, was not such as might have been expected if the 'principles of *Samhain*' were to be continued in practice at the Abbey Theatre. The objection of some of the Directors to the appointment of an Englishman as manager might be equally valid if urged against a manager trained in the naturalistic school of Shaw and Granville Barker. But Synge was dead, the brothers Fay had departed, and the time was opportune for a new orientation in the Irish dramatic movement. That new orientation was, frankly, a move in the direction of naturalism and away from the poetic drama ; and it is in this direction that the Abbey Theatre, with short interruptions, has gone under Mr. Robinson's guidance for nearly twenty years. That the change was justified at the time is certain, but the fact cannot be overlooked that it marked the end of the Irish Theatre as it had been conceived by Mr. Yeats and Lady Gregory, and of the principles which Mr. Yeats had expounded in opposition to those of Edward Martyn. The Irish Theatre would now and in the future approximate more and more to the English Repertory model, with the sole difference that the scene of its plays would be laid in Ireland and that the characters portrayed would be mainly peasants.

During the war years the Abbey Theatre was under the control of four different managers, each of whom occupied the position for about a year. In the season 1914-15 Mr. A. Patrick Wilson had control, and the only outstanding features were the production of his own play, *The Slough*, and *The Dreamers* by Lennox Robinson. On the departure of Mr. Wilson the management was assumed by Mr. St. John G. Ervine, already a dramatist of some distinction in the Theatre and favourably known to its audience. In the course of a lecture to the members of the Dublin Literary Society shortly after his appointment Mr. Ervine announced his intention to make some radical departures from the accepted tradition of the Theatre. Despite changes in acting the Theatre had remained quite definitely Irish in the themes of its plays and in the atmosphere which enveloped it, but Mr. Ervine promised to break this tradition by producing such definitely English drama as Fletcher's *Knight of the Burning Pestle* and Milton's *Samson Agonistes*. The quality of the plays that were being submitted to the Theatre was, Mr. Ervine said, very poor, and it was necessary that young dramatists should have the best models to work from. It is now plain that even at that time Mr. Ervine held the opinions which he has since expressed elsewhere that the Irish drama had ceased to be a living thing, and that the Abbey Theatre should be but one in a chain of Repertory Theatres in the British Isles (*The Organised Theatre*). Of course the real trouble was that Mr. Ervine had become quite definitely English, and that he was enamoured with his own scheme for the organisation of Repertory, without any sympathy whatever with the ideals of either the controllers or the audiences of the Abbey Theatre. But the promise of Mr. Ervine was never fulfilled, and the production of his own *John Ferguson* was the outstanding event in his short tenure of the office. When he departed the company over which he had control departed also, and its leading members have never since returned. So the new manager, Mr. J. Augustus Keogh, an actor of some distinction in England and America, had to gather a new company and to overcome the distraction of the very unsettled state of Dublin during 1916. The new management proceeded to give what was practically a repertory of Shaw plays to the apparent satisfaction of large audiences. From 1917 to 1919 the management was entrusted to Mr. Fred O'Donovan, one of the most distinguished members of the company which had departed a year earlier, and it was under his management that Mr. Robinson's popular comedy, *The Whiteheaded Boy*, was first staged. For a little while Miss Sara Allgood took control, and then Mr. Lennox Robinson returned with the title of Manager and Producer from 1919 to 1923, and later as a Director and Producer. Since 1923 the actual managership has been held by Mr. Michael J. Dolan, a leading actor of the Theatre who is also Principal of the School of Acting opened in 1927. The duties of the Producer are now separated from those of management, producing being under the control of Mr. Lennox Robinson assisted by Mr. Arthur Shields, who is also a prominent actor.

It was, perhaps, primarily the plays of Synge that brought the Irish Theatre to the notice of the world, but without the magnificent acting which those plays received it is possible that they would have escaped recognition until a much later date. It was certainly the acting that attracted most notice when the company visited London for the first time in 1903. The acting of that company did not seem to be acting at all ; it was just living, and the audience was free to participate. Realism in acting could go no further : voice, looks, gesture, movement, were all controlled as by perfect mechanism, and were all subordinated to the total effect that was sought. The individual members of the company, too, were subordinated to the team, and there were no stars, no playing for prominence. It was because of this training that Mr. C. E. Montague could write with such approval of the company. " The Irish actors from the Abbey Theatre ", he said, " have found means to come at (an) effect of spiritual austerity. More than others they leave undone the things that ought not to be done. None of them rants or flares, trumpets or booms, or frisks about when he had better be quiet, or puts on intense looks for nothing. They seem all alike to have seized on the truth that the way to do big things in an art, as it is to get into other parts of the Kingdom of Heaven, is to become as a little child, so long as you do it without thinking all the time what an engaging child you are. Without infantinism, they contrive to reach back past most of the futilities, the inexpressive apparatus of expressions, that overgrow and clog the stage ; they take a fresh, clear hold on their craft in its elements. They know how to let well alone ; they stand still when others would ' cross stage to right ' to no purpose ; when one of them has to be thrown up in high relief, the rest can fade into the background like mists at a dawn, or emit from their eyes an attention that fixes your eyes on the central figure more surely than the fiercest limelight that ever beat on an actor-manager. So each part is played in a sense by them all. One day Miss Allgood, the company's best tragedienne, is out of the cast ; her part is played by another. You find, to your wonder, how little it matters, and how much of what seemed the actress's poignancy lay in the way the rest looked at her, from simple, held-in attitudes of wonder and apprehension. The substitute, looked at in that way, seemed almost as tragic. The actors give you the force of one character through its impression on others, as Homer expressed Helen's beauty through its effect on the aged men, and as Thackeray tells you what everyone did when Beatrix entered a playhouse. In a world of things overdone, like the stage, mere quietude has the value of epigram, like a thing soberly said in a newspaper. Throughout one half of Lady Gregory's *Rising of the Moon* there is scarcely a movement : merely that no one should strut or fret tickles you. Miss Maire O'Neill as Nora, in *The Shadow of the Glen*, stands almost stock still through a scene where most English actresses would pace the stage like lionesses in a zoo. The result is that when she does move you can see the passion propel her like a screw. In Mr. Yeats' *Kathleen ni Houlihan* the average stage-manager would have thought everything under-acted ; he would have made the whole cast sweat and squirm up to the climax in a geometrical progression of muscular agonies, lest the emotion should not cross the footlights. The Irishmen keep still and white, and tragic consequence enfolds them ; set on that ground of grave and simple exposure, the slightest gesture carries you far in divination of what prompts it ; whole scenes put on a comely vesture of delicacy and containment and a haunting expressiveness, as, in the painting of some masters, every tree, you know not how, has its hamadryad " (*Dramatic Values*, pp. 51-53). No words could convey more accurately, or more adequately, the effects which the Irish company could convey in the early years of its enthusiastic ardour. Later there came a time when that team-spirit gave place to an individualism that shrieked for the spotlight of the most vain of actor-managers. But at its best the acting at the Abbey Theatre has been surpassed by no theatre of its time, and it has been equalled only, perhaps, by the acting at the Art Theatre of Moscow under Stanislavsky. The stage grouping by which attention is concentrated upon a particular actor was not, of course, an Irish discovery, nor was it exclusive to the Irish company : it was simply the tradition of the French stage which Frank Fay had absorbed and brought with him to the Irish stage.

So long as the brothers Fay led and inspired the company the group system and the French tradition dominated it, but when they left in 1908 there came a gradual reversion to the English ' star ' system by which a single actor dominated the stage. Frank Fay was primarily an elocutionist, and it was his power to give full effect to the speaking of verse which first attracted the attention of W. B. Yeats. The strength of W. G. Fay was in the creation of comedic characters. Thus Frank Fay created all the parts in the plays of W. B. Yeats

which were staged in his time, and W. G. Fay created the
principal characters in Synge's comedies. In Miss Sara
Allgood, Miss Maire O'Neill, and Miss Maire NicShuibhlaigh, were three actresses of incomparable power and
versatility : Miss Allgood· and Miss NicShuibhlaigh were
both at their best in tragedy, while Miss Maire O'Neill, who
is a sister of Miss Allgood, shone in the lighter roles. Both
Miss Allgood and Miss O'Neill were, however, equal to
playing any rôle that might be allotted to them, but Miss
NicShuibhlaigh was much more circumscribed in her powers.
When the brothers Fay left the Theatre their places were
taken by Messrs. Arthur Sinclair, J. M. Kerrigan, Fred
O'Donovan, J. A. O'Rourke, and Sydney Morgan. For
a time the group-spirit was maintained, but slowly Mr.
Sinclair secured a dominating position, while at the same time
discovering that his staccato utterance and facial manipulation
could be relied upon to make audiences laugh. He became
a great comedian, and for a time there was nothing but
comedy on the stage of the Theatre. Even the most tragic
play in the repertory of the Theatre he could make the
vehicle of laughter, and if sometimes the laughter was un-
seemly and misplaced the audience was at least as much to
blame as the actor. Arthur Sinclair was a member of the
company from the opening of the Theatre until 1916, and
during that period of nearly twelve years he played in almost
every male part from the smallest to the greatest, and no part
ever seemed to present any difficulty to him. He could give
distinction to the post-office messenger boy, Fardy Farrell,
in *Spreading the News*, as easily as to the Wise Man in *The
Hour Glass ;* and he could impersonate Scapin in Lady
Gregory's translation of Molière's *Rogueries of Scapin* as
easily as King James in *The White Cockade*. If Arthur
Sinclair is now best known as a brilliant comedian it is
because he prefers to be known in that rôle, but that he could
be a great tragedian also is known to all who have been
familiar with his work at the Abbey Theatre ; it will suffice to
mention such typical rôles as his Leum Donoghue in Fitz-

maurice's *The Pie-dish*, his Conchubar in Synge's *Deirdre*, his Shane Morrissey in Murray's *Birthright* or his John Rainey in Ervine's *Mixed Marriage*, to suggest his versatility, but only those who have actually witnessed a performance of these plays can judge of his greatness. Despite all this, however, it must be said that to Arthur Sinclair more than to any other member of the company must be ascribed the decline of the group-spirit which had been the marked feature of the earlier years : he knew he could play with his audience, and he did. That is the measure of his greatness as an actor, but it was for a time disastrous to a Theatre which had a policy differing from that of an actor-manager. To watch J. M. Kerrigan or Fred O'Donovan on the stage was at all times a delight. To see Kerrigan pass from the Ballad Singer in *The Rising of the Moon* to Michael Gillane in *Kathleen ni Houlihan*, and then to Stephen J. O'Reilly in *The Mineral Workers* or Captain Bluntschli in *Arms and the Man*, and Fred O'Donovan as Maurice in *Maurice Harte*, as Black Mike in *The Piper*, Andy O'Hea in *The Shuiler's Child*, or John Tanner in *Man and Superman*, were experiences that are unlikely to be forgotten. Both Kerrigan and O'Donovan are great actors, each great in a different way, conscientious artists whose voices are instruments upon which they can play with finished virtuosity. Only a little below these three are Sydney Morgan and J. A. O'Rourke, more limited in their range but within that range each of them is at least the equal of any actor on the contemporary stage. It was, perhaps, in Synge's plays that J. A. O'Rourke was seen to best advantage, as Michael Dara in *The Shadow of the Glen* or The Wandering Friar in *The Well of the Saints*, as it was in Murray's plays that Morgan was at his best, as Bat Morrissey in *Birthright* or Father Mangan in *Maurice Harte*. Of the leading actresses it is more difficult to speak, as the Abbey Theatre has always had at its service a more than generous supply of feminine greatness on its stage. In the more spectacularly tragic rôles Miss Sara Allgood has no peer, as her Kathleen in *Kathleen ni Houlihan*, her Deirdre in the Yeats play with that title, her Mary Cahel

in *The Gaol Gate*, and her Juno in *Juno and the 'Paycock'*
may be cited to prove. She is an actress of the first class,
capable of standing comparison with the greatest of her time,
who could pass from grave to gay as the exigencies of repertory demanded. That her great talent is not more widely
recognised must be due to the fact that she has restricted its
use almost entirely to Irish plays, and that she has not tested
it in the tragic rôles which are universally recognised by the
critics. With a voice of charming flexibility and a presence
that dominates the stage the greatest female rôles are within
her power, but how she ever consented to attempt the
futilities of English musical comedy is something that passes
understanding. She merely wastes her powers in such plays
as *The Girl Friend* or *Peg o' my Heart* when she might be
challenging the judgment of the world in *Magda* or *Phèdre*.
Sometime, perhaps, a manager of insight will provide her
with an opportunity to show her powers as C. E. Montague
saw them and recognised them many years ago ; but until
that time arrives she may continue to waste her gifts upon
futilities, if she does not return to the Abbey Theatre. In
Miss Maire O'Neill there is acting genius of a gayer and
lighter kind, which could pass from Deirdre in Synge's play
to Mirandolina in Goldoni's comedy and thence to Nora in
The Shadow of the Glen or Honor O'Donohoe in *The Work-
House Ward*. In the lighter tragic rôles she cannot be
surpassed, and she can turn to comedy with a facility that
amounts to genius. Miss Maire NicShuibhlaigh was at her
best in grim tragedy, and her greatest achievement was
undoubtedly Moll Woods in Seumas O'Kelly's *The Shuiler's
Child*, and when she abandoned the stage a really great tragic
actress was lost. In a number of the plays of the Irish
Theatre there is a kindly, pleasant, humorous, but firm,
mother, and in the portrayal of these generally middle-aged
women Miss Eileen O'Doherty was supreme. Typical of all
these women is Maura Morrissey in *Birthright*, and to the
creation of that much-worried woman Miss O'Doherty
brought a charming sympathy that will be difficult to surpass.

Of the many other actresses of great promise, and sometimes of great achievement, who have passed from the Abbey Theatre nothing need now be said except to mention that Miss Eithne Magee brought much charm and distinction to the poetic plays, and that once Miss Cathleen Nesbitt made a very poor play seem almost great. All these actors and actresses, with many others besides, have gone from the Abbey Theatre and are now playing in other countries or have retired from the stage altogether. The United States has many of them, the London stage has a greater number : some of them have added to their reputations since they left Ireland, others have failed when they left the Abbey Theatre. But of all of them it can be said that so long as they played as a company in the atmosphere and under the influence of the Abbey Theatre they constituted a group of players that any country in the world would have been proud to own. That the Irish drama is much indebted to them goes without saying, but that the stage of the world is also indebted to them must be acknowledged.

The plays and the acting have received from the Directors and the Management at all times the attention undoubtedly deserved, and both have received from audiences and critics the praise they generally merited. But there is one feature of the Theatre which has received little, if any, attention, even from the Directors. That feature is staging and stage effects. Much has been written and spoken by Mr. Yeats and others connected with the Abbey Theatre on this feature of its work, but beyond some experiments in the speaking of verse, and some very drab scenes designed by Mr. Gordon Craig, little has yet been done to improve the art of stage presentation. To the art of the theatre, as distinct from the arts of play-writing and acting, the contribution of the Abbey Theatre has been very insignificant indeed when compared with such theatres as the Art Theatre in Moscow, the Free Theatre in Berlin, or even the Lyric Theatre at Hammersmith, London. Poverty, perhaps, was the reason for this ; but when the wonderful effects achieved at, say, the Lyric Theatre at

Hammersmith are borne in mind, achieved as they were by artistic instinct rather than by lavish expenditure of money, the failure of the Abbey Theatre in this department of theatrical effort is most marked. It is true to say that the Art Theatre in Moscow, or the Lyric Theatre in Hammersmith, has done more for the art of stage production in one year than the Abbey Theatre has done throughout its entire career of nearly twenty-five years. The absence of a ' man of the theatre ' from the Abbey Theatre is very easy to detect, and even now three of its Directors are dramatists, and the fourth is a Professor of Languages added some little time ago when the Theatre received a subsidy from the Government of the Irish Free State. Throughout its career the Theatre has been under the direction and control of dramatists, and never has it had at its command the services of men such as Sir Barry Jackson or Mr. Nigel Playfair, to say nothing of such giants as Professor Reinhardt in Germany or Stanislavsky in Russia, to supervise the production and staging of its plays. So the staging had generally lacked distinction, and it has often had the appearance of mere casualness. What the genius of Lovat Fraser gave to the Lyric Theatre at Hammersmith has been missing from the Abbey Theatre, although it is probable that there was in the Art School of Dublin people who might have shown at least a talent for theatrical production had the opportunity been given to them to practise and display it. So it was that except for occasional designs and scenes by Robert Gregory the stage effects at the Abbey Theatre were never very impressive or striking, even if they were always adequate.

It is true, of course, that the peasant play did not give much scope for the impressive or the striking in the manner of its staging. In those countries where the peasantry still retains its national costume, where there is still some colour left in dress, the opportunities of the theatrical producer are very much greater than they are in Ireland. The dress of the modern Irish peasant is as dull and as drab as dress can be ; it is without distinction of any kind, except it be the distinc-

tion of tattered untidyness. The predilection in colour of the
Irish peasant farmer seems to be always for a dirty grey,
varied on some occasions of respectability by a funereal black.
On the western seaboard, and on the islands, where spinning
and weaving are still industries of the fireside, there are
splashes of colour in the local dress, particularly in the dress
of the women. There vivid red and deep blue may occasionally be glimpsed, but throughout the greater part of rural
Ireland the monotony of dress is depressing. Realism
demands that when these peasants are represented on the
stage they should be dressed as they are in ordinary life, and
so the stage of the Abbey Theatre is filled with the dim
interior of a small cottage, drab and dirty looking, with a few
pieces of primitive furniture such as a dresser, a table, chairs
and a settle by the fireside. Maybe there is a German
oleograph representing some religious subject on the wall,
and in that alone will there be colour. In Synge's plays there
was a possibility of introducing vivid colours, and *The
Playboy of the Western World* might be all the better in
representation if it were staged with some of the fantastic
colours of the western coast, but even in these plays the
possibilities were not availed of. But taken generally the
ordinary costume of the Irish peasant does not lend itself
readily to colour schemes any more than his domestic surroundings. Much might have been done by lighting had the
Theatre been equipped with some of the newer stage lighting
systems, and it is there that poverty has probably been a
handicap.

The scenery and ' sets ' are usually adequate, if never very
striking. The stage is small, and that, too, is a handicap to
the producer who would try to emulate the art of Stanislavsky in Dublin. There were occasions when the producer
had opportunities for display, in plays like Dunsany's *King
Argimenes*, the folk-history plays of Lady Gregory or the
poetic plays of W. B. Yeats, but rarely were these opportunities availed of to the full. Sometimes there was excellent
colour and bad grouping ; sometimes the grouping and

colouring were both spoiled by the lighting ; never was there staging which competed with either the words or the acting for the attention of the audience. In theatres elsewhere critics will discuss during an *entr'acte* the ' production ' as well as the play and the acting, but the groups assembled in the vestibule of the Abbey Theatre will not be heard to mention the staging. The fact is that the audience has become accustomed to drab staging, to the realistic portrayal of the peasant, and that it is shocked when Mr. Lennox Robinson tries on occasions to bring colour to his assistance. For a short time cubes designed by Mr. Gordon Craig replaced the painted scene, but these pinky-yellow slabs only made the dinginess more pronounced. There was only one play to which they seemed suited, *The Hour Glass* by W. B. Yeats, and to that play they gave a perfect setting. If the colouring of these cubes could have been varied to suit the atmosphere of different plays they might have solved the problem of thriftiness in staging which was forced upon the Directors of the Theatre, while at the same time giving a variety to the *mise-en-scène* which was usually lacking.

Since the Theatre has been in receipt of an annual subsidy from the Government of the Irish Free State there has been a considerable improvement in production and staging. A new lighting system has been installed, and there is a greater tendency to avail of the artistic talent which the Theatre has in the city, particularly in the Dublin Metropolitan School of Art. The activities of the Dublin Drama League have given these artists the opportunity to demonstrate their gifts in the theatre, and now that the little Peacock Theatre is available such demonstrations will probably be more systematic and more regular. For several years past Mr Lennox Robinson has been the appointed Producer at the Theatre, and during that time an improvement has been noticeable in the staging, but the productions which have invariably attracted most attention have been those of Mr. Arthur Shields, one of the actors who is also Assistant-Producer. It may be said that while the productions of Mr. Lennox

Robinson are striking they do not impress, but those of Mr. Shields are impressive without being striking. It is meticulous detail that seems to interest Mr. Robinson, and it is the total effect that seems to interest Mr. Shields. In Mr. Shields the Abbey Theatre seems at last to have discovered a producer who is something more than merely a stage-manager. His productions have shown him to have a sense of colour, an eye for grouping, a knowledge of the value of lighting, and sufficient attentiveness to detail not to distort the general effect he desires to give. He has shown that he knows what effect to seek, and the means by which he can secure it ; and these are, when all has been said and done, the great requirements in a producer. There has been some improvement in this important department, and it is to be hoped that Mr. Shields will be given all the scope and assistance he requires to develop the talent he has demonstrated that he possesses. If he be given that scope and assistance he may yet show that he is the ' man of the theatre ' that the Abbey requires and the staging may reach the level of the plays and the acting.

CHAPTER XIV

PLAYS AND PLAYERS OF TO-DAY

The Tendency to Depreciate the Plays and Players who Remain—The
Drain upon the Acting Resources of a Small Country—Some of the
Dramatists who Remain in Ireland—The Plays which are Popular in
the Abbey Theatre now—New Plays by Older Dramatists—And
Some New Dramatists of Promise—The Actors of To-day—Compared with the Actors of the Past—A Company that is Unexcelled in
any Repertory Theatre.

SOMETIMES it seems that only the most extreme opinions can
be entertained about Ireland, or about anything Irish ; at the
very mention of the word Ireland passions are unleashed,
tongues become spiteful, and even the mildest of ink becomes
envenomed. Thus there are those on the one side who will
contend that Yeats is the greatest poetic genius that the
theatre in the English-speaking countries has known for
generations, and that Synge is the greatest dramatist since
Ibsen, and there are others who say that ' where there is
nothing, there is W. B. Yeats ', with Miss Storm Jameson,
or with St. John Ervine that Synge has been very much over-
rated as a dramatist. The interesting thing about these
extreme opinions is that they are invariably expressed by
Irish people, and that they are not really the expression of
artistic depreciation so much as the overflow of political or
social disillusionment. For the true appreciation of Yeats as
a dramatist it is necessary that there should be some sympathy
with, or at least no active hostility to, his vaguely mystical
nationalism : and Synge requires more than an admiration
for the virtues of the *petit bourgeois* if his plays are to be
appreciated. But, perhaps, just as it lies with the younger
English novelists to decry Thackeray or sneer at Dickens, it

is now for the first time the privilege of Irish writers to attempt the belittlement of the greatest literary artists that their country has yet produced.   Thus George Moore can say in his own irresponsible way that the Irish drama began in Yeats and returns to Yeats, or St. John Ervine can say that the Irish drama has petered out.   That neither opinion is in the least degree accurate does not seem to matter, because the object of the depreciation is not the Irish drama at all, but something in or about the country itself which the critics have come to dislike and that dislike is expressed in terms of depreciation of particular persons or works.   One either loves Ireland with an ardour that is consuming, or one hates it with a hatred that distorts judgment and reduces criticism to an aspect of spite or personal spleen.   In Ireland, as in every country, will be found the Seven Deadly Sins as well as the Seven Gifts of the Holy Ghost, but there are too many Irish critics who are unable to find anything but the Sins.   The critics of other countries are more kindly, because their criticism is based upon aesthetic considerations only, and because they have no spite against the country nor any personal animosities to prejudice their judgments and embitter their words.

Since 1916, when Mr. St. John Ervine announced to his audience at the Dublin Literary Society that the supply of plays by Irish authors has almost ceased, well over one hundred original plays by Irish authors have been staged at the Abbey Theatre, and probably a greater number by other theatrical organisations throughout Ireland.   Seven years later the statement was repeated in more emphatic form in a publication which summarised the war and its effects upon the countries involved, yet since 1923 over forty new plays by Irish authors have been produced on the stage of the Abbey Theatre.   No attempt will be made to suggest that all these plays are works of genius or, indeed, even that they are works of importance, but when the quantity of very poor, and even pernicious, drama which finds its way to the stages of London theatres is borne in mind the Irish drama will be seen to be in a soundly healthy, if not in a brilliantly prolific, condition.

It is not to be expected that a Yeats, a Synge, or a Lady
Gregory, can be produced by a little country like Ireland
every month, or even every year. The population of the
entire country is only about four millions, less than half the
population of Greater London and only about two-thirds
that of New York, and the population that remains is the
residuum of the population of twice that size in the middle of
last century. No country can have its population reduced to
half its size by the emigration of its best elements without
showing some evil effects of the drain : what is remarkable
is that Ireland has been able to maintain its place in the
artistic world at all. England on one side and the United
States on the other offer inducements to the best Irish talent
against which Ireland itself is powerless. So a Shaw, a
George Moore, a Conal O'Riordan, a Lord Dunsany, and
many others will go to live in England ; and a Padraic Colum,
a Seumas O'Brien, a Joseph Campbell, amongst a horde will
go to America ; and in either country they are lost to Ireland
or to the enrichment of Irish art and Irish culture. It is the
opinion of many of the most competent critics that Ireland
has given to the world the three men whose works are the
most noteworthy in the English language to-day. The pre-
eminence of George Bernard Shaw amongst dramatists is
undoubted ; the leadership of George Moore in prose fiction
is acknowledged by all who care for style in writing ; and the
pre-eminence of W. B. Yeats as a lyric poet is unchallenged.
So that Ireland's contribution to literature and drama in the
generation that is now passing cannot fail to excite admiration.
Eugene O'Neill in America is at least as much Irish as he is
American, and it is Eugene O'Neill who has made America's
first great contribution to the drama of the world. It is
possible that all of these would have achieved a world-
reputation had they remained in Ireland, but it is certain that
they would not have received the pecuniary rewards which
the excellence of their work most certainly justifies. Ireland
is too small, and the standard of popular culture too low, to
provide the kind of appreciation that such artists demand,

and consequently it is probable that the most original Irish artists must seek abroad the applause of their peers, and the financial rewards which even excellence sometimes secures. When the education of the Irish people has been improved, and, more important, when Irish people have learned that freedom in thought and expression is at least as important as the superficial freedom of formal politics, there will be some hope that the genius of a Shaw, or a George Moore, can be retained in its native air. At present, and in the past, that native air would have stifled the first manifestations of genius, by regarding it as evil and suppressing it as immoral.

No country could withstand indefinitely the drain upon its best brains that Ireland has had to contend against for the past hundred years, and at the same time continue to produce at home work of the same quality that the best in other countries could produce. That a Shaw could be exported and a Synge produced at home in the same period is surely a great accomplishment ; that a Moore could be exported and yet have a large number of excellent novelists such as Brinsley MacNamara, Liam O'Flaherty, Daniel Corkery, and others, at home is, too, a great achievement for such a small country. Only the Irish poets have stayed at home : Yeats, Russell, O'Sullivan, to mention but three of the best, have not ventured far for many years ; but Colum, Campbell, and Austin Clarke seem to have gone for ever. Perhaps it is that the demand for Irish poets abroad is less than the demand for Irish poetry, and that, at least, is a good thing for Ireland. Irish critics leave Ireland readily, and so Ernest Boyd goes to America, and Robert Lynd goes to England to be joined later by Ireland's most fastidious essayist in John Eglinton. That Ireland has influenced the thoughts and aspirations of the English-speaking world through these men is not to be wondered at : what may be wondered at is that Ireland still retained at home some others who could affect world-thought from that little island on the edge of Europe. Belfast can send away St. John Ervine and C. K. Munro to England to enrich the poverty of the contemporary English drama, and still retain the genius of Forrest Reid. So if the Irish drama had a period of decline, and it certainly had during the past ten years, the reason for that decline is not far to seek. Synge had died in 1909, and Seumas O'Kelly a few years later ; many of the dramatists and potential dramatists lost their lives in 1916 ; many others emigrated to England or America to find the appreciation and reward that was denied them at home ; Lady Gregory and W. B. Yeats were growing old and losing the zest which they had once brought to the Irish Theatre. And then there was the aftermath of the Great War, and the disillusioning of Irish people generally in the years following 1921. The great ideals faded gradually, and little was remembered but the deeds of violence by which it was sought to realize these ideals in an imperfect world.

So the little farces and the crude melodramas had their day, but there still remained dramatists like Lennox Robinson, T. C. Murray, Daniel Corkery, George Fitzmaurice, Brinsley MacNamara and a few others amongst the younger men, while W. B. Yeats and Lady Gregory might still be looked to for good work at longer intervals. Then in 1923 came a new dramatist whose plays are now the most prominent feature in the repertory of the Theatre. Few had hoped for a new dramatist at that time, it was generally thought that some little time must elapse before another dramatist would be discovered who would contest the supremacy of those whose work was already well known. *The Shadow of a Gunman* was a very welcome surprise, and few could withhold from Sean O'Casey the praise that his work deserved. His three longer plays, *The Shadow of a Gunman*, *Juno and the 'Paycock'*, and *The Plough and the Stars*, are now easily the most popular plays which the Abbey Theatre can stage. At a performance of any one of these plays the Theatre will be filled to the fullest extent of its 650 seats, and hundreds will be turned away from the doors to try their luck another time : seats that can be booked will be all taken days before the performances, and at the cheaper parts of the Theatre long queues will stand for hours in the hope of securing admittance.   That this audience is different in kind from the audiences which built the early fame of the Theatre is admitted, it is more 'popular', less discriminating, easier to satisfy, and eager for those effects of caricature which Sean O'Casey's plays give in abundance.   O'Casey is easily the leading dramatist, if by that is meant the dramatist who is most popular with large audiences, in the Abbey Theatre to-day, and it seems that his popularity is inexhaustible, as at every revival of his plays the crowded condition of the Theatre testifies in the most eloquent manner.   Now that he has removed to London, and that his plays in the future may have London as their scene, his future as a dramatist is somewhat doubtful. Whether he can reproduce in terms of London life the effects which he can get from the dwellers of the Dublin slums is something about which even his greatest admirers express misgivings.   In his Dublin plays he was dealing with a life he knew, which he had himself lived, and with which he sympathised, and the effects which he produced depended to a large extent upon the knowledge and sympathy of his audiences.   Can he depend upon all these in London ? Certain it is that in the United States, with its big Irish population, his plays were not popular, and William Tyler who toured the Irish Players with them has stated that he lost a considerable amount of money upon the tour.   For the moment the future of Sean O'Casey is artistically a problem upon which no very decided opinion can be given, but it may be suggested that his basis is definitely localised, and that except his talent be greater than it at present appears to be his future will be as much a part of Dublin as was his past. There is one thing, however, which he has demonstrated : he has shown to those who believed that the Irish drama had reached a dead-end that new dramatists may come from the most unlikely places, as he has shown also that a new Irish drama has nowadays a new material to work upon.   He has disposed most effectively of the prophecies of George Moore and the pessimism of St. John Ervine by giving the Abbey

Theatre a new drama which is at the same time worthy of critical attention and popular applause.

Closely contesting supremacy in popular esteem are two comedies by Brinsley MacNamara, *The Glorious Uncertainty* and *Look at the Heffernans !* Neither of these plays has yet been staged outside Ireland, but there is no doubt that either of them can fill the Abbey Theatre to capacity whenever a performance is announced. With his latest play, *The Master*, MacNamara has again shown that he is equally at home with a serious play upon a theme of more than passing importance, and with a purpose that is deeper than mere laughter. Of the younger dramatists of the Abbey Theatre it is Brinsley MacNamara who seems most likely to write the ' big ' plays of the immediate future. He is intimately familiar with all aspects of Irish life, as intimate with the life of the country-man as he is with the life of Dublin slums and Dublin's literary *salons ;* his dramatic technique is equal to any strain that he may place upon it, and he is the possessor of a literary style that is as sombre and as strong as it is graceful. A novelist of considerable power, as well as a dramatist, he is one of the most interesting figures in the literary life of contemporary Ireland.

Of those who have been longer in the service of the drama in Ireland the names of Lennox Robinson and T. C. Murray immediately present themselves. To some extent they may now both be regarded as ' old masters' in the Abbey Theatre, as Robinson had his first play produced there in 1908 and Murray his first play in 1910, but both are still writing plays that show no decline in their powers even if they do not show any marked advance. It is possible that Lennox Robinson will advance in any direction at any time ; he may decide to follow the line indicated in *Crabbed Youth and Age* or he may follow his latest play, *The Big House*, with another study in the social psychology of the Irish gentry of whom too little has been seen in the Abbey Theatre. Robinson is an experimenter, keenly interested in the drama of the world, an actor of great power, as he showed in Pirandello's *Henry IV* and Strindberg's *The Father* when these plays were performed by the Dublin Drama League, so that any new play of his will be eagerly anticipated. With the more discriminating sections of the Abbey Theatre's audiences he is recognised as the leading dramatist of the time, and much is hoped from him in the future. He is still a comparatively young man with many years of work before him, and with the creditable achievement of thirteen plays behind him, so that any confidence that may be placed in his future is likely to be more than justified. He has opportunities which other Irish dramatists have been denied by birth or circumstance, in that he is familiar with the mind of the Anglo-Irish ex-Unionist in a way that no other Irish dramatist of his time can be, and that he has had a training in the actual work of the theatre that no other Irish dramatist has had. An extensive traveller with an openly receptive mind he may be relied upon to bring what is best in the drama of contemporary Europe to the stage of the Abbey Theatre. Murray, too, may be depended upon for much excellent work in the future. Already in the season of 1927-28 he broke new ground in two different directions with his plays *The Pipe in the Fields* and *The Blind Wolf*, suggesting that the eleven plays which he already has to his credit are but an earnest of some really great work yet to come. With Lennox Robinson he shares a reputation abroad that, so far, had not been achieved by any of the younger dramatists with the exception of Sean O'Casey, and that reputation rests upon achievement and a popular esteem that will probably grow considerably as the years pass and new plays are produced.

At any time Lady Gregory's wonderful vitality may break forth in a new direction, as she showed in 1927 with an adaptation of *Don Quixote* under the title of *Sancho's Master*, or in a psychological study such as *Dave*. She has left her exuberant dialogue behind with the years and the long list of her contributions to the Irish drama, but she is still a force to be reckoned with and her popularity in the Theatre shows no diminution. Mr. Yeats, too, has shown in his adaptations from Sophocles that he has lost none of his grace or his skill in the theatre, but unfortunately he is ill and his departure from Ireland to a less exacting climate is something that may be expected at any time. To Lady Gregory and to W. B. Yeats the Irish drama and the Abbey Theatre are so much indebted that anything that might be said of them would be totally inadequate. They are its creators, its inspirers, its watchful guardians, its controlling influences, and its thrifty custodians, and " without them would have been made nothing that was made ". They gave to Ireland a drama and a theatre that are sometimes the envy and sometimes the inspiration of other countries. What their actual achievement is can only be assessed by those who are intimately acquainted with Ireland and with Irish life. They had to work from nothing, and from that nothing they have given the world a new drama, a tradition in acting, and a National Theatre. " I am not yet convinced ", said Mr. Clayton Hamilton in a lecture in 1924, " that, even at the present time, we have an American drama in the positive sense in which the phrase is used when we speak of . . . even the Irish drama. I say ' even ' in the case of Ireland, because it seems astonishing that so small a country could have produced such a great drama in so short a time. The entire population of Ireland is no more numerous than that of New York City, and nine-tenths of the Irish people have never set foot inside a Theatre. . . . Yet in the short time of twenty years, the Irish have initiated, developed, and perfected a really great contribution to the drama of the world " (*Conversations on Contemporary Drama*, pp. 179-180). That is really a tribute to the great work of two people, Lady Gregory and W. B. Yeats.

During the 1926-27 season two plays were produced which gave promise of more than ordinary plays in the future ; one was the first play of a new dramatist, M. C. Madden, and the other was a new departure by a dramatist who had given two plays to the Theatre some years before. In *Parted*, which is the first play of a very young author, there is considerable achievement, but there is more promise of greater things to come. There is nothing original in the story of the play, but the firmness of its technique and the concentration of its dialogue suggest that in Mr. M. C. Madden the Abbey Theatre has discovered a new dramatist whose advent is more than welcome. *Parted* is a grim little play in one act, displaying that passion for land that has meant so much in the history of Ireland. There is nothing novel in the play, but the characters are very much alive, and on the stage it is vitality that is of greatest importance. The best play of that same season was undoubtedly a new play by John Guinan ; and this was in a season that included new plays by Lady Gregory, W. B. Yeats, and Lennox Robinson. The author of *Black Oliver*, Mr. John Guinan, had his first play produced at the Abbey Theatre as far back as 1913, and another in 1916, but neither of these plays gave any indication that their author would ever attack an abstract theme in drama. They were both melodramatic and had nothing to lift them above the average of the poor plays of their time. But in *Black Oliver* Mr. Guinan attempted, within the limits of a single act, to present a problem in metaphysics which might have daunted many of the dramatists whose names figure prominently in the contemporary theatre of Europe. If it cannot be said that Mr. Guinan's three characters quite succeeded in convincing the audience that ' believing is seeing ', he nevertheless presented a play which is novel and vital. As an attempt to place mental processes on the stage in dramatic form the play must be mentioned as one of the first of its kind to come from an Irish author. Synge hovered about the problem in *The Playboy*, but Mr. Guinan's method has more in common with Pirandello or Susan Glaspell than with Synge ; but he may owe something to Lady Gregory's *Kiltartan History*, in which it is shown how rural folk in Ireland weave legends about ordinary mortals so that they become heroic and awesome. It is to be hoped that Mr. Guinan will continue upon his new path, and that he will not revert to the mood or the method that gave *The Cuckoo's Nest* or *The Plough-Lifters* to the Abbey Theatre so many years ago. If he continues in the mood that produced *Black Oliver* he will not only enrich the Irish drama, but he will also do much to bring it into closer touch with the main currents of contemporary European drama. Upon one play alone it may be too much to predict, but when the example of Elmer Rice in America is remembered the hope is strengthened that Mr. Guinan, too, will turn from melodrama to something which is an Irish equivalent for expressionism. If this be his direction the Irish Theatre will have discovered a dramatist who will give the younger, and the potential, Irish dramatists a new interest and a new direction.

The Abbey Theatre has always been noted for the excellence of its acting, and despite many changes in the personnel of the Company the standard has been maintained. Twice in the history of the Theatre has the entire, or at least the leading members of the company, left its service in a body: in 1908 when the brothers Fay and their company left, and in 1916 when the company since known in England and America as the Irish Players departed in a body. The Second Company which was to be formed from Mr. Nugent Monck's School of Acting in 1912 never really came into being, but it did contribute one or two members to other companies. After the departure of Arthur Sinclair and his colleagues in 1916 a company that was somewhat heterogeneous was gathered together; it was not a good company and gradually its individual members left the Theatre, so that only a few survive in the present company. This 'scratch' company had none of the traditional technique of the Theatre, and for some time the programmes presented might have come direct from any of the English Repertory Theatres. But slowly new members were added and incompetent members were dropped, so that by 1923, when Mr. Lennox Robinson relinquished the Management to Mr. Michael J. Dolan, there had been assembled a company which was more than a collection of individual actors and actresses. Some members of this company have been in the Theatre for a very long period, notably Mr. Dolan himself, Mr. Barry Fitzgerald, and and Mr. Eric Gorman. For a time Mr. Dolan was absent playing in other companies on tour in England and elsewhere, and for a time he was a soldier on the battlefields of Flanders, but at the end of the war he returned to the Theatre where he rapidly assumed his present position as the leading character actor. Since the earliest days of the Theatre's existence audiences have been familiar with Messrs. Barry Fitzgerald and Eric Gorman, for many years playing the small parts and getting little chance to make anything more than their names familiar. But since the departure of Arthur Sinclair his place as a comedian has been more than capably filled by Barry Fitzgerald, who, when the opportunity came to him, revealed himself as one of the most droll of modern comic actors. Never likely to be an actor of outstanding quality Mr. Eric Gorman is nevertheless very painstaking, and occasionally, when he is exceptionally cast, gives a performance that is equal to anything that the Theatre has known. Sharing extreme popularity during the past few years with Barry Fitzgerald is the actor who is in many respects the most brilliant member of the company, Mr. F. J. MacCormick. A comparative newcomer when compared with a few of his colleagues, Mr. MacCormick has had a long and varied experience on the stage, for a time even touring with *Paddy-the-next-best-thing* in many parts of the world, and he is an actor who can generally be relied upon to give a brilliantly finished performance in a wide variety of rôles. In Mr. Arthur Shields is an actor who combines the duties of Assistant-Producer with an occasionally fine performance on the stage. Of the other male members of the company little need be said except that they are invariably competent if never much more. A couple of young men, J. Stephenson and M. Scott, both of whom graduated in amateur dramatic societies in Dublin, give promise of developing into something more then mere competence, but at present it is impossible to express any considered opinion on their abilities. The Theatre was never so poor in acting ability amongst its female members than it is at present, as with the exception of Miss Eileen Crowe none of the ladies is above the average of a good amateur company. For some years now, except in the odd months when Miss Sara Allgood returns for some special performance, Miss Eileen Crowe has been the leading actress in the Theatre, and that her lead is more than merely titular is generally only too obvious. Always capable of a finished performance, Miss Crowe often rises to supreme heights, and if she never quite challenges comparison with the great actresses of the older companies she is nevertheless an actress of the first class. Of her colleagues only Miss Maureen Delany and Miss May Craig are anything more than mediocre, and both these ladies are capable on occasions of magnificent performances. A very young girl has recently joined the company, Miss K. Curling, and the few appearances she has made upon the stage suggest that she will develop into an actress of supreme ability.

It is when the performances of the present company are compared with those of its predecessor, in the same plays, that the superiority of what may be called the Sinclair company becomes manifest ; but when the performances of the present company in new plays are witnessed the general competence, and occasional brilliance, is easily recognised. For example, there is no group of actors in the world which could improve upon the present Abbey Theatre Company's acting in *Juno and the ' Paycock'* or in *The Plough and the Stars*. Messrs. Barry Fitzgerald and F. J. MacCormick as the two Dublin loafers in *Juno* are well worth travelling long distances to see ; in their impersonations there is little or no caricature, yet by their very fidelity to the originals they can keep a crowded house in laughter for hours. To see M. J. Dolan in *Autumn Fire*, *The Blind Wolf*, or *The Two Shepherds* would be an equally unforgetable experience ; in each of these widely different rôles he presents a portrait which is as convincingly real as it is sympathetic. At sight Miss Eileen Crowe does not look a person who would be a success as Nora Helmer in *A Doll's House*, yet she played that part in a manner which challenged comparison with the great actresses who have played it in all parts of the world. And when she turns from the seriousness of Ibsen to Brinsley MacNamara in his lighter mood of *Look at the Heffernans !* she shows herself a comedy actress of great ability. It is in *The White-headed Boy* that Arthur Shields shows to greatest advantage ; and probably Uncle Peter in *The Plough and the Stars* is Eric Gorman's greatest achievement. Miss May Craig shows best in *The Country Dressmaker*, and Miss Maureen Delany has given of her best in *John Bull's Other Island*. It is when the members of the Sinclair company and the present company are individually compared that the older company shows its great superiority. Compare Sinclair with Barry Fitzgerald, J. M. Kerrigan with Michael Dolan, Fred O'Donovan with F. J. MacCormick or Arthur Shields, J. A. O'Rourke with Eric Gorman, or Sydney Morgan with P. J. Carolan ! From any such comparison the individual members of the older company must be adjudged very greatly superior to the individual members of the present company. And when any attempt is made to compare the ladies individually the comparison becomes almost ludicrous. Yet as a company the present is little inferior to the past, and generally speaking the new plays are acted with a finish that would be difficult to excel in any theatre in Great Britain or America. Occasionally there is a very bad preformance by which a new play is almost ruined, as the recent performance of Guinan's *Black Oliver* or Brinsley MacNamara's *The Master* may be cited to prove, but these are more than counterbalanced by such a brilliant performance as was given to the first production of Murray's latest play *The Blind Wolf*.

So when all the comparisons have been made it remains to be said that in the present company the Abbey Theatre has a group of actors and actresses that will compare favourably with any similar group in any country of the world. No little country and no little theatre can keep on producing actors of the highest class for a period of more than thirty years. It would be too much to expect that Ireland from its one little theatre could supply the stages of England and America with some of their greatest and most brilliant actors, and at the same time continue to have at home a company of equal greatness and individual brilliance. For the present the flow has been stemmed, and it may be expected that the present company will be permanent, with continuous recruitment from promising pupils of the new School of Acting. If this be so the future acting in the Theatre may well surpass the great standards of the past, and potential Irish dramatists will be assured of an interpretation equal to that of any stage in the world. Ireland has nothing to fear, even now, from comparison with Moscow, or Prague, or Liverpool, or Greenwich Village.

CHAPTER XV

THE FUTURE OF THE IRISH DRAMA

Has the Irish Drama a Future ?—Pessimists of Many Kinds—The Prophecies of George Moore and St. John Ervine—Prejudice displaces the Critical Faculty—The Basis of The Past—Irish Drama in Two Languages—A Break with Tradition—The Necessity for a Liberal Policy—The Vindication of the Founders.

HAS the Irish Drama any future ? Pessimists will be found even in Dublin to say that it has not, as there are Irishmen in England and in Ireland to deny that it even has a past. Some there are in Ireland who still maintain that the drama which is called Irish is in reality but a sub-division of the English drama, and that a real Irish drama would have been written in the Irish language. All these may be discounted without much consideration. The Dublin pessimists are invariably people who are doleful about the entire future of the country, people who are disillusioned and mourning for a past that will never return they are unable to see the good in the present or the great potentialities of the future. Fortunately such people are not very numerous, and such influence as they may have is confined within a narrow circle of aged folk who are incapable of controlling events. Of those who deny that the Irish drama has a past or that it can have a future Mr. St. John Ervine may be taken as a typical specimen. He is firmly convinced that nothing good can ever come, or ever did come, out of Southern Ireland, by which name he designated the Irish Free State, and that all the good in Ireland is in Ulster, which name he usurps for the six counties of that province which make Northern Ireland. The Catholic Church, as he has said, may be " ultimately unsuitable to the spiritual needs of a gentleman, although adequate to the needs of servant girls and actors " (*Some Impressions of my Elders*, p. 23), but it must be admitted to have been the faith of some of the best dramatists, and all of the best actors, in the Abbey Theatre. Such a pre-occupation with the merely sectarian bigotry of Belfast Orangeism is not one of the best qualifications of a critic of either the past or the future of the drama of any country, and consequently the doleful forebodings of Messrs. George Moore and St. John Ervine may be dismissed as the results of prejudice rather than the exercise of critical faculties in this particular case. The criticism of those in Ireland who maintain that the achievements of the dramatists of the Abbey Theatre are contributions to English, rather than to a genuinely Irish, drama has greater weight and must be given more attention. If one accepts language as the *only* distinctive mark of a nation such criticism must be very damaging, if not entirely destructive, to the claim that the plays of the Abbey Theatre bore definitely national traits, and were in fact an expression of nationality. But language is not the *only* distinctive mark of a nation, nor can it ever be. The nation is a spiritual thing, ' a community of memories and of hopes ' as Anatole France said, and it is the spiritual differences that make nations of groups of people. In Ireland the English language has so firmly established itself that all effort to eradicate it in the future must prove vain, and it is in the English language that the spiritual difference between the people in Ireland and the people in all other geographical entities will of necessity be best expressed. That is not to deny that there can exist simultaneously a drama in the Irish language which is also Irish, though perhaps in a lesser degree because it must express the spirituality of a smaller number of people. In fact, since the first play in the Irish language was staged in 1901 there has been a growing movement to write plays in Irish, and this movement has culminated in the formation of a Gaelic Drama League which is subsidised by the Free State Government. This Gaelic Drama League is gathering strength, so much so that in the season 1927-28 it actually produced ten new plays as compared with

the nine of the National Theatre Society. Both organisations use the Abbey Theatre, but while the Drama League
gives only two performances monthly the National Theatre
Society's company plays continuously for at least ten months
every year. So the claim of the Abbey Theatre dramatist to
the use of the national adjective is substantiated by the
overwhelming number of plays staged, by their inherent
superiority, by the fact that they could have been written by
none but Irish people, and by their acceptance by the Irish
people. Since the opening of the Abbey Theatre in December
1904 to the end of the 1927-28 season in May 1928 the
National Theatre Society has presented 241 plays by 92
authors, and of these authors no less than 77 were Irish, and
only a fractional proportion of the plays produced were by
foreign authors. The figures alone show the hollowness of
the denial that the Theatre and the Drama were and still
remain Irish. Nevertheless, the growth of a drama in the
Irish language is an encouraging sign of the times, and a sign
that will be heartily welcomed by all who love the drama in
whatever language it may be presented.

The Irish drama most certainly has a future. It will in the
future be a drama in two languages, and criticism in the future
will be compelled to take note of the drama in the Irish
language when it has grown beyond the infantinism of the
present. When the pessimists seemed likely to be justified in
their doleful prophecies the emergence of Sean O'Casey
shattered them, and since then a succession of excellent plays
from the older and some of the newer dramatists has smashed
them completely. Glance at the list of the authors from
whom much good work may still be expected with confidence,
and then say that the Irish drama has petered out ! Lady
Gregory and W. B. Yeats are still capable of excellent
dramatic work, but much reliance must not be placed upon
them for the future. But there still remains George Fitzmaurice, John Guinan, J. Bernard MacCarthy, Brinsley
MacNamara, T. C. Murray, Lennox Robinson, and George
Shiels among the older dramatists.   And in the ranks of the

newer dramatists there is Dorothy Macardle, M. C. Madden, F. J. H. O'Donnell, Sean O'Casey, Arthur Power, Kenneth Sarr, and many others who have plays waiting to be produced. Of course, it will not be said that all these are capable of writing plays of the highest class, or even that many of the plays awaiting production will be other than mediocre ; but that is so in every country, and if the banalities of London and New York be accepted as a standard the future of the Irish drama looks like being very brilliant by comparison. There is no appreciable reduction in the number of potential dramatists, and at any moment another Sean O'Casey may burst forth from a Dublin tenement, a Synge may come from the glens of Wicklow, another Padraic Colum or Brinsley MacNamara from the Midland plains, a George Moore, Lady Gregory, or Edward Martyn from the fastnesses of Connacht, or a Lennox Robinson, T. C. Murray, or Daniel Corkery from the prolific county of Cork. Truly the wind bloweth where it listeth, and just as thirty years ago some of those who since made the name of the Abbey Theatre famed throughout the world were obscure and unknown as dramatists, so to-day there are probably living in the same obscurity bearers of names which will be famous in the next quarter of a century. No one can say to-day who these dramatists may be, or whence they are likely to come, but it is certain that in the future it will be more difficult to achieve fame as a dramatist in Ireland than it has been in the past. There are now standards which were lacking twenty-five years ago, and there is now a repertory adequate for the normal requirements of most theatres, and so the standards to which the new dramatist will be required to conform will be more exacting than they were in the past. But still the apprentice must be given his chance, and the policy which Mr. Lennox Robinson outlined in 1927 (see p. 124) must not be too rigorously enforced. Better a poor play from a new author who shows promise, and who may learn from seeing his work actually staged, than continued production of the plays of established dramatists whose work shows no advance. The Directors in the future must show at least the same hospitality to the new dramatist that the Directors in the past have shown : it will not be sufficient that new dramatists are given over to the little Peacock Theatre to stage their plays to an audience of their friends at their own expense. In that direction lies stagnation, of which there are some few signs at present, and which must be avoided at all costs. The subsidy which the Abbey Theatre receives from the Irish Free State Government must be used for the·discovery of new dramatists and new actors no less than for the equipment and decoration of the Theatre.

It is certain, however, that the Irish drama of the future will be very different from that of the past. In England and America, apparently, the audiences still expect nothing from anything labelled as Irish drama but the buffooneries of Handy Andy. In Ireland itself all that has been killed by the efforts of the National Theatre Society, which has demonstrated that in order to be Irish drama need not necessarily be absurd. But even in the Abbey Theatre itself the type of drama upon which it flourished in the past is found to be out of date. The ' peasant play ' upon which the foundation of its success was laid is now found to be insufficient to interest audiences. A new Ireland is in the process of formation, and that new Ireland will not be so morbidly concentrated upon its nationality as was the Ireland of the past. If Bernard Shaw's metaphor may be used, the broken arm has been re-set and it no longer absorbs all the attention of its owner. The Irish drama of the future will be not so much an expression of Irish nationality as of the Irish view of human nature. Already Lennox Robinson and T. C. Murray have broken with the traditions of the Theatre, and even the scene of Murray's latest play, *The Blind Wolf*, is not laid in Ireland, but in Hungary. True, Murray's Hungarians are not noticeably different from Murray's Cork peasants, but the change of location is significant in a Theatre where all the plays by Irish authors have had their scene in Ireland or in the land of mythology. This change suggests that in the future the problems of the world, and the peoples of the world, may be staged in the Irish Theatre, and that themes which were barred in the past by the restrictive policy of the Directorate will not be barred in the future. This widening will give the new dramatists opportunities which were either denied or unsought in the past, and will line the Irish theatre with the theatre of the world; it will make the Abbey Theatre one with the theatre of Europe, at least, rather than a brilliant, if somewhat eccentric, example of a national folk-theatre.

From its earliest days the Abbey Theatre has been a little hospitable to some plays from famous foreign dramatists. As early as 1907 Maeterlinck's *Interior* was presented on its stage, and since then the plays of some of the more notable European and American dramatists have been produced. In recent years that hospitality has grown more cordial, and the tendency to stage the plays of famous dramatists has become more marked. It is probable that in the future this tendency will be still further emphasised, and that the Theatre may encroach upon the province of the excellent Dublin Drama League. There is no doubt that the best plays that are being written must be produced in Dublin if Irish dramatists are to be kept informed of the changes in outlook and technique of the leading contemporary dramatists, and if that be not done the introspective and incestuous practices of the not very remote past may again manifest themselves. This must be guarded against as carefully as the alleged tendency to restrict productions to those who have had plays produced in the past if the Irish drama is to continue in a healthy state. No one can complain of the undue national prejudice which has staged plays by Hauptmann, Maeterlinck, Strindberg, Ibsen, Tchechov, Evreinov, Mazaud, Tagore, Romain, and Sierra, while at the same time the Dublin Drama League was giving Dublin an opportunity to witness the plays of leading dramatists of to-day even before London had seen them on the stage. It is this practice of showing the best that is being written for the theatre to-day that is producing the new tendencies now to be observed in the plays of some Irish dramatists, and it is to a continuance of the practice that the stimulation of the Irish drama must be looked for in the immediate future. There must be a liberal outlook on the part of the Directorate, both in the direction of discovering and encouraging new dramatists and in the staging of examples of the best plays that the world is staging. Only in that way can the future of the Irish drama be assured. The Abbey Theatre has achieved adult status and must behave as an adult.

From the very day it opened its doors the Abbey Theatre has been a model and an inspiration to everyone interested in the theatre and in the development of the drama. It has survived its period of experiment and of political stress and excitement. It has come safely through a political revolution, and it is now secure for the future. Its repertory system has proven its worth by giving to Ireland a national drama which has attracted the attention of the world. It has made drama possible to Irishmen at home, and has produced dramatists and actors of whom the world has been glad to take note. Before Mr. Yeats created his dream in the reality of the Abbey Theatre Ireland had no place in the history of the drama, although it had a place in the history of the stage ; now that has been so much altered that every book on the drama has a section devoted to Ireland. To all who have ideas for the development of folk-drama, too, the Abbey Theatre offers a model and a repertory of plays that is unequalled elsewhere. Every community has possibilities for the dramatist, but every region does not tempt the commercial theatre, and if regional drama is to have the opportunities that its importance deserves, only the method of the Abbey Theatre, and the repertory system, will be available for guidance and inspiration. Efforts are being made in the United States and in many parts of Great Britain to foster national and local drama, and these efforts have been to some extent successful. So the drama is enriched by a Eugene O'Neill or a Paul Green in America, and by a Stanley Houghton, a John Drinkwater, a James Gregson, or a John Brandane, in England or Scotland,

and by a Caradoc Evans and a Hughes in Wales. That is the great contribution of the repertory theatre system to the life of its district and of its time. The great dramatists of the past twenty-five years have all been nurtured in repertory theatres : Synge in the Abbey Theatre in Dublin, Tchechov in the Art Theatre in Moscow, the brothers Capek in Prague, Eugene O'Neill in Greenwich Village, John Drinkwter in Birmingham, not to mention Ibsen, Shaw, Hauptmann, and Strindberg of an earlier day. Whatever the commercial theatre may be prepared to do to amuse the populace it will do nothing with experimental drama, or with drama that is revolutionary either in its idea or in its technique. There is no hope for a Toller, a Kaiser, or a Hofmannsthal in the commercial theatre, for such as they small theatres are necessary, and there must be the driving force of enthusiastic interest in the drama and in the theatre as an institution. Great funds and elaborate organisations are unnecessary. The Abbey Theatre grew from an idea backed by enthusiasm and energy. It has grown from very small beginnings, as other similar theatrical enterprises as the Provincetown Players in America and the Repertory Theatre in Birmingham yet it has done more for drama, and more for the people in whose midst it is established, than the commercial theatres of the large and populous towns where there are many theatres but little drama. The Abbey Theatre has now entered upon its maturity, secure in the support of the Government of the Irish Free State, and no less secure in the affectionate regard of its audiences. It is the only State-subsidised theatre in the English-speaking world, a fact which marks it as a pioneer in yet another direction which will ultimately be followed by theatres in the other Dominions, and perhaps in Britain itself. That its dramatists can still attract the attention of the outer world the success of plays by Sean O'Casey, Lennox Robinson, and T. C. Murray, recently in London and New York, stands as proof. Its acting is still up to the best that may be seen in any theatre in the world, and it may be hoped that soon the Theatre will have several companies in its service, some of which will tour regularly in the smaller Irish towns, or even abroad, while one would remain permanently in Dublin. When this has been done the great faith and energy of Lady Gregory and W. B. Yeats will have been completely vindicated, " and the ancient dreams come true ".

APPENDIX I

NUMBER OF FIRST PRODUCTIONS EACH YEAR OF THE IRISH LITERARY THEATRE AND THE ABBEY THEATRE.

1899.	2 Productions.	1914.	14 Productions
1900.	3 "	1915.	6 "
1901.	2 "	1916.	10 "
1902.	6 "	1917.	12 "
1903.	5 "	1918.	9 "
1904.	5 "	1919.	13 "
1905.	5 "	1920.	13 "
1906.	8 "	1921.	8 "
1907.	10 "	1922.	10 "
1908.	11 "	1923.	10 "
1909.	10 "	1924.	10 "
1910.	11 "	1925.	7 "
1911.	9 "	1926.	8 "
1912.	14 "	1927.	12 "
1913.	16 "	1928.	3 "

Total Number of Plays Produced from May 1899 to May 1928 - - - - - - - - - - - 262

Irish Literary Theatre Productions, May 1899 to November 1904 - - - - - - - - - 21

Abbey Theatre Productions, December 1904 to May 1928   241

Number of Authors whose Plays were Produced, 1904-1928   92

Number of Non-Irish Authors whose Plays were Produced, 1904-1928 - - - - - - - - 15

Plays Translated from Languages other than Irish, 1904-1928 - - - - - - - - - 19

The First Performances at the Abbey Theatre were given on 27th December, 1904.

APPENDIX II

DATE OF FIRST PRODUCTION OF EVERY PLAY PRODUCED BY THE IRISH LITERARY THEATRE AND THE ABBEY THEATRE.

Date.	Name of Play.	Author.
1899.		
May 8th.	The Countess Cathleen.	W. B. Yeats.
„ 9th.	The Heather Field.	Edward Martyn.
1900.		
Feb. 19th.	The Bending of the Bough.	George Moore.
„ 19th.	The Last Feast of the Fianna.	Alice Milligan.
„ 20th.	Maeve.	Edward Martyn.
1901.		
Oct. 21st.	Diarmuid and Grania.	Yeats and Moore.
„ 21st.	The Twisting of the Rope (In Irish).	Douglas Hyde.
1902.		
April 2nd.	Deirdre.	G. W. Russell ('A.E.').
„ 2nd.	Kathleen ni Houlihan.	W. B. Yeats.
Oct. 29th.	The Sleep of the King.	James Cousins.
„ 29th.	The Laying of the Foundations.	Fred Ryan.
„ 30th.	A Pot of Broth.	W. B. Yeats.
„ 31st.	The Racing Lug.	James Cousins.
1903.		
Mar. 14th.	The Hour-Glass.	W. B. Yeats.
„ 14th.	Twenty-Five.	Lady Gregory.
Oct. 8th.	The King's Threshold.	W. B. Yeats.
„ 8th.	In the Shadow of the Glen.	J. M. Synge.
Dec. 3rd.	Broken Soil.	Padraic Colum.
1904.		
Jan. 14th.	The Shadowy Waters.	W. B. Yeats.
„ 14th.	The Townland of Tamney.	S. MacManus.
„ 25th.	Riders to the Sea.	J. M. Synge.

ABBEY THEATRE.

Date.	Name of Play.	Author.
Dec. 27th.	On Baile's Strand.	W. B. Yeats.
,, 27th.	Spreading the News.	Lady Gregory.
1905.		
Feb. 4th.	The Well of the Saints.	J. M. Synge.
Mar. 25th.	Kincora.	W. B. Yeats.
April 25th.	The Building Fund.	William Boyle.
June 9th.	The Land.	Padraic Colum.
Dec. 9th.	The White Cockade.	Lady Gregory.
1906.		
Jan. 20th.	The Eloquent Dempsey.	William Boyle.
Feb. 19th.	Hyacinth Halvey.	Lady Gregory.
April 16th.	The Doctor in Spite of Himself.	Molière–Gregory.
Oct. 20th.	The Gaol Gate.	Lady Gregory.
,, 20th.	The Mineral Workers.	William Boyle.
Nov. 24th.	Deirdre.	W. B. Yeats.
Dec. 8th.	The Canavans.	Lady Gregory.
,, 8th.	The Shadowy Waters. (Revised.)	W. B. Yeats.
1907.		
Jan. 26th.	The Playboy of the Western World.	J. M. Synge.
Feb. 23rd.	The Jackdaw.	Lady Gregory.
Mar. 9th.	The Rising of the Moon.	Lady Gregory.
,, 16th.	Interior.	M. Maeterlinck.
April 1st.	The Eyes of the Blind.	W. M. Letts.
,, 3rd.	The Poorhouse.	Gregory–Hyde.
,, 27th.	Fand.	Wilfrid S. Blunt.
Oct. 3rd.	The Country Dressmaker.	George Fitzmaurice.
,, 31st.	Dervorgilla.	Lady Gregory.
Nov. 21st.	The Unicorn from the Stars.	Yeats–Gregory.
1908.		
Feb. 3rd.	The Man Who Missed the Tide.	W. F. Casey.
,, 13th.	The Piper.	Conal O'Riordan.
Mar. 10th.	The Pie-dish.	George Fitzmaurice.
,, 19th.	The Golden Helmet.	W. B. Yeats.
,, 19th.	Teja.	H. Sudermann.
April 4th.	The Rogueries of Scapin.	Molière–Gregory.
,, 20th.	The Workhouse Ward.	Lady Gregory.

Date.	Name of Play.	Author.
May 29th.	The Scheming Lieutenant.	R. B. Sheridan.
Oct. 1st.	The Suburban Groove.	W. F. Casey.
„ 8th.	The Clancy Name.	Lennox Robinson.
„ 15th.	When the Dawn is Come.	Thomas MacDonagh.
1909.		
Jan. 21st.	The Miser.	Molière–Gregory.
Mar. 11th.	Stephen Gray.	D. L. Kelleher.
April 1st.	The Cross Roads.	Lennox Robinson.
„ 1st.	Time.	Conal O'Riordan.
„ 29th.	The Glittering Gate.	Lord Dunsany.
May 27th.	An Imaginary Conversation.	Conal O'Riordan.
Aug. 25th.	The Shewing-up of Blanco Posnet.	Bernard Shaw.
Sep. 16th.	The White Feather.	R. J. Ray.
Oct. 14th.	The Challenge.	W. M. Letts.
Nov. 11th.	The Image.	Lady Gregory.
1910.		
Jan. 13th.	Deirdre of the Sorrows.	J. M. Synge.
Feb. 10th.	The Green Helmet.	W. B. Yeats.
„ 24th.	Mirandolina.	Goldoni–Gregory.
Mar. 2nd.	The Travelling Man.	Lady Gregory.
May 12th.	Thomas Muskerry.	Padraic Colum.
„ 26th.	Harvest.	Lennox Robinson.
Sep. 28th.	The Casting-out of Martin Whelan.	R. J. Ray.
Oct. 27th.	Birthright.	T. C. Murray.
Nov. 10th.	The Full Moon.	Lady Gregory.
„ 24th.	The Shuiler's Child.	Seumas O'Kelly.
Dec. 1st.	Coats.	Lady Gregory.
1911.		
Jan. 5th.	The Nativity Play.	Douglas Hyde.
„ 12th.	The Deliverer.	Lady Gregory.
„ 26th.	King Argimenes and the Unknown Warrior.	Lord Dunsany.
„ 26th.	Land of Heart's Desire.	W. B. Yeats.
„ 30th.	Mixed Marriage.	St. J. G. Ervine.
Nov. 23rd.	The Interlude of Youth.	Anon.
„ 23rd.	The Second Shepherd's Play.	Anon.
„ 30th.	The Marriage.	Douglas Hyde.
Dec. 7th.	Red Turf.	Rutherford Mayne.

Date.	Name of Play.	Author.

1912.

Jan.	4th.	The Annunciation.	Anon.
,,	4th.	The Flight into Egypt.	Anon.
,,	11th.	MacDonough's Wife.	Lady Gregory.
,,	15th.	The Tinker and the Fairy (In Irish).	Douglas Hyde.
,,	29th.	The Worlde and the Chylde.	Anon.
Mar.	28th.	Family Failing.	William Boyle.
April	11th.	Patriots.	Lennox Robinson.
,,	15th.	Judgment.	Joseph Campbell.
June	20th.	Maurice Harte (Court Theatre, London).	T. C. Murray.
July	4th.	The Bogie Man. (Court Theatre, London).	Lady Gregory.
Sep.	26th.	The Countess Cathleen (Revised).	W. B. Yeats.
Oct.	17th.	The Magnanimous Lover.	St. J. G. Ervine.
Nov.	21st.	Damer's Gold.	Lady Gregory.
Dec.	26th.	A Little Christmas Miracle.	E. H. Moore.

1913.

Jan.	13th.	The Cuckoo's Next.	John Guinan.
,,	23rd.	The Dean of St. Patrick's.	S. Paternoster.
Feb.	20th.	Hannele.	G. Hauptmann.
Mar.	6th.	There are Crimes and Crimes.	A. Strindberg.
April	10th.	The Homecoming.	Gertrude Robins.
,,	17th.	The Stronger.	A. Strindberg.
,,	24th.	The Magic Glasses.	George Fitzmaurice.
,,	24th.	Broken Faith.	S. R. Day and C. D. Cummins.
May	17th.	The Post Office.	R. Tagore.
June	30th.	The Gombeen Man.	R. J. Ray.
Sep.	11th.	Sovereign Love.	T. C. Murray.
Oct.	2nd.	The Mine Land.	Joseph Connolly.
,,	16th.	My Lord.	Mrs. Bart Kennedy.
Nov.	20th.	The Critics.	St. J. G. Ervine.
,,	16th.	Duty.	Seumas O'Brien.
,,	18th.	The Bribe.	Seumas O'Kelly.

1914.

Jan.	29th.	David Mahony.	V. O'D. Power.
Mar.	13th.	The Orangemen.	St. J. G. Ervine.
,,	13th.	The Lord Mayor.	Edward McNulty.
April	2nd.	Kinship.	J. B. MacCarthy.

Date.	Name of Play.	Author.
April 15th.	The Cobbler.	A. P. Wilson.
Aug. 27th.	A Minute's Wait.	M. J. MacHugh.
Sep. 3rd.	The Supplanter.	J. B. MacCarthy.
„ 9th.	The Dark Hour.	R. A. Christie.
„ 23rd.	The Crossing.	Con O'Leary.
„ 30th.	The Prodigal.	Walter Riddall.
Oct. 13th.	The Cobweb.	F. Jay.
„ 20th.	The Jug of Sorrow.	W. P. Ryan.
Nov. 3rd.	The Slough.	A. P. Wilson.
Dec. 26th.	The Critic.	R. B. Sheridan.
1915.		
Jan. 27th.	By Word of Mouth.	Moore and Flanagan.
Feb. 2nd.	The Dreamers.	Lennox Robinson.
April 5th.	The Bargain.	William Crone.
„ 5th.	The Philosopher.	M. J. MacHugh.
„ 8th.	Shanwalla.	Lady Gregory.
Nov. 30th.	John Ferguson.	St. J. G. Ervine.
1916.		
Jan. 4th.	Fraternity.	Bernard Duffy.
Feb. 8th.	The Coiner.	Bernard Duffy.
Mar. 28th.	The Plough Lifters.	John Guinan.
Sep. 25th.	John Bull's Other Island.	Bernard Shaw.
Oct. 9th.	Widower's Houses.	Bernard Shaw.
„ 16th.	Arms and the Man.	Bernard Shaw.
„ 25th.	Nic.	William Boyle.
Nov. 15th.	Partition.	D. C. Maher.
Dec. 11th.	The Counter Charm.	Bernard Duffy.
„ 13th.	The Whiteheaded Boy.	Lennox Robinson.
1917.		
Jan. 8th.	Tommy-Tom-Tom.	M. J. MacHugh.
„ 19th.	The Crusaders.	J. B. MacCarthy.
Feb. 2nd.	Fox and Geese.	S. R. Day and G. D. Cummins.
„ 26th.	Man and Superman.	Bernard Shaw.
Mar. 12th.	The Inca of Perusalem.	Bernard Shaw.
April 25th.	The Strong Hand.	R. J. Day.
May 26th.	The Doctor's Dilemma.	Bernard Shaw.
Sep. 24th.	The Parnellite.	Seumas O'Kelly.
Oct. 30th.	The Bacac.	J. Barnewell.
Nov. 20th.	Friends.	H. Farjeon.
„ 13th.	The Spoiling of Wilson.	R. J. Purcell.
Dec. 11th.	Blight.	Alpha and Omega.

Date.	Name of Play.	Author.
1918.		
Jan. 8th.	Spring.	T. C. Murray.
„ 22nd.	When Love Came Over the Hills.	Fcaron and Nesbit.
„ 29th.	Hanrahan's Oath.	Lady Gregory.
Mar. 12th.	Aliens.	Rose McKenna.
Feb. 9th.	The Lost Leader.	Lennox Robinson.
May 28th.	A Little Bit of Youth.	C. Callister.
Sep. 16th.	Sable and Gold.	Maurice Dalton.
Nov. 12th.	The Grabber.	E. F. Barrett.
Dec. 17th.	Atonement.	Dorothy Macardle.
1919.		
Mar. 11th.	The Rebellion in Ballycullen.	Brinsley MacNamara.
April 21st.	The Dragon.	Lady Gregory.
Aug. 4th.	Brady.	Sadie Casey.
„ 19th.	The Fiddler's House.	Padraic Colum.
„ 19th.	A Serious Thing.	G. Ousley.
Sep. 2nd.	The Saint.	Desmond Fitzgerald.
„ 2nd.	A Night at an Inn.	Lord Dunsany.
„ 30th.	The Labour Leader.	Daniel Corkery.
Oct. 7th.	Meadowsweet.	Seumas O'Kelly.
„ 14th.	Queer Ones.	Con O'Leary.
Nov. 4th.	Androcles and the Lion.	Bernard Shaw.
„ 25th.	The Enchanted Trousers.	G. Ousley.
Dec. 9th.	The Player Queen.	W. B. Yeats.
1920.		
Jan. 6th.	The Golden Apple.	Lady Gregory.
Feb. 10th.	The Devil's Disciple.	Bernard Shaw.
„ 17th.	The Daemon in the House.	F. Barrington.
April 27th.	The Good-Natured Man.	Oliver Goldsmith.
May 4th.	The Yellow Bittern.	Daniel Corkery.
„ 24th.	The Tents of the Arabs.	Lord Dunsany.
Aug. 9th.	The Wooing of Julia Elizabeth.	James Stephens.
Sep. 7th.	The Drifters.	F. J. H. O'Donnell.
„ 21st.	A Royal Alliance.	Fergus O'Nolan.
Oct. 5th.	The Serf.	Stephen Morgan.
„ 12th.	The Island of Saints.	St. J. G. Ervine.
Nov. 30th.	The Land for the People.	Brinsley MacNamara.
Dec. 27th.	Candle and Crib.	K. F. Purdon.

Date.	Name of Play.	Author.
1921.		
Jan. 6th.	Bedmates.	George Shiels.
Feb. 24th.	The Revolutionist.	Terence MacSwiney.
Mar. 17th.	Aristotle's Bellows.	Lady Gregory.
Oct. 18th.	The Perfect Day.	Emile Mazaud.
,, 18th.	A Merry Death.	Nicholas Evreinov.
Nov. 8th.	The Courting of Mary Doyle.	Edward MacNulty.
,, 15th.	The Piper of Tavran.	Bernard Duffy.
Dec. 13th.	Insurance Money.	George Shiels.
1922.		
Jan. 10th.	Aftermath.	T. C. Murray.
,, 31st.	The Round Table.	Lennox Robinson.
Mar. 9th.	The Man of Destiny.	Bernard Shaw.
April 6th.	The Young Man from Rathmines.	M. M. Brennan.
,, 6th.	Ann Kavanagh.	Dorothy Macardle.
Aug. 29th.	The Moral Law.	R. J. Ray.
Sep. 5th.	A Lepracaun in the Tenement.	M. M. Brennan.
Oct. 3rd.	Paul Twyning.	George Shiels.
,, 24th.	The Grasshopper (Adapted).	Padraic Colum.
Nov. 14th.	Crabbed Youth and Age.	Lennox Robinson.
1923.		
Jan. 9th.	The Long Road to Garranbraher.	J. B. MacCarthy.
Mar. 8th.	'Twixt the Giltenans and the Carmodys.	George Fitzmaurice.
,, 22nd.	A Doll's House.	Henrik Ibsen.
April 9th.	The Shadow of a Gunman.	Sean O'Casey.
,, 22nd.	She Stoops to Conquer.	Oliver Goldsmith.
Sep. 3rd.	Apartments.	Fand O'Grady.
Oct. 1st.	Cathleen Listens-in.	Sean O'Casey.
Nov. 27th.	The Glorious Uncertainty.	Brinsley MacNamara.
Dec. 26th.	First Aid.	George Shiels.
,, 31st.	The Old Woman Remembers.	Lady Gregory.
1924.		
Feb. 12th.	The Two Shepherds.	G. M. Sierra.
Mar. 3rd.	Juno and the ' Paycock '.	Sean O'Casey.
April 8th.	Never the Time and the Place.	Lennox Robinson.
,, 14th.	The Story Brought by Brigit.	Lady Gregory.

Date.	*Name of Play.*	*Author.*
May 12th.	The Retrievers.	George Shiels.
Sep. 8th.	Autumn Fire.	T. C. Murray.
„ 29th.	Nannie's Night Out.	Sean O'Casey.
Nov. 3rd.	The Kingdom of God.	G. M. Sierra.
Dec. 16th.	The Passing.	Kenneth Sarr.
„ 22nd.	Old Mag.	Kenneth Sarr.
1925.		
Feb. 24th.	The Old Man.	Dorothy Macardle.
Mar. 17th.	Anti-Christ.	F. J. H. O'Donnell.
„ 31st.	Portrait.	Lennox Robinson.
April 21st.	Fanny's First Play.	Bernard Shaw.
„ 28th.	The Proposal.	Anton Tchechov.
Sep. 14th.	Professor Tim.	George Shiels.
Oct. 12th.	The White Blackbird.	Lennox Robinson.
1926.		
Jan. 4th.	The Would-be Gentleman.	Molière–Gregory.
Feb. 8th.	The Plough and the Stars.	Sean O'Casey.
„ 16th.	Doctor Knock.	Jules Romaine.
April 12th.	Look at the Heffernans !	Brinsley MacNamara.
Aug. 16th.	Mr. Murphy's Island.	Elizabeth Harte.
Sep. 6th.	The Big House.	Lennox Robinson.
Nov. 6th.	The Importance of Being Earnest.	Oscar Wilde.
Dec. 6th.	Œdipus the King.	Sophocles–Yeats.
1927.		
Jan. 24th.	The Emperor Jones.	Eugene O'Neill.
„ 24th.	Trifles.	Susan Glaspell.
Mar. 14th.	Sancho's Master.	Lady Gregory.
April 5th.	Parted.	M. C. Madden.
May 9th.	Dave.	Lady Gregory.
„ 16th.	Black Oliver.	John Guinan.
July 8th.	The Round Table (Revised).	Lennox Robinson.
Sep. 12th.	Œdipus at Colonnus.	Sophocles–Yeats.
Oct. 3rd.	The Pipe in the Fields.	T. C. Murray.
„ 24th.	Caesar and Cleopatra.	Bernard Shaw
Nov. 29th.	Cartney and Kevney.	George Shiels.
Aug. 22nd.	The Drapier Letters.	Arthur Power.
1928.		
Mar. 6th.	The Master.	Brinsley MacNamara.
April 3rd.	John Gabriel Borkman.	Henrik Ibsen.
„ 30th.	The Blind Wolf.	T. C. Murray.

APPENDIX III

ALPHABETICAL LIST OF AUTHORS, WITH PLAYS AND DATES OF FIRST PRODUCTIONS.

Anonymous.
The Interlude of Youth - - - November 23rd, 1911.
The Second Shepherd's Play - - November 23rd, 1911.
The Annunciation - - - - January 4th, 1912.
The Flight into Egypt - - - January 4th, 1912.
The Worlde and the Chylde - - January 29th, 1912.

Alpha and Omega.
Blight - - - - - - December 11th, 1917.

Barnewall, John.
The Bacac - - - - - October 30th, 1917.

Barrett, E. F.
The Grabber - - - - November 12th, 1918.

Barrington, F.
The Daemon in the House - - February 17th, 1920.

Blunt, Wilfrid Scawen.
Fand - - - - - - April 27th, 1907.

Boyle, William.
The Building Fund - - - April 25th, 1905.
The Eloquent Dempsey - - June 20th, 1906.
The Mineral Workers - - - October 20th 1906.
Family Failing - - - - March 28th, 1912.
Nic - - - - - - October 25th, 1916.

Brennan, M. M.
The Young Man from Rathmines - April 6th, 1922.
A Lepracaun in the Tenement - September 5th, 1922.

Callister, C.
A Little Bit of Youth - - - May 28th, 1918.

Campbell, Joseph.
Judgment - - - - - April 15th, 1912.

Casey, W. F.
 The Man Who Missed the Tide - February 13th, 1908.
 The Suburban Groove - - - October 1st, 1908.

Casey, Sadie.
 Brady - - - - - - August 4th, 1919.

Christie, R. A.
 The Dark Hour - - - - September 9th, 1914.

Colum, Padraic.
 Broken Soil - - - - December 3rd, 1903.
 The Land - - - - June 9th, 1905.
 Thomas Muskerry - - - May 12th, 1910.
 The Fiddler's House (F.P. elsewhere
  1907) - - - - - Aug. 19th, 1919.
 The Grasshopper - - - October 24th, 1922.

Connolly, Joseph.
 The Mine Land - - - October 2nd, 1913.

Corkery, Daniel.
 The Labour Leader - - - September 30th, 1919.
 The Yellow Bittern - - - May 4th, 1920.

Crone, William.
 The Bargain - - - - April 5th, 1915.

Cousins, James.
 The Sleep of the King - - - October 29th, 1902.
 The Racing Lug - - - October 31st, 1902.

Dalton, Maurice.
 Sable and Gold - - - September 16th, 1918.

Day, S. R., and Cummins, G. D.
 Broken Faith - - - April 24th, 1913.
 Fox and Geese - - - February 2nd, 1917.

Duffy, Bernard.
 Fraternity - - - - January 4th, 1916.
 The Coiner - - - - February 8th, 1916.
 The Counter Charm - - - December 11th, 1916.
 The Piper of Tavran - - - November 15th, 1921.

Dunsany, Lord.
 The Glittering Gate - - - April 29th, 1909.
 King Argimenes and the Unknown
  Warrior - - - - January 26th, 1911.
 A Night at an Inn - - - September 2nd, 1919.
 The Tents of the Arabs - - - May 24th, 1920.

Ervine, St. John G.
Mixed Marriage - - - - - March 30th, 1911.
The Magnanimous Lover - - October 17th, 1912.
The Critics - - - - - November 20th, 1913.
The Orangeman - - - - March 13th, 1914.
John Ferguson - - - - November 30th, 1915.
The Island of Saints - - - October 12th, 1920.

Farjeon, Herbert.
Friends - - - - - November 20th, 1917.

Fearon, W. R., and Nesbitt, Roy.
When Love Came Over the Hills - January 22nd, 1918.

Fitzgerald, Desmond.
The Saint - - - - - September 2nd, 1919.

Fitzmaurice, George.
The Country Dressmaker - - October 3rd, 1907.
The Pie-dish - - - - - March 10th, 1908.
The Magic Glasses - - - April 24th, 1913.
'Twixt the Giltenans and the Carmodys March 8th, 1923.

Glaspell, Susan.
Trifles - - - - - - January 24th, 1927.

Goldsmith, Oliver.
The Good-Natured Man - - April 27th, 1920.
She Stoops to Conquer - - - April 22nd, 1923.

Gregory, Lady Augusta.
Twenty-Five - - - - March 14th, 1903.
Spreading the News - - - December 27th, 1904.
Kincora - - - - - March 25th, 1905.
The White Cockade - - - December 9th, 1905.
Hyacinth Halvey - - - - February 19th, 1906.
The Doctor in Spite of Himself (*Trs.*
    Molière) - - - - April 16th, 1906.
The Gaol Gate - - - - October 20th, 1906.
The Canavans - - - - December 8th, 1906.
The Jackdaw - - - - February 23rd, 1907.
The Rising of the Moon. - - March 9th, 1907.
The Poorhouse (*With* Douglas Hyde) April 4th, 1907.
Dervorgilla - - - - - October 31st, 1907.
The Unicorn from the Stars (*With*
    W. B. Yeats) - - - - November 21st, 1907.
Teja (*Trs.* Sudermann) - - - March 19th, 1908.
The Rogueries of Scapin (*Trs.* Molière) April 4th, 1908.

Gregory, Lady Augusta—contd.

The Workhouse Ward - - - April 20th, 1908.
The Miser (*Trs.* Molière) - - January 21st, 1909.
The Image - - - - - November 11th, 1909.
Mirandolina (*Trs.* Goldoni) - - February 24th, 1910.
The Travelling Man - - - March 2nd, 1910.
The Full Moon - - - - November 10th, 1910.
Coats - - - - - - December 1st, 1910.
The Nativity Play (*Trs.* Douglas Hyde) January 5th, 1911.
The Deliverer - - - - January 12th, 1911.
McDonough's Wife (*Later* McDar-
    ragh's Wife) - - - - January 11th, 1912.
The Bogie Man (Court Theatre, London) July 4th, 1912.
Damer's Gold - - - - November 21st, 1912.
Shanwalla - - - - - April 8th, 1915.
Hanrahan's Oath - - - - January 29th, 1918.
The Dragon - - - - April 21st, 1919.
The Golden Apple - - - January 6th, 1920.
Aristotle's Bellows - - - March 17th, 1921.
The Old Woman Remembers
    (*Dramatic Poem*) - - - December 23rd, 1923.
The Story Brought by Brigit - - April 14th, 1924.
The Would-be Gentleman (*Trs.* and
    Adapted Molière) - - - January 4th, 1926.
Sancho's Master - - - - March 14th, 1927.
Dave - - - - - - May 9th, 1927.

Guinan, John.

The Cuckoo's Nest - - - January 13th, 1913.
The Plough Lifters - - - March 28th, 1916.
Black Oliver - - - - May 16th, 1927.

Harte, Elizabeth.

Mr. Murphy's Island - - - August 16th, 1926.

Hyde, Douglas.

The Twisting of the Rope (*In Irish*) - October 21st, 1901.
The Poorhouse (*With* Lady Gregory) April 3rd, 1907.
The Nativity Play (*Trs.* Lady Gregory) January 5th, 1911.
The Marriage - - - - November 30th, 1911.
The Tinker and the Fairy (*In Irish*)- January 15th, 1912.

Jay. F.

The Cobweb - - - - October 13th, 1914.

Kelleher, D. L.

Stephen Gray - - - - March 11th, 1909.

Kennedy, Mrs. Bart.
My Lord - - - - - October 16th, 1913.

Letts, W. M.
The Eyes of the Blind - - - April 1st, 1907.
The Challenge - - - - October 14th, 1909.

Macardle, Dorothy.
Atonement - - - - - December 17th, 1918.
Ann Kavanagh - - - - April 6th, 1922.
The Old Man - - - - February 24th, 1925.

MacDonagh, Thomas.
When the Dawn is Come - - October 15th, 1908.

MacNamara, Brinsley.
The Rebellion in Ballycullen - - March 11th, 1919.
The Land for the People - - November 30th, 1920.
The Glorious Uncertainty - - November 27th, 1923.
Look at the Heffernans - - - April 12th, 1926.
The Master - - - - March 6th, 1928.

MacSwiney, Terence.
The Revolutionist - - - - February 24th, 1921.

MacCarthy, J. Bernard.
Kinship - - - - - April 2nd, 1914.
The Supplanter - - - - September 3rd, 1914.
The Crusaders - - - - January 19th, 1917.
The Long Road to Garranbraher - January 9th, 1923.

MacManus, Seumas.
The Townland of Tamney - - January 14th, 1904.

Madden, M. C.
Parted - - - - - - April 5th, 1927.

McHugh, Martin J.
A Minute's Wait - - - - August 27th, 1914.
The Philosopher - - - - April 5th, 1915.
Tommy-Tom-Tom - - - January 8th, 1917.

Maher, D. C.
Partition - - - - - November 15th, 1916.

McKenna, Rose.
Aliens - - - - - - March 12th, 1918.

McNulty, Edward.
The Lord Mayor - - - - March 13th, 1914.
The Courting of Mary Doyle - - November 8th, 1921.

Martyn, Edward.
The Heather Field - - - May 8th, 1899.
Maeve - - - - - - February 20th, 1900.

Mayne, Rutherford.
Red Turf - - - - - December 17th, 1911.

Milligan, Alice.
The Last Feast of the Fianna - - February 19th, 1900.

Moore, George.
The Bending of the Bough - - February 19th, 1900.
Diarmuid and Grania (*With* W. B.
Yeats) - - - - - October 21st, 1901.

Moore, E. Hamilton.
A Little Christmas Miracle - - December 26th, 1912.

Moore, F. C., and Flanagan, W. P.
By Word of Mouth - - - January 27th, 1915.

Morgan, Stephen.
The Serf - - - - - October 5th, 1920.

Murray, T. C.
Brithright - - - - - October 27th, 1910.
Maurice Harte - - - - June 20th, 1912.
Sovereign Love - - - - September 11th, 1913.
Spring - - - - - January 8th, 1918.
Aftermath - - - - - January 10th, 1922.
Autumn Fire - - - - September 8th, 1924.
The Pipe in the Fields - - - October 3rd, 1927.
The Blind Wolf - - - - April 30th, 1928.

O'Brien, Seumas.
Duty - - - - - - November 16th, 1913.

O'Casey, Sean.
The Shadow of a Gunman - - April 9th, 1923.
Cathleen Listens-in - - - October 1st, 1923.
Juno and the ' Paycock ' - - - March 30th, 1924.
Nannie's Night Out - - - September 29th, 1924.
The Plough and the Stars - - February 8th, 1926.

O'Donnell, F. J. H.
The Drifters - - - - September 7th, 1920.
Anti-Christ - - - - - March 17th, 1925.

O'Grady, Fand.
Apartments - - - - - September 3rd, 1923.

O'Kelly, Seumas.
The Shuiler's Child - - - November 24th, 1910.
The Bribe - - - - - November 18th, 1913.
The Parnellite - - - - September 24th, 1917.
Meadowsweet - - - - October 7th, 1919.

O'Leary, Con.
The Crossing - - - - September 23rd, 1914.
Queer Ones - - - - - October 14th, 1919.

O'Neill, Eugene.
The Emperor Jones - - - January 27th, 1927.

O'Nolan, Fergus.
A Royal Alliance - - - - September 21st, 1920.

O'Riordan, Conal.
The Piper - - - - - February 13th, 1908.
Time - - - - - - April 1st, 1909.
An Imaginary Conversation - - May 27th, 1909.

Paternoster, G. Sidney.
The Dean of Saint Patrick's - - January 23rd, 1913.

Power, Arthur.
The Drapier Letters - - - August 27th, 1927.

Power, Victor O'D.
David Mahony - - - - January 29th, 1914.

Purcell, R. J.
The Spoiling of Wilson - - - November 13th, 1917.

Purdon, K. F.
Candle and Crib - - - - December 27th, 1920.

Ray, R. J.
The White Feather - - - September 16th, 1909.
The Casting-out of Martin Whelan September 29th, 1910.
The Gombeen Man - - - June 30th, 1913.
The Strong Hand - - - - April 25th, 1917.
The Moral Law - - - - August 29th, 1922.

Riddall, Walter.
The Prodigal - - - - - September 30th, 1914.

Robins, Gertrude.
The Home-Coming - - - April 10th, 1913.

Robinson, Lennox.
The Clancy Name - - - - October 8th, 1908.
The Cross Roads - - - - April 1st, 1909.
Harvest - - - - - - May 26th, 1910.

Robinson, Lennox—contd.

Patriots - - - - - - April 11th, 1912.
The Dreamers - - - - February 2nd, 1915.
The Whiteheaded Boy - - - December 13th, 1916.
The Lost Leader - - - - February 19th, 1918.
The Round Table - - - - January 31st, 1922.
Crabbed Youth and Age - - November 14th, 1922.
Never the Time and the Place - April 8th, 1924.
Portrait - - - - - March 31st, 1925.
The White Blackbird - - - October 12th, 1925.
The Big House - - - - September 26th, 1926.
The Round Table (*Revised*) - - July 18th, 1927.

Russell, George W. ('A.E.').

Deirdre - - - - - April 2nd, 1902.

Ryan, Fred.

The Laying of the Foundations - October 29th, 1902.

Ryan, W. P.

The Jug of Sorrow - - - - October 20th, 1914.

Sarr, Kenneth.

The Passing - - - - - December 16th, 1924.
Old Mag - - - - - December 22nd, 1924.

Shaw, G. Bernard.

The Shewing-up of Blanco Posnet - August 25th, 1909.
John Bull's Other Island - - - September 25th, 1916.
Widower's Houses - - - - October 9th, 1916.
Arms and the Man - - - - October 16th, 1916.
Man and Superman - - - - February 26th, 1917.
The Inca of Perusalem - - - March 12th, 1917.
The Doctor's Dilemma - - - May 26th, 1917.
Androcles and the Lion - - - November 4th, 1919.
The Devil's Disciple - - - February 10th, 1920.
The Man of Destiny - - - March 9th, 1922.
Fanny's First Play - - - - April 21st, 1925.
Cæsar and Cleopatra - - - October 24th, 1927.

Sheridan, Richard Brinsley.

The Scheming Lieutenant - - May 29th, 1908.
The Critic - - - - - December 26th, 1914.

Shiels, George.

Bedmates - - - - - January 6th, 1921.
Insurance Money - - - - December 13th, 1921.
Paul Twyning - - - - October 3rd, 1922.
First Aid - - - - - December 26th, 1923.

Shiels, George—contd.

The Retrievers - - - -	May 12th, 1924.
Professor Tim - - - -	September 14th, 1925.
Cartney and Kevney - - -	November 29th, 1927.

Stephens, James.

The Wooing of Julia Elizabeth -	August 9th, 1920.

Synge, John M.

In the Shadow of the Glen - -	October 8th, 1903.
Riders to the Sea - - - -	February 25th, 1904.
The Well of the Saints - - -	February 4th, 1905.
The Playboy of the Western World	January 26th, 1907.
Deirdre of the Sorrows - - -	January 13th, 1910.

Tagore, Rabindranath.

The Post Office - - - -	May 17th, 1913.

Wilde, Oscar.

The Importance of Being Earnest -	November 8th, 1926.

Wilson, A. P.

The Cobbler - - - -	April 15th, 1914.
The Slough - - - - -	November 3rd, 1914.

Yeats, W. B.

The Countess Cathleen - - -	May 8th, 1899.
Diarmuid and Grania (*With* George Moore) - - - - -	October 21st, 1901.
Kathl. 'n ni Houlihan - - -	April 2nd, 1902.
The Pot of Broth - - - -	October 13th, 1902.
The Hour-Glass (*Prose Version*) -	March 14th, 1903.
The King's Threshold - - -	October 8th, 1903.
The Shadowy Waters - - -	January 14th, 1904.
On Baile's Strand - - - -	December 27th, 1904.
Deirdre - - - - - -	November 24th, 1906.
The Shadowy Waters (*Revised*) -	December 8th, 1906.
The Unicorn from the Stars (*With* Lady Gregory) - - -	November 21st, 1907.
The Golden Helmet - - -	March 19th, 1908.
The Green Helmet (*Verse*) - -	February 10th, 1910.
The Land of Heart's Desire - -	February 26th, 1911.
The Countess Cathleen (*Revised*) -	September 26th, 1912.
The Hour-Glass (*Verse*) - - -	November 21st, 1912.
The King's Threshold (*Revised*) -	October 13th, 1913.
The Player Queen - - - -	December 9th, 1919.
Œdipus the King (*Trs.* Sophocles) -	December 6th, 1926.
Œdipus at Colonnus (*Trs.* Sophocles)	September 12th, 1927.

Play Announced but never Produced.

The Spancel of Death.   T. H. Nally.   April 25th, 1916.

The date upon which this play was to have been produced was the Easter Monday of the Insurrection in Dublin in 1916. No attempt was afterwards made to stage the play.

Translations not Otherwise Listed.

Interior.	*Maurice Maeterlinck.*	March 16th, 1907.
Teja.	*Herman Sudermann.*	March 19th, 1908.
Hannele.	*Gerhart Hauptmann.*	Feb. 20th, 1913.
There are Crimes and Crimes.	*August Strindberg.*	March 6th, 1913.
The Stronger.	*August Strindberg.*	April 17th, 1913.
The Perfect Day.	*Emile Mazaud*	Oct. 18th, 1921.
The Merry Death.	*Nicholas Evreinov.*	Oct. 18th, 1921.
A Doll's House.	*Henrik Ibsen.*	March 22nd, 1923.
The Two Shepherds.	*G. M. Sierra.*	Feb. 2nd, 1924.
The Kingdom of God.	*G. M. Sierra*	Nov. 3rd, 1924.
The Proposal.	*Anton Tchechov.*	April 26th, 1925.
Doctor Knock.	*Jules Romains.*	Feb. 16th, 1926.
John Gabriel Borkman.	*Henrik Ibsen.*	April 3rd, 1928

INDEX

345